Black Music in the
Harlem Renaissance

A Collection of Essays

EDITED BY
Samuel A. Floyd, Jr.

Contributions in Afro-American and African Studies, Number 128

GREENWOOD PRESS
New York • Westport, Connecticut • London

Library of Congress Cataloging-in-Publication Data

Black music in the Harlem Renaissance : a collection of essays /
    edited by Samuel A. Floyd, Jr.
        p.   cm. — (Contributions in Afro-American and African
    studies, ISSN 0069-9624 ; no. 128)
      Bibliography: p.
      Includes index.
    ISBN 0-313-26546-1 (lib. bdg. : alk. paper)
        1. Afro-Americans—New York (N.Y.)—Music—History and criticism.
2. Music—New York (N.Y.)—20th century—History and criticism.
3. Harlem Renaissance. I. Floyd, Samuel A. II. Series.
ML3556.8.N5B6   1990
780′.89′9607307471—dc20   89-11985

British Library Cataloguing in Publication Data is available.

Copyright © 1990 by Samuel A. Floyd, Jr.

Library of Congress Catalog Card Number: 89-11985
ISBN: 0-313-26546-1
ISSN: 0069-9624

First published in 1990

Greenwood Press, 88 Post Road West, Westport, CT 06881
An imprint of Greenwood Publishing Group, Inc.

Printed in the United States of America

The paper used in this book complies with the
Permanent Paper Standard issued by the National
Information Standards Organization (Z39.48-1984).

10 9 8 7 6 5 4 3 2

Black Music in the
Harlem Renaissance

Recent Titles in
Contributions in Afro-American and African Studies

Class and Consciousness: The Black Petty Bourgeoisie in South Africa,
1924 to 1950
Alan Gregor Cobley

Black Novelist as White Racist: The Myth of Black Inferiority in the
Novels of Oscar Micheaux
Joseph A. Young

Capital and the State in Nigeria
John F. E. Ohiorhenuan

Famine in East Africa: Food Production and Food Policies
Ronald E. Seavoy

Archetypes, Imprecators, and Victims of Fate: Origins and Developments
of Satire in Black Drama
Femi Euba

Black and White Racial Identity: Theory, Research, and Practice
Janet E. Helms, editor

Black Students and School Failure: Policies, Practices, and Prescriptions
Jacqueline Jordan Irvine

Anne, the White Woman in Contemporary African-American Fiction:
Archetypes, Stereotypes, and Characterizations
Anna Maria Chupa

American Policy and African Famine: The Nigeria-Biafra War, 1966-1970
Joseph E. Thompson

Wines in the Wilderness: Plays by African American Women from the
Harlem Renaissance to the Present
Elizabeth Brown-Guillory, editor and compiler

Education of the African American Adult: An Historical Overview
Harvey G. Neufeldt and Leo McGee, editors

The Wealth of Races: The Present Value of Benefits from Past Injustices
Richard F. America, editor

Contents

List of Illustrations

Preface

This book began as a special issue of *Black Music Research Journal* devoted to music in the Harlem Renaissance. When, in the course of the work's coming together, the project grew to be larger than planned, it was developed into this volume. Even so, aspects of the subject remain uncovered, with Renaissance activities in France and other parts of Europe as well as in the British and French colonies remaining absent, although England is covered in Jeffrey Green's essay. Additionally, the relationships among the arts, as portrayed in the essays by Richard Long and Allan Gordon, must be more fully explored. But with this volume the doors have been opened; perhaps a later treatment can bridge these gaps.

Credit and thanks go to the editorial board of *Black Music Research Journal*, who performed their functions as reviewers and editors, and especially to Marsha J. Reisser who, in addition to her duties as an associate editor of *BMRJ*, prepared the camera-ready copy on the desk-top publishing system of the Center for Black Music Research. Special thanks also go to the administration of Columbia College Chicago, particularly President Mike Alexandroff and Executive Vice President Bert Gall, whose support of the Center for Black Music Research made this work possible.

CHAPTER 1

Music in the Harlem Renaissance:
An Overview

Samuel A. Floyd, Jr.

It is a rare and intriguing moment when a people decide that they are the instruments of history-making and race-building. It is common enough to think of oneself as part of some grand design. But to presume to be an actor and creator in the special occurrence of a people's birth (or rebirth) requires a singular self-consciousness. In the opening decades of the Great Depression, black intellectuals in Harlem had just such a self-concept. These Harlemites were so convinced that they were evoking their people's "Dusk of Dawn" that they believed that they marked a renaissance (Huggins 1971, 3).

The primary artistic leaders of the Harlem Renaissance were a group of intellectuals that David Levering Lewis has dubbed "The Six"—Jessie Redmond Faucet, Charles S. Johnson, Casper Holstein, Alain Locke, Walter White, and James Weldon Johnson (Lewis 1981, 119ff).[1] These individuals thought of themselves as "thinkers, strivers, doers, and . . . cultured"; they "aspired to high culture as opposed to that of the common man, which they hoped to mine for novels, plays and symphonies" (Huggins 1971, 5). They put a high premium on the rediscovery and promotion of folk materials for the sake of documenting and celebrating the black cultural heritage and for the use of these materials as sources of inspiration and points of departure for artistic creation (Huggins 1971, 72–83).

Some writers set the beginning of the movement in 1921, when Noble Sissle and Eubie Blake's *Shuffle Along* opened on Broadway. Others set it in 1925, the year in which Alain Locke's book *The New Negro* appeared (Lewis 1981, 117). Eileen Southern sets the "official" beginning in 1917, when James Weldon Johnson's *Fifty Years and Other Poems* was published (Southern 1983, 396). Let it suffice to say that, by the mid-twenties, and probably several years before, the Renaissance was under way.

It should be remembered, however, that although Harlem's literary movement "began to be recognized in 1924" (Anderson 1981, 68), black *music* was in ascendancy much earlier, as we shall see.

At bottom, the Renaissance was an effort to secure economic, social, and cultural equality with white citizens, and the arts were to be used as a means of achieving that goal. Charles S. Johnson, for example, perceived the arts as a primary area of advancement for black people, as "a crack in the wall of racism" (Lewis 1981, 48). It was believed that once black artists made their mark, equality would emerge on all fronts. At the same time, the black heritage was to remain central to the effort. To this end, The Six encouraged the aristocratic adaptation of folk materials in the creation of "high art" with the purpose of replacing existing values with their newly formulated ones (Bone 1968, 412). These ideals were articulated in lectures and discussions and in the pages of periodicals that helped to create and spread Renaissance credo. Lewis (1981, 50) tells us that "from 1923 onward, the skies shimmered from Charles Johnson's ambitious program to promote racial advancement through artistic creativity."

To advance the movement, Johnson and Locke issued a call for artists to come to Harlem (Lewis 1981, 6). The lure of success brought young artists from all parts of the country—the writers Langston Hughes and Zora Neal Hurston, the painter Aaron Douglas, and many others. Musicians came to the city in numbers, if not in response to the "call" of Johnson and Locke, to that of the city and its opportunities. Eubie Blake came from Baltimore; Duke Ellington from Washington, D.C.; Fletcher Henderson from Atlanta; other musicians came from a variety of locations. The lure was the potential for success in an exciting environment.

In 1918, W. C. Handy, bandleader and composer, as he tells it,

> headed for Harlem. And what a Harlem it was! Big old good-looking, easy-going, proud-walking Harlem. I strolled through the principal streets of Harlem and on 135th Street, near the old Lincoln Theater, I saw a sign on the door. It read: "Harlem Musicians' Association." I paused to listen to a saxophone sextette and walked in, wondering whom I would meet and if anyone would know me. I was instantly recognized and, instead of a group of mediocre musicians, met the cream of New York's leaders at that time. Will Vodery, arranger of numerous Ziegfeld musical scores, invited me as his guest to the Cocoanut Grove on the Century Roof. And on the following night I was the guest of Ford Dabney at the Ziegfeld Roof (Handy 1941, 194–95).

Handy established his publishing firm, Handy Brothers, in the Gaiety Theater building, together with (or before and after) two other black songwriter-publishers—Clarence Williams and Perry Bradford (Kirkeby 1966, 86).

In 1920, composer William Grant Still moved into a brownstone on 127th Street. He lived in a middle-class, predominantly white neighborhood and played downtown in Will Vodery's orchestra (Redd 1981).[2] In 1923, Duke Ellington moved to New York with a band called The Washingtonians (Ellington 1973, 69). Music was flourishing everywhere. Tin Pan Alley was in its heyday; cabarets did a booming business with prohibition liquor and popular music; concert life was active and stimulating. The common black folk were frequenting the cabarets, and so were the intellectuals after attending concerts of the New York Philharmonic Orchestra and the Metropolitan Opera (Redd 1981). But Harlem was the center of the movement.

The white show world of downtown New York, where a few black musicians performed and where black shows were also presented, was active; but after hours everyone, white and black, went to Harlem to hear black music. The following excerpt from Nathan Huggins's interview of Eubie Blake is both informative and provocative:

> N. H. You are saying that white people were coming uptown following the music. And it was the sense of the music that was at the center of the Renaissance?
> E. B. The music and the entertainment (Huggins 1976, 339–40).

This brief exchange is important because it provides a perspective whose implications are not treated in most accounts of the movement. The Harlem Renaissance has been treated primarily as a literary movement, with occasional asides, contributed as musical spice, about the jazz age and the performances of concert artists.[3] But music's role was much more basic and important to the movement. In fact, the stance of the black leadership and scattered brief comments about music during the period suggest the primacy of music to Renaissance philosophy and practice. The idea that black music was America's only distinctive contribution to American and world musical culture was accepted and emphasized by Renaissance leaders and by some of the rank and file. The cultural environment created by Renaissance leaders promoted only literature, but it stood as a network of physical elements that consisted of nightlife, cocktail parties, literary discussions, and strategy sessions—an environment in which all the arts were supported, albeit some only indirectly.

Generally, however, the Harlem Renaissance used and was supported and accompanied by music. The music of the black theater shows, the dance music of the cabarets, the blues and ragtime of the speakeasies and the rent parties, the spirituals and the art songs of the recital and concert halls all created an ambiance for Renaissance activity and contemplation. Furthermore, the pre-Renaissance activities of black musicians had created a climate in which the movement could take root and receive sustenance. On the other hand, as we shall see, the music of the Renaissance period was also the source of certain ambivalent attitudes on the part of the black leadership.

THE NEW NEGRO

Renaissance leaders aspired to create a "New Negro," one who would attend concerts and operas and would be economically and socially prepared to enter an ideally integrated American society. He would not "crawl nor cringe" and would not turn the other cheek, for he would be "equal" (Lewis 1981, 24). He would not frequent musical dens of iniquity, for he would then tarnish the image that was to be presented to the world as evidence of his preparedness. So, at first, the "lower forms" of black music were frowned upon by those of this outlook. These leaders realized that a new stereotype was developing simultaneously with their efforts to destroy the old ones. Jazz and show entertainers were being viewed by whites as symbols of primitive indulgence, as symbols "of that freedom from restraint for which the white intellectual longed so ardently." This stereotype was reinforced by the "discovery of primitive African sculpture and the ascendancy of jazz" in the Renaissance years (Bone 1968, 416).

The Harlem Renaissance was a youth movement, despite the ages of leaders such as W.E.B. Du Bois and James Weldon Johnson. Most of the writers, artists, and musicians were in their twenties during the 1920s. The New Negro was typically a young, talented, and newly arrived Harlemite who was seeking to make his mark in the world and was proud of his new status. Arna Bontemps remembers:

> It did not take long to discover that I was just one of many young Negroes arriving in Harlem for the first time and with many of the same thoughts and intentions. Within a year or two we began to recognize ourselves as a "group" and to become a little self-conscious about our "significance." When we were not busy having fun, we were shown off and exhibited and presented in scores of places to all kinds of people. And we heard the sighs of wonder, amazement and sometimes admiration when it was whispered or announced that here was one of the "New Negroes" (quoted in Locke [1925] 1968b, x).

In the New Negro's attempt to define and build a culture, music provided much of the movement's color, spirit, and quality. It provided a base for the general aesthetic ethos and a style for the intellectual climate of the time. This fact is reflected in some of the writings of Renaissance literary figures, as, for example, when Hughes refers to jazz as "the tom-tom of the revolt" (Bone 1968, 416). In this adventure, music played an important and perhaps indispensable role, while being taken for granted by most of the participants. This is not surprising, since music had always been a critical part of the existence of all individual Afro-Americans, while literature had not. Although prior to the Renaissance there may have been quite a flood of literature by a number of writers, the literary output of Afro-Americans did not begin to match, for sheer volume, that of the music.

For music, there had been no slow incubatory and developmental period. Black music had spread throughout the world by the 1920s, receiving international acceptance and acclaim, although there were Renaissance leaders who, like most middle-class white Americans during this period, "steadfastly refused to give credence to the merits of almost any music that deviated from the accepted norms of European musical standards. To these people, blues and jazz were strictly primitive expressions of an uncivilized people" (Nelson 1973, 72–73).

The necessity of Renaissance leaders to extol some aspects of black culture while denying and suppressing others was natural, since the idea was to integrate with white society by selling black people and black culture to the larger society as worthy and equal. The fact was, however, that the "primitive" and "degenerate" secular music of the period manifested the aesthetic of the movement better than any other resource available. But, as we shall see, this dilemma would resolve itself in time.

MUSICIANS AND THE MUSIC

Although the musical aspects of the Renaissance were built upon the rich source of black folk music, all such music was not entirely appropriate fare for the New Negro. The spirituals were an exception; but the secular music of the black masses was rejected by New Negro leaders in favor of music that was not stereotypical or "vulgar." To at least some Renaissance leaders, most secular music of the black underclass would be acceptable only as it could be used as a basis for a higher "art music."

Apparently, Renaissance leaders did not understand, or would not acknowledge, the fact that all of the black musical genres belonged to a single cultural and aesthetic tradition, that they were all bound together by a common body of musico-aesthetic principles and characteristics. By 1920 it was certainly clear that polymeter, multimeter, call-and-response patterns, certain pitch collections and inflections, and all of the sound devices and techniques of Afro-American music performance practices were common traits, to some degree, of all the music that had emanated from black culture in the United States, and that these traits defined this body of music as Afro-American. Being of the culture, this music mirrored and expressed Afro-American life-styles—the struggles and the fulfillments of living in a land and an environment that was both hostile and promising, binding and free. Apparently, however, the elements that defined the music of the black folk communicated the very stereotypes and values that Renaissance leaders wanted to eradicate.

In spite of such contradictions, Renaissance thinkers believed that the building of a culture required a foundation on which to build the new ideas and institutions. For this foundation, black thinkers and artists reached back to the artistic forms of the "old Negro" and his forebears in Africa. This approach was reasonable and appropriate. It was left only for the musicians to convert the folk forms into high art. Actually, the ideal had been realized to some degree as early as 1921, with the completion and premiere of Robert Nathaniel Dett's oratorio *The Chariot Jubilee,* an extended work for chorus and orchestra that is based on the spiritual "Swing Low, Sweet Chariot."

IMPORTANT COMPOSERS AND PERFORMERS OF POPULAR MUSIC

Between 1900 and 1930, there were three groups of musicians whose works were of revolutionary significance. The members of these groups did transform, to some degree, "primitive" black musical genres into "higher forms," although these forms were not quite the same as those envisioned by New Negro thinkers. Not necessarily directly influenced by intellectual theory, these musicians, through their individual works, ensured that the inherited black music genres, and elements thereof, were developed into extended and more complex forms.

For convenience, and at the risk of banality, I will group and label these musicians as follows. The first is The Group of Four that included Ford Dabney (1883–1958), James Reese Europe (1881–1919), Will Marion Cook (1869–1944), and William Christopher Handy (1873–1958). The second group, The Jazzmen, was comprised of Fletcher Henderson (1897–1952) and Duke Ellington (1894–1974). The final group is that of The Pianists that includes James P. Johnson (1894–1955), Willie "The Lion" Smith (1897–1973), and Thomas "Fats" Waller (1904–1943).

The Group of Four

Alain Locke has pointed out that Dabney, Europe, Cook, and Handy "organized Negro music out of a broken, musically illiterate dialect and made it a national and intellectual music" (Locke [1936] 1968a, 65–66). In spite of the "New Negroese" character of the statement, Locke is correct in the most general sense. Specifically,

Dabney revolutionized the Negro dance orchestra and started the musical

fortunes of Florenz Ziegfeld. . . . Jim Europe . . . organized the famous
"Clef Club Orchestra" and music center in 1910. . . . Europe was to . . .
make [Negro music] preferred for its rhythm and accord in the new dance
vogue of the American stage started by the celebrated Vernon and Irene
Castle (who insisted on Negro orchestras for their accompanists).

· · · · ·

Marion Cook not only gave Negro music its first serious orchestral ambitions, but with his "syncopated orchestra" surprised and converted the
European music centers by his concerts. . . . Handy . . . championed Simon
pure and despised Mississippi folk music and . . . loosed the overwhelming flood of the "Blues" (Locke [1936] 1968a, 66–67).

Primarily, these men—The Group of Four—were pre-Renaissance figures whose accomplishments were recognized as significant and provocative by New Negro leaders and rank and file, and they no doubt
cited them as examples that musical aspirants of the 1920s were to build
upon. In fact by 1915 *Crisis* magazine, the "voice" of the New Negro
movement, was already carrying favorable writings about Handy's
work (Handy 1941, 236). From our present-day perspective, however,
we can see that without the achievements of Dabney, Europe, Cook, and
Handy, those of their immediate successors would have been much
more difficult to achieve, especially those of Ellington, Henderson,
James P. Johnson, and Eubie Blake.

The Jazzmen

The primary pioneers of Renaissance jazz were Fletcher Henderson
and Duke Ellington. In 1921 Henderson formed a band that, for the duration of the Renaissance period, served as the house band at the Rose-
land Ballroom on Broadway (Kirkeby 1966, 82), an establishment that
had a whites-only policy. With arranger Don Redman primarily responsible for the Henderson sound, the band was a pioneer of both "hot"
and "sweet" music in New York; its "Sugar Foot Stomp" became "the
classic model of the New York style" (Lewis 1981, 171). Henderson's
style and his highly influential band were imitated by almost all of the
emerging jazz bands and became a standard against which later bands
would be measured. The "prissy and important" Henderson, educated
at Atlanta University, cultured, and of impeccable character, was primarily responsible, Lewis tells us, for "the sufferance if not the approval
of jazz by some of the Talented Tenth" (Lewis 1981, 173).

Second in both popularity and importance to the Henderson band
was Ellington's. Based at the famed Cotton Club, another whites-only
establishment, this group, with its use of blue notes, growls, and hot
rhythms, was a jazz band as well as a commercial dance orchestra. The
band's performances of the pop and dance tunes of the day may have

been influenced by the examples of Will Vodery and Will Marion Cook, two musicians whom Ellington greatly admired and from whom he had picked up pointers on technique and orchestration. From his contact with these older men, Ellington gained theoretical knowledge that together with his inimitable sense of the tonal palette, helped him develop into a jazz *artist*—the first of a breed—and a composer. In the 1920s Ellington wrote more than fifty compositions, among them "Black and Tan Fantasy" (1927), "Rent Party Blues" (1929), "Saturday Night Function" (1929), "Harlem Flat Blues" (1929), and "Dicty Glide" (1929), all of which are in some way commentary on the Harlem culture of the period. Among his early 1930s pieces are "Mood Indigo" (1931), "It Don't Mean a Thing If It Ain't Got That Swing" (1932), "Sophisticated Lady" (1933), "Solitude" (1934), "In a Sentimental Mood" (1935), and "Harlem Speaks" (1935) (Ellington 1973, 493–95).

While his "jungle" music at the Cotton Club surely did not endear him to Renaissance leaders, his position in the entertainment world and his commitment to the "cause," together with his courtly assertiveness, aristocratic bearing, and charming aloofness probably made him an acceptable New Negro. His *Creole Rhapsody*, an extended composition written during 1931, was regarded by Europeans even then as "the first real jazz composition" (Collier 1978, 245–46). In 1936 Locke was touting Ellington as "the pioneer of super-jazz," pointing to "Reminiscing in Tempo" and *Creole Rhapsody* as evidence of his potential greatness as a composer (Locke [1936] 1968a, 99).

The Pianists

After 1912—the height of ragtime's popularity—Harlem's ragtime composers began to experiment with new ideas. The primary black composers in the movement were Charles Luckeyth "Luckey" Roberts (1887–1968) and James P. Johnson. They created the New York school of stride ragtime, a style that was more difficult to render than the traditional and novelty styles, a style that would greatly influence the development of jazz piano. Roberts does not seem to have been very active in the 1920s, and Blake had turned his attention to composition and show music. But Thomas "Fats" Waller emerged to join Johnson and Willie "The Lion" Smith to form a group of three pianists who were to change the course of American popular piano music and virtually create jazz piano style. As the best and most advanced ragtime pianists in New York and the entire country, these men set the standards for all pop and jazz pianists who would follow. Roberts's "Nothin," Johnson's "Carolina Shout," and Waller's "Handful of Keys" served as proving pieces for all the pianists of the period; they were three of the most important rent party/cuttin' contest pieces of the 1920s. James P. Johnson was generally regarded as *the* master of stride piano; he codified the style and served as a model for the younger men.

The pianists were not interested in the approval of the Renaissance leaders. Their lives, their livelihoods, and their interests were bound up with the show-music/cabaret/rent-party world. However, as the Renaissance progressed this would change, as we shall see.

The popular music and jazz of the Renaissance period were introduced, developed, and promoted primarily by these three groups of musicians. To a large extent, they charted the course of popular music during the Renaissance and beyond, ever maintaining the continuity of the human expressions of the Afro-American experience. In their pursuits they were publicly defended, supported, and encouraged by only one intellectual literary voice of the period—that of Langston Hughes. To Talented Tenth rhetoric regarding the race putting its best foot forward, Hughes retorted:

> Let the blare of Negro jazz bands and the bellowing voice of Bessie Smith singing Blues penetrate the closed ears of the colored near-intellectuals until they listen and perhaps understand. . . . We younger Negro artists who create now intend to express our dark-skinned selves without fear or shame. If white people are pleased we are glad. If they are not, it doesn't matter. We know we are beautiful. And ugly too. The tom-tom cries and the tom-tom laughs. If colored people are pleased we are glad. If they are not, their displeasure doesn't matter either. We build temples for tomorrow, strong as we know how, and we stand on top of the mountain, free within ourselves (quoted in Lewis 1981, 191).

Such youthful and eloquent defiance harmonized with the ambiance of the Renaissance and surely must have exerted a positive influence.

MUSICAL SHOWS AND SHOW MUSIC

While Renaissance thinkers were theorizing about the future of black culture and the nature of its art products and while Hughes was taking them to task about their ideas, black musical theater (which had a previous blossoming in the closing decade of the nineteenth century) was in the midst of a revival, celebrating black culture with some of the old stereotypes and the new aspirations. In the world of the show musical, there was truly a renaissance of the great show years of the 1890s.

The decades of the 1920s and 1930s saw produced at least forty black musical shows and revues. After Sissle and Blake's 504 Broadway performances of *Shuffle Along*, there were no fewer than two and as many as five or more such shows produced each year in New York alone during the next ten years. Johnson and Waller, together with Blake and Noble Sissle, made black musical theater what it was in the 1920s, producing among them the following hit shows: *Shuffle Along* (Sissle and Blake 1921), *The Chocolate Dandies* (Sissle and Blake 1924), *Runnin' Wild* (Johnson 1924), *Keep Shufflin'* (Waller and Johnson 1928), and *Hot Chocolates* (Waller 1929) (Bordman 1968, 359–452). Other black composers and lyricists writing the music and the books for black shows included Luckey Roberts, Henry Creamer, Turner Layton, Maceo Pinkard, Porter Grainger, Fred Johnson, Clarence Williams, Donald Heywood, Ford Dabney, Joe Jordan, and Clarence Todd. Among the principal performers were the team of Flournoy Miller and Aubrey Lyles; Florence Mills; the actor and composer Shelton Brooks; Ethel Waters; Buck and Bubbles; and Eva Taylor. Also making appearances were entertainers and concert artists such as Louis Armstrong, Butterfly McQueen, Moms Mabley, Bessie Smith, Jules Bledsoe, Will Vodery, and the Cecil Mack Choir.

Most of these musicals and revues featured comedy sketches, rent-party skits, and singing, dancing, and high-stepping. *Shuffle Along* set the vogue. "It was a revue, acted and produced by Negroes for Negro audiences. . . . It did not bother to make concessions to white taste or to theater cliches" (Isaacs 1947, 63, 66). The entire score was stunning, featuring the later-to-be hit songs "I'm Just Wild About Harry" and "Love Will Find a Way." *Spice of 1922*, with a racially mixed cast, introduced Turner Layton's "Way Down Yonder in New Orleans." *Plantation Revue*, also of 1922, included in its cast Shelton Brooks (composer of "Walkin' the Dog," "Darktown Strutters Ball," and other hit songs of the day), Florence Mills, and Will Vodery. On November 27, 1922, Maceo Pinkard's *Liza* was produced; it was a "zesty," "vital," and worthwhile successor to *Shuffle Along* (Bordman 1968, 376). The next year, *Runnin' Wild* came close to duplicating the success of *Shuffle Along*, introducing the Charleston, the dance that was to help change both American musical theater and American popular society. The score was written by James P. Johnson; Miller and Lyles starred, as they had in *Shuffle Along*. *The Chocolate Dandies* was also produced in 1923. Sissle and Blake's score and the production itself were both lavish and of high quality. *The Chocolate Dandies* ran to ninety-six performances. *Dixie to Broadway* allowed black actors to imitate white performers such as George M. Cohan and others. Florence Mills starred in its eight-week run.

The white-cast musical *Deep River* (1926), in which Jules Bledsoe, the only black performer in the cast, had a minor but effective role, was a "native opera." Set in New Orleans in 1835, it was complete with quadroon balls, Place Congo, and a Voodoo ceremony. The black revue *Rang Tang* was produced on July 12, 1927. Starring Miller and Lyles, the music was written by Ford Dabney. The first black musical of the year 1928 was *Keep Shufflin'*, the music by Fats Waller and James P. Johnson, the words by Henry Creamer and Andy Razaf.

Two of the 1929 black musicals were *Pansy* and *Hot Chocolates*. *Pansy*, "a Negro collegiate musical," was composed and produced by Maceo Pinkard; Bessie Smith made at least one appearance in its three-performance run. *Hot Chocolates*, written by Fats Waller and Andy Razaf, ran for more than six months, with Louis Armstrong in the orchestra and featured as a soloist. The show's music, including the hit song "Ain't Misbehavin'," suggested "the stylings of the music that would come out of Broadway for the next few years" (Bordman 1968, 452). *Hot Rhythm* ran for eight-and-a-half weeks on 42nd Street. The score for this stereotypical black musical of the day was written by Donald Heywood and Porter Grainger. The score for *Brown Buddies* was written by Joe Jordan, with interpolations by Porter Grainger and Victor Young. That show's 111 performances featured the singing of Adelaide Hall and the dancing of Bill "Bojangles" Robinson.

The music of the 1930 version of *Lew Leslie's Blackbirds*, unlike that of the original 1928 version, was written by black composers—primarily by Eubie Blake—with lyrics by Andy Razaf. It featured Ethel Waters, Flournoy Miller, and Buck and Bubbles spoofing the Broadway hit *Green Pastures*. *Blackbirds* included the later-to-be hits "Memories of You" and "You're Lucky to Me."

The stars of these shows were impressive. Miller and Lyles, a veteran vaudeville act, had "packed them in" at the vaudeville houses and in the nightclubs and theaters of Harlem. Unlike other such teams of the period, Miller and Lyles were versatile performers who had in their repertoire a number of skits on which they improvised freely. The team also wrote scripts for *Runnin' Wild* and several other Broadway shows. Florence Mills was a critically acclaimed actress, both in the United States and abroad, having been hailed as being "by far the most artistic person London has had the good fortune to see" (Isaacs 1947, 69). Bill "Bojangles" Robinson was widely known as the best tap dancer in the world, as "a tap dancer without peer" (Isaacs 1947, 71). With his dancing, Robinson served as cement for more than 500 performances of *Blackbirds of 1928*, then went on to perform in a number of musicals and revues, including *Brown Buddies* (1930) and *Hot Mikado* (1939).

While the names of these and other stars appear again and again in the chronicles of black musical theater, many lesser-known and now-unknown talents held forth during the period, as they did in *Deep Harlem*, a 1929 revue that was "written by and filled with unknown names" (Bordman 1968, 447). And there were experiments with various theatrical forms, as with Donald Heywood's *Africana*—of 1933, not his 1927 revue by the same name—an operetta that ran for just three performances.

As noted, black musicals generally employed dancing and high-stepping, primarily featuring new jazz dances such as the Charleston, Black Bottom, Shimmy, and others. For whites, the dancing was apparently the most appealing aspect of the shows, since it was the feature the critics commented on most. It was both impressive and influential. Bordman points out that in *Runnin' Wild*, for example, the Charleston "pronounced the beat for 'the lost generation' and liberated the jazz movement." It "typified the black inspired high-stepping of the era" (Bordman 1968, 382).

The rent-party skits, reflecting the always operative struggles and fulfillments of black culture, were surely quite meaningful and effective for the black spectators since such affairs were a regular part of the real-life social scene in Harlem. Comedy sketches had been a staple of black entertainment for decades, having had their genesis in the minstrel tradition. In many of the black musicals, the characters of Sam and Peck—specialties of Miller and Lyles—made appearances or played major parts. They appeared in *Shuffle Along* and *Sugar Hill* of 1931, among others.

It is interesting to note that whenever black musicals departed from stereotypical presentations, whites were offended. White critics especially "seemed to resent a black musical that strove to emulate costly white mountings" (Bordman 1968, 391) as did, for example, *The Chocolate Dandies*. One critic referred to such efforts as "unwarranted attempts to imitate white musicals" (Bordman 1968, 452). But it was acceptable, apparently, for whites to imitate black productions and to use black ideas. *Lady Be Good* (1924), for example, was created by black writers, but was "given a cerebral white interpretation by George Gershwin." With this show, Bordman tells us, "the rhythms, tensions, and color of stage jazz was defined" (Bordman 1968, 395). It ran in New York for 330 performances.

Black music maintained its continuity and influence in the black and white musical traditions of the 1920s and the 1930s; its characteristics, power, intensity, and irresistibility substantially affected the music of the show world and, consequently, American popular music in the decades to come.

CLASSICAL MUSIC

But it was in the realm of concert music that Renaissance thinkers hoped for great achievement, expecting that black folk music would serve as the basis for great symphonic compositions that would be performed by accomplished black musicians. A number of black composers and performers of the period followed this credo.

Eileen Southern has most appropriately identified as black nationalist composers such figures as Harry T. Burleigh, Clarence Cameron White,

Robert Nathaniel Dett, Harry Lawrence Freeman, Florence Price, J. Harold Brown, and William Levi Dawson, writing that they all "consciously turned to the folk music of their people as a source of inspiration for their compositions, . . . placed special emphasis upon Negro performance practices, and made efforts to reflect the individualities of these practices for their composed music" (Southern 1983, 266).[4] And Lewis appropriately describes as "break-throughs in serious music" Roland Hayes's December 1923 Town Hall "Concert of Lieder and Spirituals"; Jules Bledsoe's April 21, 1924, Aeolian Hall concert; the organization of the Hall Johnson Choir in 1924; and the "First American Jazz Concert" performance at Aeolian Hall on February 12, 1924 (Lewis 1981, 163).

As college-educated individuals interested in "elevating the music of their race" while establishing themselves as artists in the European tradition, these composers and performers were prime Talented-Tenth material. They were committed strivers who represented the New Negro credo in action. Many of the artists were as philosophical as the theorizers. Robeson, for example, stated in 1926:

> Whether singing or acting, race and color prejudices are forgotten. Art is one form against which such barriers do not stand (Paul Robeson, quoted in Schlosser 1965, 87).

And William Grant Still maintained that his purpose was "to elevate Negro musical idioms to a position of dignity and effectiveness in the field of symphonic and operatic music" (Haas 1975, 134).

What all the vocal recitalists had in common was their use of Afro-American spirituals in their performances. This, too, conformed to Renaissance thinking, for W.E.B. Du Bois, the prime exponent of the Talented-Tenth concept, is credited with the "rediscovery of the spirituals" and with having given them credence through a serious and proper interpretation as "the peasant's instinctive distillation of sorrow and his spiritual triumphs over a religious ecstasy and hope." Locke viewed the spirituals as works of "an epic intensity and tragic depth of religious emotion," maintaining that they "stand out . . . as one of the great classic expressions of all times of religious emotion and Christian moods and attitudes" (Locke [1936] 1968a, 20, 23–25). With such noble sentiments and sanctions from two powerful Renaissance leaders, the work of "serious" musicians of the Renaissance period was perfectly sanctioned. Critic and theorist that he was, Locke was promulgating New Negro propaganda as late as 1936, touting the "sorrow songs" as "more than a priceless heritage from the Negro past, promising material for the Negro music of the future." He felt that "they are caught in the transitional stage between folk-form and art form." The danger was that the

"Negro composers have been too much influenced by formal European idioms in setting them" (Locke [1936] 1968a, 23–25).[5]

Not only did these classically trained musicians make use of spirituals, but as composers and performers of art songs, they set and sang for Renaissance audiences poems by contemporary poets such as Langston Hughes and James Weldon Johnson, as well as texts by older black writers such as Paul Laurence Dunbar. The instrumental music that was performed for Renaissance audiences made use of "plantation themes" (e.g., Burleigh's *Plantation Melodies for Violin and Piano* [1916] and White's *From the Cotton Fields* for violin [1925]); symphonic music celebrated the race (e.g., Still's *Darker America* [1924] and *Africa* [1930]); stage works—operas and oratorios—made use of both spirituals and race themes (e.g., Freeman's *Vendetta* [1923] and *Voodoo* [1928], Dett's *The Chariot Jubilee* [1921], and White's *Ouanga* [1930–1931]); and African and Haitian life provided the subjects for Still's two Renaissance ballets: *La Guiablesse* (1927) and *Sahdji* (1930). Dett's piano suites, *Enchantment* and *The Cinnamon Grove*, were also in the black tradition (Southern 1983, 271–77, 423–27). New-Negro audiences must have been thrilled by it all, for although many of the composers of these works were not Harlemites or New Yorkers, most of their compositions were performed in New York. For example, Freeman's *Vendetta* was produced at the Lafayette Theater in Harlem in 1923; his opera *The Tryst* had been performed in New York in 1911 (Southern 1971, 448–49). White's violin compositions were performed by leading white violinists of the period and surely by leading black violinists such as Felix Weir and Arthur Boyd, both of whom were members of the Negro String Quartet.

For black concert and recital music, the decade of the 1920s was one of significant musical progress, stimulated in part by the newly formed National Association of Negro Musicians. Organized in 1919, the group's avowed purpose paralleled that of the New Negro leadership: to stimulate "progress, to discover and foster talent, to mold taste, to promote fellowship, and to advocate racial expression" (Hare [1936] 1974, 242).

For the nationwide musical activity of which these individuals and groups are but a few examples, there had been no parallel in literature or the arts. Nor in 1919, when NANM was founded, was there activity in literature to parallel, in quantity at least, that of music. Could it be that Charles Johnson and Alain Locke took the NANM as a general model for their later and much more loosely knit literary movement? Was it the example of music that gave initial impetus to the Renaissance's artistic philosophy? The question, while rhetorical, is at least provocative.

Whatever the case, it seems that music officially and unequivocally became a part of the Renaissance no later than 1923, when Roland Hayes presented his Town Hall concert.

> After that night Black performers, particularly Black singers, became a regular part of the concert scene. Five months later Marian Anderson sang her initial Town Hall recital and Jules Bledsoe made his debut in Aeolian Hall, and a year after that Paul Robeson sang his famous first concert of spirituals (Abdul 1977, 74–75).

Talented-Tenth leaders and their followers must have been continuously ecstatic. Such accomplishments had certainly signaled the arrival of the New Negro. Other, equally impressive events quickly followed. Among them, there stand out the following: Taylor Gordon and J. Rosamond Johnson's 1927 concert tour of America and Europe; Abbie Mitchell's 1927 appearance at Steinway Hall; the premiere of James P. Johnson's *Yamekraw* at Carnegie Hall in 1928; and Edward Matthews's 1931 debut at Town Hall. In the preparation and performance of *Yamekraw*, a rhapsody for symphony orchestra and piano, James P. Johnson and Thomas "Fats" Waller teamed up with William Grant Still and W. C. Handy in a performance that surely satisfied the intellectuals. Composed by Johnson, orchestrated by Still, conducted by Handy, with the piano solo played by Waller, the piece employed "spirituals and blues tunes," among others, and was played in that performance by a symphony orchestra made up of Harlem musicians. This was Renaissance style—exactly in keeping with the dreams and goals of Renaissance leadership and masses. Following this premiere, *Yamekraw* was played a number of times on other occasions.

Among the concert pianists of the period was the widely acclaimed Hazel Harrison. In opera, Caterina Jarboro and Lillian Evanti reigned supreme among black operatic artists. And it should be noted that Roland Hayes (tenor) and Jules Bledsoe (baritone) ranked among the few top male singers in the world. The Negro String Quartet accompanied Roland Hayes in concert at Carnegie Hall in 1925 (Abdul 1977, 217–19). This group, whose members were all conservatory-trained musicians, had been founded in 1919 and was active in New York and in Philadelphia in the 1920s and the 1930s. Its members were Felix Weir (first violin), Arthur L. Boyd (second violin), Hall Johnson (viola), and Marion Cumbo (cello). Versatile musicians all, Johnson, Weir, and Cumbo had played in the *Shuffle Along* road orchestra in 1923. In addition to standard works by European composers, the quartet performed compositions by contemporary black composers. In its repertoire, for example, were Edward Margetson's *String Quartet* (1928) and Clarence Cameron White's *Quartet in C Minor*. The Negro String Quartet's Lenten Concert of March 21, 1926, presented music by Haydn, Beethoven, Cui,

Tschaikovsky, Svendsen, and Pochon. Featured guest musicians on the program were baritone G. Willard McLean, accompanied by Frederick J. Work. McLean sang, among other pieces, spiritual arrangements by Burleigh and Hall Johnson (see figure 1.1).

The orchestra that premiered James P. Johnson's *Yamekraw* was probably the Harlem Symphony Orchestra. As early as December 5, 1925, this organization, under the leadership of E. Gilbert Anderson, presented a concert, its third of the season.[6] On December 27, 1925, the orchestra presented another concert, performing music by Weber, Beethoven, Mendelssohn, and Nicolai, along with Coleridge-Taylor's four-movement *Scenes from "An Imaginary Ballet."* The printed program for the latter event advertises that the orchestra's next concert would be held on February 14, 1926. The personnel roster, printed on the back of the program, lists ten first violins, eight second violins, five violas, six cellos, four double basses, one tuba, two oboes, three flutes and one piccolo, four clarinets, four bassoons, two horns, five trumpets, four trombones, four percussion, and one piano ("Printed Program" 1925).

The Renaissance years were a proving period for black composers and performers, and they more than measured up. The rewards were pleasant and considerable. Between 1925 and 1932, a number of awards and prizes were established, or already available, to encourage the development of the arts: The Holstein Prize, the Spingarn Achievement Award, the Wanamaker Music Contest Prizes, the Juilliard Musical Foundation Fellowship, the David Bispham Medal, the Guggenheim Fellowships, the Julius Rosenwald Awards, and the Harmon Foundation Awards. Of these, the Holstein, Harmon, and Wanamaker prizes are especially notable since they included prizes for musical composition. Among the recipients of such awards were Edmund T. Jenkins, Florence B. Price, Camille Nickerson, J. Harold Brown, N. Clark Smith, Margaret Bonds, Harry Lawrence Freeman, Hall Johnson, William Grant Still, Harry T. Burleigh, Clarence Cameron White, and Robert Nathaniel Dett (Hare [1936] 1974, 260–64).

Most of these composers had been followers of Dvořák's brand of romantic nationalism (Locke [1936] 1968a, 107) or had been inspired and influenced by the Anglo-African composer Samuel Coleridge-Taylor. That is, they had been influenced either by Dvořák's aesthetic theories, which to some degree paralleled, validated, supported, and perhaps even influenced those of Renaissance thinkers, or by Coleridge-Taylor's musical output. The works of Dett, Burleigh, Still, and Dawson are the most accessible evidence of this. However, Locke tells us, Hall Johnson and Edmund Jenkins "broke with this school . . . and joined forces with the realistic school that discovered classical jazz by trailing the lowly footpaths of folk jazz" (Locke [1936] 1968a, 107). Evidently, Jenkins's *Af-*

PROGRAM

1. QUARTET IN D MAJOR ....Haydn

   Allegro Moderato
   Adagio Cantabile
   Menuetto
   Finale

2. SONGS

   (a) Yesterday and Today.. Spross
   (b) I Love Life... Mana Zucca
   (a) Invictus...Bruna Huhn

3. QUARTET

   (a) Minuet..Beethoven
   (b) Moto Perpetuo ....Cui
   (c) Andante Cantabile ....Tschaikowsky

4.—SONGS

   (a) Wade in de Water ....Burleigh
   (b) Were You There ....Burleigh
   (c) Jesus, Lay Yo' Head in de Winder ....Hall Johnson

5.—QUARTET

   (a) Andante from A minor quartet ....Svendsen
   (b) Deep River (Negro Spiritual) ....Pochon
   (c) Emperor Variations..Haydn

Figure 1.1. Concert program of the Negro String Quartet, March 21, 1926

rican War Dance, the 1925 Holstein first prize winner, and his *Charlestonia: A Negro Rhapsody for Orchestra*, performed in Brussels and Paris in 1924, and Johnson's *Sonata*, the 1927 prize winner, are examples of this music of Locke's "realistic school." It would be interesting to know if the works of this persuasion were related in any way to those of Cook's Southern Syncopated Orchestra which toured the United States and Europe in 1919–1920 and which Hare claims was "the finest aggregation of musicians ever before heard in what is termed distinctly Negro music" (Hare [1936] 1974, 165).

Unfortunately, we know little about the quantity and the quality of the bulk of the works produced by Renaissance composers; we know even less about the conditions, number, and quality of their performances. But it appears that, comparatively speaking, the activity was feverish, the atmosphere charged and optimistic. And this black music-inspired productivity was not limited to black composers. Hare lists 150 pre-1936 compositions by seventy-seven composers, most of them white, as being "among many serious works written in various forms, the spirit of which is Negro" (Hare [1936] 1974, 282). Among the composers listed are Ernest Bloch, John Alden Carpenter, George Chadwick, Aaron Copland, Morton Gould, Ernesto Lecuona, Darius Milhaud, Frances Poulenc, Wallingford Riegger, Erik Satie, Leo Sowerby, Igor Stravinsky, Edgar Varèse, George Antheil, Frederick Delius, Charles Ives, Ernest Krenek, Maurice Ravel, and Ferde Grofe (Hare [1936] 1974, 182–94).

So the works produced during, and inspired by, the Harlem Renaissance and by pre-Renaissance musical activity, and the aesthetic on which they were based, represented the extension, at least, of a significant break with the Euro-American tradition which, until this period, had looked to German romanticism for its models (Locke [1936] 1968a, 110–11). Black folk music and its derivatives were the catalyst. The use of Afro-American stylistic devices and performance practices in the works of European and American white composers and by American black composers ensured the spreading of the expressions of black culture, mirroring the struggles and the fulfillments of black folk culture, of the New Negro, and consequently, of the continuity of Afro-American music.

CULTURE AND CLASS

In the early years of the Renaissance, there was a sharp line dividing intellectuals from "show people" (Redd 1981). As far as creative artists were concerned, literary writers, classical musicians, and actors in the legitimate theater were in the former category, while the latter category comprised jazz and pop musicians and other entertainers. Willie "The Lion" Smith reminds us that Renaissance "strivers" rebelled against the

"Negro image created in the South and constantly given a showcase by both white and colored show business" (Smith 1975, 312). Some of the antics of black jazzmen who helped perpetuate the stereotype with actions and posturings inherited from the minstrel tradition were embarrassing to the intelligentsia; many of the musicians themselves must have experienced ambivalence, at least. On the other hand, for jazz and show musicians, the intellectuals were a source of amusement. Known as the "dicty" set, they served as inspiration for Henderson's "Dicty's Blues" (1923) and Ellington's "Dicty Glide" (1929), both of which were meant to poke fun at Talented Tenth types.

While there was a firm class structure in Harlem, interaction did take place between these two groups—interaction that was to lead, in later years, to their merger in a rather classless society. George Redd's observations imply that it was the more educated jazz musicians who helped to bring the two camps together. He points out that Duke Ellington, Fletcher Henderson, and others presented an image that was acceptable to the intellectuals (Redd 1981). Redd is probably right. Ellington's dignified bearing, his aristocratic flair, and his self-assurance in any company exemplified the New Negro in and outside the jazz world. But other developments also contributed to the elimination of class distinctions. Initially, the spirituals, in spite of Du Bois's position in favor of them, had been unacceptable to many New Negroes. Until Harry T. Burleigh and others began to perform spirituals in public concerts (an acceptable environment, perhaps) and until the Johnson brothers (James Weldon and J. Rosamond) first anthologized them (Johnson and Johnson 1925; Johnson and Johnson 1926), "second generation respectability" prevented Renaissance leaders from promoting them (Crawford 1940, 39). This public activity and the reception it won from educated Afro-Americans prompted a change. In addition, the world of the Savoy Ballroom, where the "high-brows" and the "low-brows" fraternized, and the general climate it helped to create contributed to the merger of the two "cultural universes." Du Bois, the leader of the intellectuals, was also influenced by his association with show musicians. At the Black Swan Phonograph Company, for example, William Grant Still and Du Bois served on the board of directors (Southern 1971, 399).

The Renaissance ambiance itself affected the world of jazz and show music. The new sense of self-worth, the optimistic climate, and the new self-confidence certainly affected people from all walks of life, especially musicians and entertainers. In the final analysis, the eventual blurring of class distinctions "contributed something to the style of the New Negro" (Redd 1981). But the initial class distinctions were reflected in the housing patterns of Renaissance participants. For the affluent—doctors, lawyers, and successful businessmen—there was Sugar Hill, where also resided W.E.B. Du Bois, Roy Wilkins, Walter White, Jules Bledsoe, and other Renaissance leaders and artists who lived at 409 Edgecombe Avenue in one of the nation's first high-rise apartment buildings. Just below Sugar Hill was Strivers' Row, where successful middle-class New Negro artists and writers such as Paul Robeson, Countee Cullen, Clarence Cameron White, W. C. Handy, and Fletcher Henderson lived in the classy Paul Dunbar Apartments which stood at 7th Avenue and 150th Street (Redd 1981). James Weldon Johnson lived at 185 West 135th Street, and Fats Waller lived next door (Smith 1975, 132). Then there was The Valley, which contained the black working classes and "sporting types" (Lewis 1981; Redd 1981).

This separateness also prevailed socially. For the intellectuals, for example, there was "The Dark Tower," the third floor of A'lelia Walker's city home, where literary personages and aspirants gathered each evening for relaxation, intellectual discourse, and strategy discussions relating to progress, publication, and promotion of Renaissance philosophy. Contrasting with The Dark Tower was the social world of the Rhythm Club, where jazz musicians and entertainers gathered and where after-hours jam sessions took place nightly.

> The Rhythm Club was a hanging-out place for musicians around 1924 and 1925. They served food for reasonable prices and jazz men could come in any time and play whatever they wanted without bothering the usual singers or floor shows. It became the place where young musicians would go to learn and be heard. Many jazz figures were at first heard at the Rhythm Club and leaders like Henderson, Ellington, Elmer Snowden, and Charlie Johnson would go there to hire their side-men.
>
> . . . . .
>
> On one visit, you could hear playing, one after the other, The Lion, Luckey Roberts, Fats, James P., and Duke, all working on individual interpretations of some popular tune of the day, like "Tea for Two" (Smith 1975, 159–60).

These two social worlds—those of The Dark Tower and the Rhythm Club—contrasted sharply, but they both provided means that would ensure the continuing elaboration of Afro-American music: opportunity for discussion and exchange of ideas about those aesthetic principles on which the music was based. These worlds came together at the Savoy Ballroom, where Fletcher Henderson's band often played. The Savoy was frequented by those of both social worlds, for it "belonged to two different cultural universes [which were] also two versions of the same phenomenon—the upsurge of Afro-American self-confidence and creativity" (Lewis 1981, 169). And it was at the Savoy and other places like it that the ideals of both worlds had opportunity to meet and interact. For example, Harlem society was organized around the fraternities and sororities that held "high class dances" at the Renaissance Casino and other locations. Here, too, the two groups came together to form, in Redd's words, "very polite associations." While dance music prevailed at these affairs, it was at a Kappa Alpha Psi dance in 1921 that Marian Anderson was first heard in New York. At the intermission, she gave her first performance there before a large number of people (Redd 1981).

An entirely different social world was that of the house-rent party. Also known by the terms "rent party," "parlor social," "Saturday night function," and other appropriately descriptive names, these events were held and frequented primarily by residents of The Valley (Kirkeby 1966, 39). Organized for the purpose of raising money for the exorbitant rents that Valley residents were charged, these funky, down-home affairs "began after midnight, howling and stomping sometimes well into dawn in a miasma of smoke, booze, collard greens and hot music" (Lewis 1981, 107). As far as creativity is concerned, such affairs served as the proving ground for the pianists. Dominating this creative world were James P. Johnson, Willie "The Lion" Smith, Thomas "Fats" Waller, Luckey Roberts, and Duke Ellington. It was in this world that these and other musicians honed their artistic tools and worked out their ideas for presentation in the world of show business.

So, while the social worlds were sharply divided, there was interaction among them. And the cabarets were frequented by all. Harlem's cabaret society was culturally productive in that it provided the environment in which the dances of the period were invented. It was at the Savoy, for example, that "the lindy, black bottom, shimmy, truckin', snake hips, [and] suzy Q" were all created and developed (Southern 1983, 434). In addition to the Savoy there were Happy Rhone's, Pod's & Jerry's, Basement Brownies, Leroy's, Banks', Barron's, Edmond's, The Bucket of Blood, Haynie's Oriental, Smalls' Paradise, the Renaissance Casino, and the Rockland Palace, among others. Performing at these clubs were the better bands and pianists of the period—the Ellington and Henderson bands, along with others, the keyboard men mentioned above, and their lesser counterparts. Lewis is correct when he writes that by the mid-twenties, Harlem's "clubs were . . . rapidly becoming laboratories of a new type of jazz, attracting even the great jazz masters of New Orleans and Chicago as well as hordes of excited, uninstructed whites" (Lewis 1981, 156).

CULTURE AND RACE

The social interaction between black and white musicians was intense and took place on all social levels. George Gershwin frequented the Harlem rent parties, especially those at which The Pianists performed. He later invited these pianists to downtown soirees, including a party celebrating the first performance of his *Rhapsody in Blue*. The Pianists readily attended Gershwin's parties and, through them, secured gigs for themselves on the downtown circuit (Vance 1977, 40–41). For one of Gershwin's birthday parties, Paul Whiteman hired Waller and Smith to provide the music. For white musicians, including Gershwin, the process of learning black music was osmotic. A contemporary observer reports that

> by 1920 [Fats Waller] had met, and knew well, some of the leading lights of Tin Pan Alley. Irving Berlin, Paul Whiteman, and George Gershwin—especially the last—were uptown incessantly, making the rounds and drinking in all there was to be seen and heard. Gershwin wrote down the jazz forms that came at him from the horns, drums and pianos, penetrating even the lowest of the low-down clubs. He invaded the rent parties and socials and was often to be seen sitting on the floor, agape at the dazzling virtuosity and limitless improvisation that clamored around him (Kirkeby 1966, 53).

It was in this and related ways that the continuity of Afro-American music spread to middle- and upper-class white musical culture and began to become a part of the American musical tradition (although many of those who would enjoy the resulting fruits would not know from whence they sprang). In this connection, it is well known among black-music scholars that "Summertime," from Gershwin's opera *Porgy and Bess*, is an adaptation of the Afro-American spiritual "Sometimes I Feel Like a Motherless Child," and that his melody "I Got Rhythm," used in the beginning measures of the scherzo of William Grant Still's *Afro-American Symphony*, was a long-time signature motive for William Grant Still in his improvisations and his compositions.

We get a sense of the downtown social scene when we read W. C. Handy telling of "that evening when I dined at the home of a friend in the company of Gershwin, Cadman and Whiteman, and . . . how we discussed the great potentialities and possibilities of American music" (Handy 1941, 298). And a typical evening at the home of a Renaissance leader or one of the movement's patrons would see rubbing shoulders such diverse personalities as Roland Hayes, Carl Van Vechten, George Gershwin, Heywood Hale Broun, John Dewey, Sinclair Lewis, and a host of other such celebrities and intellectuals.

Such relationships were far-reaching. In 1927 Dorothy and Dubose Heywood's *Porgy* was produced, and the Jenkins' Orphanage Band had a role, appearing in the third and fourth scenes of the New York production. Apparently, they were with the show for the duration, with their music helping, again, to ensure the continuing elaboration of black musical performance practices. In 1928 Paul Robeson joined the cast as

Crown. This racial and musical accommodation among musicians also prevailed in cabaret circles. Harlem nightclubs were frequented by white musicians who would later become famous in the swing era—Benny Goodman, Artie Shaw, and a host of others. At the Hollywood Club, Duke Ellington relates, "Paul Whiteman came often" (Ellington 1973, 71). Aaron Copland, Darius Milhaud, and other composers of classical works also found their way to Harlem's cabarets, and just as modernists in painting—Picasso, Matisse, Brancusi, and others—had used black art as a basis for composition, the process was duplicated in music to some extent by Copland, Stravinsky, Virgil Thompson, and others. The spread and the impact of black music increased, its devices and practices becoming more effectively integrated into American and European music but at the same time becoming less recognizable *as black* by the general public. The impact was aesthetically vital, however.

At bottom, nearly all the black/white relationships were in some degree exploitative, no matter how genuine. The exploitation was not only artistic and economic but also psychological, for the suspicion prevailed that these friends and patrons of the New Negro valued "Negro-ness, not talent. Nor was the Negro artist assumed to be the final judge of quality and appropriateness" where his own work was concerned (Huggins 1971, 129). The resulting quality was mixed. As it happened, Paul Whiteman became the "King of Jazz" and Benny Goodman the "King of Swing," both by way of Fletcher Henderson, and Gershwin became "the first jazz composer," in spite of Duke Ellington. The borrowings and verisimilitude were great, and had it not been for those well-known intangibles of Afro-American musical performance practices, who knows what might have happened.

SUMMARY

The Talented-Tenth expectation that the Renaissance would spawn a genius to transform black folk genres into high art was never realized on a broad scale. Although there were a few more or less successful efforts, the expectation was unrealistic for several reasons. For example, the tremendous freedom to create during the Renaissance years apparently siphoned off some of the best minds and deprived the musicians of the kind of discipline and preparation necessary for written composition in extended forms. It also happened that the Renaissance ended before composers could fully develop their skills. But jazz did create a climate for and make contributions to the movement by making possible the production of works consistent with the Renaissance credo. It provided a nationalistic context in which black artists could "join together to discover, reflect upon, and experiment with their roots and heritage through the arts" (Blum 1974, 75).

Jazz had "an epochal significance—it [was] not superficial, it [was] fundamental" (Locke [1936] 1968a, 95), Locke was to say, and it was to play the decisive role in launching "The Afro-American Epoch" in music history, that period so dubbed by Henry Pleasants (1969, 90) and which, he suggests, started in the 1940s, but which actually, I would suggest, began even earlier. During the Renaissance period, jazz and European music had considerable influence on one another, but the direction of influence was mostly from the former to the latter. Jazz had its own aesthetic standards, and the jazzmen were unconcerned about meeting those of classical music.

What bound all Renaissance music together was generic black folk music both in its uses and its possibilities—black folk music as stimulus, a basis for, and a result of the nationalistic and self-discovery efforts of the New Negro. It was all based on the prevailing black aesthetic, unexplicated but extremely evident, that bound in social interaction diverse musicians and diverse life-styles. Dvořák perceived the aesthetic (he did not invent it), being aware of it as early as the 1890s, when he composed his *New World Symphony*. As we have seen, black composers were to produce works in this aesthetic through the middle to late stages of the Renaissance period. And the aesthetic was as universal as it was specific. Du Bois would say that music is the expression of a soul that "loves and hates . . . toils and tries . . . laughs and weeps" (Du Bois [1903] 1979, 144). Surely he would have recognized that the struggle-fulfillment idea was at the heart of Afro-American art. Since such dualities got their most extensive and eloquent treatment in the writings of philosopher John Dewey, Du Bois surely had discussions with Dewey about these very ideas since they socialized together and were both on the board of directors of the NAACP.

Nineteen twenty-five was the peak year for the Harlem Renaissance. A study of *The New York Times Index* reveals a slow start in 1921 with two Renaissance-related items in music, while there appeared at least eighteen such items in 1925. The years 1926, 1927, and 1928 are almost equally good years; 1929 and 1930 reflect a significant decline in activity. The end of the Renaissance is usually set at 1929 or 1930, or with the onset of the Great Depression. Southern (1983, 396–456) apparently carries it through the 1930s or later. De Lerma (1981, 11) suggests that it never ended. But my reading of the evidence suggests that by 1932 it was clear that the end of the Renaissance as a *social* phenomenon was near. The crash of Wall Street had negatively affected every aspect of American life, and black musicians had begun to travel to Europe to meet the demand there for entertainment, especially in Paris and Berlin (Lewis 1981, 24). As early as 1924, the migration had started as a trickle. De Lerma reminds us that:

France was becoming more familiar with Afro-American music, thanks to Sousa, Will Marion Cook, Jim Europe, and others, while the entertainment scene obligates notice of Ada "Bricktop" Smith Du Conge, who began to appear in Montmartre in 1924, and of Josephine Baker, who made her 1925 entrance at the Théâtre des Champs Elysées dressed in feathers. It was in the same neighborhood in 1928 that Noble Sissle attracted the ardent attention of Jascha Heifitz, Béatrice Lilli, Tallulah Bankhead, Lord and Lady Louis Montbatten, Lee Schubert, Polga Negri, Cole Porter, Elsa Maxwell, and the Baroness de Rothschild. Edmund Jenkins's *Charlestonia*, an orchestral rhapsody had been heard four years earlier in Paris and Brussels (de Lerma 1981, 10).

In addition, the end of prohibition was to bring radical changes in cabaret society and, consequently, in the economic structure in Harlem. Furthermore, the end could be seen, according to Lewis, in a more "rigidly-divided racist society" and in "butchers' rotten meat and gouging landlords, . . . economic exploitation by absentee whites, and . . . moral decay fostered by those who 'do their dirt in Harlem'" (Lewis 1981, 23). Apparently, it was the resulting 1935 riot in Harlem that sealed the fate of Harlem's nightlife. The refusal of white merchants to hire black Harlemites, while profiting from their purchases, brought about conditions that were inimical to the "good times." A contemporary observer tells us that "the 1935 riot had left only a trickle of the money which poured into Harlem during the 1920s" (Malcom X, quoted in Haley 1966, 114). In addition, with the arrival of the talking pictures in 1927, audiences were drawn from the theaters into the movie houses, lessening the need for musicians in the numbers in which they had previously been in demand. It is evident that these conditions ended the socio-musical aspects of the Harlem Renaissance, although the movement's legacy was to continue as new struggles and new fulfillments emerged and as new modes of expression were created.

NOTES

1. Some readers may view this formulation as a deliberate but poor analogy to the French composers known as *Les Six* and may even question Lewis's inclusion of Holstein and omission of individuals such as W. C. Handy or James Schuyler. But Lewis's formulation is useful, and it does serve its purpose.

2. While a student at Columbia University, George Redd lived in the Still's home.

3. See, for example, Huggins (1971) and Lewis (1981). Southern has chronicled the movement's musical activity quite thoroughly. My purpose, however, is to explain the philosophy and intellectual content of

that activity and to further delineate the role of black music in the movement.

4. For further discussion also see Southern (1983) pages 266–80 and 415–27.

5. Although Locke's statement was published in 1936, there is no evidence to indicate that his thinking was any different in the 1920s.

6. I have not been able to determine dates for the first two concerts of that season; nor have I located information about previous seasons.

REFERENCES

Abdul, Raoul. 1977. *Blacks in classical music: A personal history.* New York: Dodd, Mead.

Anderson, Jarvis. 1981. That was New York: Harlem, III—what a city. *The New Yorker,* July 13:38–79.

Blum, Martin. 1974. Black music: Pathmaker of the Harlem Renaissance. *Missouri Journal of Research in Music Education* 3, no. 3:72–79.

Bone, Robert A. 1968. The background of the Negro Renaissance. In *Black history: A reappraisal,* Melvin Drimmer, ed., 408–21. Garden City, N.Y.: Doubleday & Company.

Bordman, Gerald. 1968. *American musical theater.* New York: Oxford University Press.

Collier, James Lincoln. 1978. *The making of jazz: A comprehensive history.* Boston: Houghton Mifflin.

Crawford, Lucile H. 1940. The musical activities of James Weldon Johnson. Master's thesis, Fisk University, Nashville, Tenn.

De Lerma, Dominique-René. 1981. Music and the Harlem Renaissance. Unpublished manuscript.

Du Bois, W. E. Burghardt. [1903] 1979. *The souls of black folk: Essays and sketches.* Nashville, Tenn.: Fisk University Press.

Ellington, Edward Kennedy. 1973. *Music is my mistress.* Garden City, N.Y.: Doubleday.

Haas, Robert Bartlett, ed. 1975. *William Grant Still and the fusion of cultures in American music.* Los Angeles: Black Sparrow Press.

Haley, Alex. 1966. *The autobiography of Malcom X.* New York: Grove Press.

Handy, W. C. 1941. *Father of the blues: An autobiography of W. C. Handy.* New York: Macmillan.

Hare, Maude Cuney. [1936] 1974. *Negro musicians and their music.* New York: Da Capo Press.

Huggins, Nathan Irvin. 1971. *Harlem Renaissance.* New York: Oxford University Press.

————. 1976. Interview with Eubie Blake. In *Voices from the Harlem Renaissance,* Nathan Irvin Huggins, ed., 336–40. New York: Oxford University Press.

Isaacs, Edith. 1947. *The Negro in the American theater.* New York: Theatre Arts.

Johnson, James Weldon, and J. Rosamond Johnson. 1925. *The book of American Negro spirituals.* New York: Viking Press.

————. 1926. *The second book of Negro spirituals.* New York: Viking Press.

Kirkeby, Ed. 1966. *Ain't misbehavin'.* New York: Dodd, Mead.

Lewis, David Levering. 1981. *When Harlem was in vogue.* New York: Alfred A. Knopf.

Locke, Alain. [1936] 1968a. *The Negro and his music.* Kennikat Press Series in Negro Culture and History. Port Washington, N.Y.: Kennikat Press.

————. [1925] 1968b. *The New Negro.* New York: Atheneum.

Nelson, Sheldon Lee. 1973. The Harlem Renaissance, 1920–1932. Master's Thesis, Eastern Michigan University.

Pleasants, Henry. 1969. *Serious music and all that jazz.* New York: Simon and Schuster.

Printed program. 1925. Third symphony concert of the Harlem Symphony Orchestra. December 27. Photocopy held by the Center for Black Music Research, Columbia College Chicago.

Redd, George Nathaniel. 1981. The Harlem Renaissance remembered. Interview with Betty Leonard. Audio tape, Fisk University, January 8.

Schlosser, Anatol I. 1965. Paul Robeson's mission in music. In *Paul Robeson: The great fore-runner*, edited by The Editors of *Freedomways*, 87–93. New York: Dodd, Mead.

Smith, Willie "The Lion." 1975. *Music on my mind: The memoirs of an American pianist*. New York: Da Capo Press.

Southern, Eileen. 1971. *The music of black Americans: A history*. 1st ed. New York: W. W. Norton.

——. 1983. *The music of black Americans: A history*. 2d ed. New York: W. W. Norton.

Vance, Joel. 1977. *Fats Waller: His life and times*. Chicago: Contemporary Books.

CHAPTER 2

Vindication as a Thematic Principle in the Writings of Alain Locke on the Music of Black Americans

Paul Burgett

The concept of vindication is a persistent theme in Locke's writings about the music of black Americans, and an examination of this theme is instructive of certain early thinking on the issue of a black aesthetic.

An initial observation in this matter holds that the Negro intelligentsia, from the Civil War through the Negro Renaissance, according to Crane (1971, 28) were essentially elitist in relation to the black population. Those comprising the Negro Renaissance, by virtue of their education and cosmopolitanism—many spent time abroad and their interactions at home were expanded to include a wide-ranging interracial spectrum of people—made up a new class of persons who did not have, to use Nathan Huggins's words, "a grass roots attachment." This elitism remained an intact principle despite certain philosophical differences among disparate perspectives—for example, Du Bois's devotion to a referential or propaganda theory of art vis-à-vis Locke's espousal of a more absolutist perspective, i.e., art for art's sake.

Despite such differences, there clearly was a tendency among the Negro intelligentsia that sought the cultural transformation of black folk culture into a formal or high culture—an art of greater value. Huggins (1971, 5) points out that most "aspired to *high* culture as opposed to that of the common man, which they hoped to mine for novels, poems, plays, and symphonies."

Huggins observes further, by way of example, that, except for poet Langston Hughes, none of the Harlem intellectuals took jazz seriously. While people like James Weldon Johnson and Alain Locke respected jazz as an example of folk music, their greatest expectations lay in its transformation into serious music of high culture by some race genius in the tradition of a Dvorák or a Smetana.

The theme of vindication in Locke's thinking can perhaps best be seen and understood by looking briefly at black musical history as he saw it and by analyzing the philosophical perspective that emerges from that framework.

The framework, developed by Locke, and reported, essentially, in his book *The Negro and His Music* ([1936] 1969), is embodied in three categories of music, all derived from folk origin, which embrace both sacred and secular types.

The first category is folk music. Produced without formal musical training or intention, Negro folk music is a product of emotional creation. This type, according to Locke, "has produced the most characteristic Negro musical idiom,—sad but not somber, intense but buoyant, tragic but ecstatic . . . a unique and paradoxical combination of emotional elements." The second type is that derived from original folk music. It is, however, diluted; a form "imitatively exploited by both white and Negro musicians, it has become the principal source and ingredient of American popular music" (Locke [1936] 1969, 8).

The third type, according to Locke ([1936] 1969, 9), is a strictly formal or classical type of music, which can be "properly styled Negro music only when obviously derived from folk music idioms or strongly influenced by them."

Incidental to these three categories is another type of music composed by blacks which Locke mentions only in passing. It is what he calls music in the universal mode without trace of folk idiom or influence. It is, to use Locke's words, "in the general mainstream of cosmopolitan or classical music." According to Locke ([1936] 1969, 9), music of this sort, composed by Negro musicians, in no sense can be called "Negro music."

It is the original folk music of the Negro, the spirituals and the secular songs that Locke uses as a base in organizing his views of Negro musical development. Several observations about his views of Negro folk music deserve further elaboration here.

First of all, despite Locke's insistence about the great worth of this music, one senses in his writing that their degree of worth is directly related to the value the music has as potential for some "higher" development. In other words, folk music is valuable at a specific level. Its value, however, increases when elements of this music can be used to influence the music of some higher level.

For example, Locke makes the statement that the spirituals received the "highest possible recognition" when they were used as thematic material for symphonic music in Dvorák's symphony *From The New World*.

Specifically, he points to the theme of the slow movement as expressing the true atmosphere of a Negro spiritual, and he says of the Scherzo movement that it was "nose close to jazz, for Dvořák took his rhythms and tone intervals from the shout type of Negro dance" (Locke [1936] 1969, 106). Locke asserts that Dvořák chose spirituals to represent the atmosphere of America. Because of this symphony, Locke goes on to say ([1936] 1969, 20–21):

> the spirituals and even the secular Negro folk melodies and their harmonic style have been regarded by most musicians as the purest and most valuable musical ore in America; the raw materials of a native American music. So gradually ever since, their folk quality and purity of style have been emphasized by real musicians.

It is important to pursue this particular example because the findings establish important implications for Locke's theories about black music.

Despite claims by Locke and others that Negro folk tunes as well as American Indian tunes were used in Dvořák's symphony to represent American atmosphere, Dvořák himself indicated that this was untrue. In a letter to a friend he states:

> I send you Kretzschmar's analysis of the symphony but omit that nonsense about my having made use of "Indian" and "Negro" themes—that is a lie. I tried to write in the spirit of those folk melodies ("Jacket notes" n.d.).

Furthermore, and again by Dvořák's own admission, any suggestion of the Negro spiritual idiom in the symphony is actually original material created by the composer (Clapham 1966, 87).

There is no doubt that Dvořák heard and was influenced by spirituals. Harry T. Burleigh, a black singer and student at the National Conservatory of Music in New York at the time Dvořák was its director, was known to have sung spirituals for Dvořák on several occasions (Clapham 1966, 87). A curious and somewhat ironic aside concerning Burleigh is Locke's condemnation of Negro composers' abuse of the spirituals by affecting their settings with too much influence from formal European idioms and mannerisms. He cites Burleigh as one composer responsible for such abuses (Locke [1936] 1969, 23).

At this point, a look at specific parts of the symphony involving questions of Dvořák's use of spirituals will be helpful. In the first movement, the second theme, in G major, is played by solo flute (see example 2.1). The first four measures of this theme have been likened to the spiritual melody, "Swing Low, Sweet Chariot." Actually, the shape of Dvořák's melody would encompass roughly only the words of the spiritual, ". . . chariot, coming for to carry me home." The first phrase of the spiritual

Example 2.1. *"New World" Symphony*, Antonín Dvořák, first movement, second theme

melody is shown in example 2.2 (Work [1915] 1969, 21). The asterisks identify the melodic intervals that appear in the Dvořák symphony.

Example 2.2. "Swing Low, Sweet Chariot," Negro spiritual

Swing low,   sweet char - i - ot.   Com - ing for to car - ry me   home.

The English horn melody of the Largo movement is another salient example (see example 2.3). Several sources suggest that this melody was inspired by Dvořák's interest in Longfellow's "Song of Hiawatha" and that the Largo theme describes the burial of Minnehaha in the forest. Clapham and Evans cite the Longfellow inspiration; but both concede, however, that the melody has an unmistakable Negro flavor about it (Clapham 1966, 88; Evans 1970, 87). Clapham goes on to suggest, on the basis of clearly speculative evidence, that the reason Dvořák may have chosen the English horn as solo instrument was because it resembled the quality of Burleigh's singing (Clapham 1966, 90).

Example 2.3 *"New World" Symphony*, Antonín Dvořák, second movement, first theme

This writer could find no evidence either in other sources or from his own examination of the music to support Locke's thesis that the Scherzo movement is "nose close to jazz" in its rhythms. In fact, Edwin Evans observes (1970, 87):

> We may dismiss the suggestions that the Scherzo is an Indian dance asso-
> ciated with Hiawatha, or that its rhythmic insistence has Negro affinities
> for neither has much relation to its true character, which is, as fundamen-
> tally Slavonic as that of most of Dvořák's Scherzi.

These are probably the most obvious examples involving the issue of Dvořák's use of Negro folk music materials. Despite the fact that the composer used no specifically Negro melodies, his own or the original, there can be no doubt that the Negro folk idiom, at times, permeates the symphony very subtly.

In view of the facts, it seems to this writer that to subscribe to Locke's suggestions of the presence, in part, of the spiritual "Swing Low, Sweet

Chariot" or of inspiring Negro influence in the English horn melody of the second movement or to insist on the presence of jazz rhythms in the Scherzo is to unduly belabor what are, at best, tenuous theories.

Disapproval of the theories of Locke and others in this instance is, however, not the central issue. Had Dvořák literally employed Negro spirituals in the symphony, the issue would be no less obscured. The real issue seems to involve an attitude about Negro music. In this instance, that attitude is reflected in Locke's attempts to vindicate the value of Negro folk music, especially the spirituals, by pointing out their use in a musical form not endemic to the spiritual's culture of origin but, rather, a highly valued form of western European culture, i.e., the symphony, composed by a renowned and respected individual.

There are two other points to be made relative to Locke's ideas about Negro folk music. One senses that the Negro spirituals hold a position of superior value over the secular music. Locke ([1936] 1969, 18) describes the former as

> the most characteristic product of Negro genius to date. The spirituals are its great folk-gift, and rate among the classic folk expressions in the whole world because of their moving simplicity, their characteristic originality, and their universal appeal.

Locke ([1936] 1969, 28) does assign the secular folk songs to the status of folk classics but he refers to them as being "second . . . to the spirituals."

The second point relates to the musicians mentioned in Locke's discussion of the Dvořák symphony. He asserts that "most musicians" regard Negro folk music as the purest and most valuable musical ore in America. Further, he maintains that the folk quality and purity of style of Negro folk music have been emphasized since the twentieth century by "real musicians." The musicians of whom he speaks are clearly not those engaged in the creation of folk music.

The second category of Negro music that Locke treats is that derived from original folk music. He calls it a diluted form, "the petty dialect," as opposed to the great dialect of the spirituals. It is this second type of Negro music that served as the principal ingredient of American popular music including minstrelsy, ragtime, and jazz (Locke [1936] 1969, 9). For Locke, this type of Negro music spanned a significant period of history—from about 1850 to 1936, the year *The Negro and His Music* was published.

It is in his treatment of jazz, especially, that one obtains a clearer picture of the vindication theme in Locke's treatment of the music of this second category. Locke asserts that jazz eventually took up more or less permanent residence in two places. "Chicago became the reservoir of the rowdy, hectic, swaggering style of jazz that has since become known as 'hot jazz.'" (Locke devotes relatively little attention in his writings to the "hot jazz" of Chicago.) "New York (and Paris and London)," on the other hand, "has furnished the mixing bowls for the cosmopolitan style of jazz notable for stressing melody and flowing harmony known as 'sweet jazz.'" Locke clearly places much greater emphasis on this style ([1936] 1969, 84).

Of the early New York school of jazz (1905–1915), Locke singles out four Negro musicians for special consideration. The four—Ford Dabney, James Reese Europe, Will Marion Cook, and W. C. Handy—are called "arrangers of genius" by Locke ([1936] 1969, 66) because they

> organized Negro music out of a broken, musically illiterate dialect and made it a national music with its own peculiar idioms of harmony, instrumentation, and technical style of playing.

As Locke saw it, the chief common contribution of these men was the "vindication" of Negro music. These four men were the "ambassadors who carried jazz to Europe and the haughty citadels of serious music." Since New York jazz was more polished and sophisticated whereas its Chicago counterpart was rougher and more crude, Locke felt that it was more appropriate and fortunate that the New Yorkers' "smoother, more mellow jazz was the first to become world famous and to have international influence" ([1936] 1969, 85). Further contributions of these men included the "vindication" of Negro music as the preferred dance vogue on the American stage ([1936] 1969, 66–67).

The activities of the early New York jazz people culminated in an event of significant historical proportions. In May of 1912 a jazz orchestra of 125 Negro musicians performed at Carnegie Hall under the direction of James Reese Europe. Locke's comments about this event are worth reporting.

> The formal coming-out party was at Carnegie Hall, the audience, the musical elite of New York, the atmosphere and the comparison challenged that of any concert of "Classical music," and the compositions conducted by their own composers or arrangers. . . . That night the Cinderella of Negro folk music found royal favor and recognition and under the wand of Negro musicians put off her kitchen rags. At that time ragtime grew up to full musical rank and the golden age of jazz really began ([1936] 1969, 68).

Locke's perspective on the role of white jazz performers is especially important here. In his view, the musical techniques of early jazz, rooted as they were in a distinctive Negro style that was characterized by a unique racial intensity of mood and a peculiar style of technical performance, were capable of being imitated, making jazz the property of a universal audience. To quote Locke ([1936] 1969, 82):

> White performers and arrangers and conductors had learned the new tricks and were feverishly and successfully competing in carrying jazz style to a rapid perfection.
>
> • • • • •
>
> The white musicians studied jazz, and from a handicap of first feeble imitation and patient hours in Negro cabarets listening to the originators finally became masters of jazz, not only rivaling their Negro competitors musically but rising more and more to commercial dominance of the new industry.

Locke ([1936] 1969, 72) observes finally that although jazz is basically Negro, "fortunately, it is also human enough to be universal in appeal and expressiveness." Such an extraordinary statement and those that precede it establish Locke's democratic views regarding aesthetic experience: that in the matter of Negro musical materials, he allowed for no distinctions in perception based on race.

The third of Locke's three categories of Negro music is what he calls strictly formal or classical type. This category actually includes three types: "jazz classics," "classical jazz," and "modern American music." The first two types are what Locke calls "worthwhile jazz as distinguished from the trashy variety" ([1936] 1969, 96). The latter refers primarily to the commercial efforts of Tin Pan Alley.

A "jazz classic" is a work that,

> rising from the level of ordinary popular music, usually in the limited dance and song-ballad forms, achieves creative musical excellence (Locke [1936] 1969, 96).

The "jazz classics" were products of the jazz orchestras that were emerging in the late 1920s. Locke admits as principal figures in the creation of these classics such big-time Negro figures as Fletcher Henderson, Earl Hines, Luis Russell, Claude Hopkins, "Fats" Waller, Cab Calloway, Louis Armstrong, Don Redman, Jimmie Lunceford, and, of course, Duke Ellington. White bands singled out for recognition include those of Jean Goldkette, Paul Whiteman, Ben Pollack, Red Nichols, Ted Lewis, The Casa Loma Orchestra, Jimmy Dorsey, and Benny Goodman ([1936] 1969, 98).

Locke saw one of the major efforts, indeed responsibilities, of these musicians as the exploitation of Negro folk materials. In the hands of these skilled musicians, jazz was to be "harnessed and seriously guided . . . to new conquests" ([1936] 1969, 97). It was the Negro musician, especially, who had the greater responsibility. Jazz, says Locke ([1936]

1969, 101), is the spirit child of the Negro musician and its artistic vindication rests in its sound development by these musicians.

It was Duke Ellington whom Locke viewed with greatest critical admiration. Of Ellington, Locke says ([1936] 1969, 99):

> In addition to being one of the great exponents of pure jazz, Duke Ellington is the pioneer of super-jazz and one of the persons most likely to create the classical jazz toward which so many are striving. He plans a symphonic suite and an African opera, both of which will prove a test of his ability to carry native jazz through to this higher level.

Locke saw the work of Ellington as especially important to the placing of intuitive music under control, as restraining and refining crude materials. In Locke's words ([1936] 1969, 100), "Someone had to devise a technique for harnessing this shooting geyser, taming this wild well."

In making his break between "jazz classics" and the "trashy variety" of popular music, Locke had decisively steered Negro music out of the progressive stages of a maturing folk music onto the early plane of what he would call "art" music, the universal and timeless quintessence of the composer's creative efforts.

"Classical jazz," the second type of Locke's third category, is music

> which successfully transposes the elements of folk music, in this case jazz idioms, to the more sophisticated and traditional musical forms ([1936] 1969, 96).

"Classical jazz" and "modern American music" are related types, if not the same thing. They represent yet a further development upward of Negro music. The most obvious medium for the development of classical jazz was what Locke refers to as symphonic jazz—a form derived from but ultimately divorced from dance jazz and popular song ballads ([1936] 1969, 112).

It is not altogether easy to understand clearly just what symphonic or classical jazz is. By his own admission, Locke calls it ([1936] 1969, 112) "a somewhat unstable and anaemic hybrid." It does seem to be inclusive of all sorts of symphonic music. The works Locke discusses include Gershwin's *Rhapsody in Blue* and *Porgy and Bess*, William Grant Still's *Afro-American Symphony*, Edmund Jenkins's *Charlestonia: A Negro Rhapsody for Full Orchestra*, and William Dawson's *Negro Folk Symphony* ([1936] 1969, 110–12). Locke saw the work of these composers as pioneering efforts in elevating jazz to the level of the classics.

There is a curious comment that Locke makes regarding such cultural elevation in the work of the black composer Florence E. Price. Concerning her *Symphony in E Minor* and her *Piano Concerto,* Locke says ([1936] 1969, 115):

> In the straight classical idiom and form, Mrs. Price's work vindicates the Negro composer's right, at choice, to go up Parnassus by the broad high road of classicism rather than the narrower, more hazardous, but often more rewarding path of racialism. At the pinnacle, the paths converge, and the attainment becomes, in the last analysis neither racial nor national, but universal music.

Locke does not offer many clues about what he means, but he concludes his discussion of black music with some observations about its ultimate achievement.

He suggests first that "Negro idioms will never become great music nor representative national music over the least common denominators of popular jazz or popular ballads that are in common circulation today." Locke goes on to say that "neither America nor the Negro can rest content as long as it can be said: 'Jazz is America's outstanding contribution, so far, to world music'" ([1936] 1969, 130).

He speculates that "classical jazz" may indeed itself be no more than a transitional stage of American musical development. "Eventually," says Locke, "the art music and the folk-music must be fused in a vital but superior product" ([1936] 1969, 130). Locke was not specific about what this superior product would be because he himself did not know. He did point to appropriate prototypes elsewhere in the world that have successfully blended the folk with the formal.

Locke cites Russian, Hungarian, and Bohemian composers who were confronted with this problem and who

> widened the localisms of their native music to a universal speech; they were careful, in breaking the dialect, to reflect the characteristic folk spirit and preserve its unique flavor. What Glinka and his successors did for Russian music, Liszt and Brahms for Hungarian music, and Dvořák and Smetana for Czech music, can and must be done for Negro music (quoted in Butcher 1972, 91).

Because of his desire for cultural reciprocity, it is clear that Locke sought to fashion an aesthetic alliance between European culture and American Negro culture. Central to this alliance was the vindication of Negro musical materials. Essential to vindication was the use of these materials as inspiration in European musical monuments such as the symphony, opera, and ballet.

It is difficult to understand fully what Locke's real motivation was in urging these efforts at vindication. On the one hand, his language suggests a psychological undercurrent of cultural inferiority about Negro music. His statement, "Fortunately, [jazz] is also human enough to be universal in appeal and expressiveness," raises serious questions about how Locke really felt about the value of jazz. His observations about the use of Negro materials in the Dvořák E-minor symphony reveal a pitiable straining for respectability. Locke's reliance on white arbiters of taste is revealing when he cites the following critics of "jazz of the better sort" as names "certainly authoritative enough": Kreisler, Rachmaninoff, Koussevitsky, and Stokowski. Other white critics of jazz whom Locke cites as among the most authoritative include Henri Prunières and Robert Goffin of Paris, Constant Lambert of England, and Hugues Panassié, author of *Le Jazz Hot*.

Locke's aesthetic perspective, to some extent, was affected by a vindication syndrome which, in fact, was dissimilar from the efforts of late nineteenth-century western European Nationalist composers with whom he invites comparison. The disturbing thread of cultural inadequacy implied in Locke's language about the music suggests the inexorable pull on him of western monism which, despite its uncompromisingly racist posture, simply may have been too irresistible in the end.

An alternative interpretation, however, treats the issue of vindication from another perspective. Perhaps Locke was absolutely convinced of the efficacy of its integration, on an equal basis, within the white cultural mainstream. However, Negro music, as well as Negro culture generally, was viewed by the white and much of middle-class black American culture as inferior. Considering the strong anti-Negro sentiment that prevailed within the American mainstream about black folk music materials, the use of these materials or even the suggestion of their use, for example, by so eminent a composer as Dvořák, must have seemed to Locke a significant step forward toward the goal of greater recognition and use by "serious" composers, black and white. It may have been that vindication was essential—not in the sense that Negro folk music needed such exploitation to prove its worth but, rather, such use was the only way that the worth of this music ever would be recognized. In other words, Locke's perspective may have been politically motivated. He understood only too well the inexorable tendency of western European cultural hegemony on American culture. He also understood the racist posture of American culture, and as a black American and philosopher, he could not expose himself to the indignities of the dehumanization, the pain and suffering wrought by western monistic thought. In the words of Kallen (1957, 123),

> As a human being with an individuality of his own, [Locke] knew that no commitment or obligation could be laid on him heavier than anybody else's, and that the necessities of vindicating his integrity and realizing his own potentialities in his own way had the first claim and the last.

In the end, then, it would seem that Alain Locke was a victim of conflicting forces. On the one hand there were the powerful influences of his education: twice a Harvard graduate (magna cum laude and Phi Beta Kappa honors, 1907; Ph.D., philosophy, 1918), where, in his own words,

> [he] was exposed to the Golden Age of liberalism and, deeply influenced by Barrett Wendell, Copeland, Briggs, and Baker, shed the Tory restraints for urbanity and humanism, and under the spell of Royce, James, Palmer, and Santayana, gave up puritan provincialism for critical-mindedness and cosmopolitanism (Kunitz and Haycraft 1942, 837).

He was the first black Rhodes scholar to Oxford; was a student of philosophy at the University of Berlin where he studied under Brentano and Meinong, and under Bergson in Paris.

On the other hand, there loomed the exigent harshness of the racial experience in America. This towering intellect would have preferred to embrace a monist or universal perspective. His educational background and training disposed him favorably to its elegant logic and, as Kallen points out, this preference interposed an active reservation to the actuality of the plural and long kept Locke from completely committing himself to the philosophy of cultural pluralism.

From the perspective of the 1980s, there may be a tendency to be confused by this conflict and to criticize the efforts of Locke as naive, myopic, elitist, and bourgeois. One needs, however, to understand Locke's efforts in their proper context. The Negro Renaissance was a phenomenon of another time.

In order to be understood fairly and correctly, Locke must be viewed not from a perspective of the 1980s but from the perspective of his own time. To that end, as Huggins (1971, 6) has so astutely observed, the historical analyst's task, when negotiating the efforts of the men and women of that era, requires "a humanism that will modulate . . . his own ego and self-consciousness enough to perceive theirs."

The thinking of Alain Locke and other members of the Negro Renaissance was, in its day, startlingly new and, considered by many, even radical.

The theme of vindication, whatever criticism it might sustain, was supported by its own special and not uncomplicated logic and was an appropriate response to conditions of the time. In whatever light this thinking may be viewed today, criticism of Locke's efforts needs to be tempered by the humanity of which Huggins writes.

REFERENCES

Butcher, Margaret Just. 1972. *The Negro in American culture*. 2d ed. New York: Alfred A. Knopf.

Clapham, John. 1966. *Antonín Dvořák*. New York: St. Martin's Press.

Crane, Clare Bloodgood. 1971. Alain Locke and the Negro Renaissance. Ph.D. diss., University of California, San Diego.

Dvořák, Antonín. [1903] n.d. *Symphony no. 5 in E minor, op. 95, "New World."* Scarsdale, N.Y.: E. F. Kalmus Orchestra Scores.

Evans, Edwin. 1970. The symphonies and concertos. In *Antonín Dvořák*, Victor Fischl, ed., 71–95. Westport, Conn.: Greenwood Press.

Huggins, Nathan Irvin. 1971. *Harlem Renaissance*. New York: Oxford University Press.

Jacket notes. n.d. Antonín Dvořák. *Symphony no. 9, "From the new world."* Columbia 31809.

Kallen, Horace Meyer. 1957. Alain Locke and cultural pluralism. *The Journal of Philosophy* 54 (February):119–27.

Kunitz, Stanley J., and Howard Haycraft, eds. 1942. *Twentieth century authors*. New York: H. W. Wilson Co.

Locke, Alain. [1936] 1969. *The Negro and his music*. New York: Arno Press and the New York Times.

—————. 1942. Pluralism and intellectual democracy. In *Conference on science, philosophy, and religion, second symposium*, 196–212. New York: The Conference.

Vivas, Eliseo, and Murray Krieger, eds. 1953. *The problems of aesthetics*. New York: Rinehart and Company.

Work, John Wesley, ed. [1915] 1969. *Folk song of the American Negro*. New York: Negro Universities Press.

CHAPTER 3

Vocal Concert Music in the Harlem Renaissance

Rawn Spearman

The cultural flux characterizing the peak years of the Harlem Renaissance (ca. 1926–1930) found both black thinkers and artists compelled to see themselves afresh. Culturally, this black artist, the "New Negro," seeing anew and seen by some as worthy of unprecedented esteem, had begun conceiving of himself in broad, indeed, international terms. Black musicians proved no exception: composers and performers alike turned toward the musical stuff of "high" culture and steeped themselves in European musical traditions.

But the Afro-American spiritual proved an important point of contact between the Afro-American folk tradition and the concert and recital music that was influenced by the philosophies of the Harlem Renaissance. For composers, the results were seen in sophisticated arrangements of spirituals and in newly composed works that incorporated the older tradition into their fabric. For concert singers, while the German Lied, the French mélodie, the Italian aria, and other "art song" equivalents had become standard repertoire on the recital programs of such soloists as Roland Hayes, tenor (1887–1976), and Marian Anderson, contralto (b. 1902), spirituals were presented on their concerts as the equal of the standard European repertoire. Paul Robeson, bass-baritone (1898–1976), proved rather exceptional in that he often sang entire programs of spirituals and folk songs.

That these and many other black artists in the 1920s reveled in "renascent feelings of race pride and group solidarity" (Spear 1968, vi) goes without saying. At times the older generation of black intellectuals, such as W.E.B. Du Bois and James Weldon Johnson, thought the young Renaissance leaders to be a bit too feisty, as the latter refused in many instances to follow or even to imitate the "genteel cultural tradition which held a firm grip on both white and black creative artists" (Spear 1968, ix). The young black artists particularly wanted both to proclaim that a new artistic day was at hand and to search their older, African heritage for solutions to setting artistic standards and finding a personality for the New Negro (Suthern 1952, 3).

The contributing authors to one of the earliest black art quarterlies, *Fire!!* (Wirth 1982, [1]). Indeed, many of these Harlem mavericks, wanting on one hand to shed an old, seemingly burdensome image, often called upon what they thought to be salient features of their past as a means to serve the image of the New Negro.

Wallace Thurman, one of the seven *Fire!!* collaborators, nicknamed the group "The Niggerati."

> The word fit their concept of themselves: clever, cultured, talented, perhaps a bit pretentious, but urbane enough to recognize the fact and to find their own pretense amusing (Wirth 1982, [1]).

Hence *Fire!!* differed from two earlier black publications—*Crisis*, which originated in the NAACP, and *Opportunity*, which originated in the Urban League. *Fire!!* remained independent of sponsoring organizations—wealthy and white—with "larger" political and social objectives.

The contributors to *Fire!!* thus enjoyed considerable freedom of choice in terms of content, style, and voice. And they took advantage of this freedom, however brief. Wirth suggests that theirs was a freedom to

> pursue and achieve the objective which united them in their diversity of intentions, sensibilities and styles: excellence. Excellence for its own sake. And excellence to show that the breadth and depth of talent existed among younger Negro artists to produce a literary magazine of the first rank (Wirth 1982 [2]).

Though short-lived, having published only one issue, the magazine proved itself first-rate, boasting as contributors an imposing group of artists (though none of them were musicians). Writers Thurman, Zora Neal Hurston, and Langston Hughes contributed works, as did artist/illustrator Aaron Douglas and several others.

It is clear, then, that the young black intellectuals or artists, whether a figure like Thurman, Hayes, or Hughes, had much to do with keeping up the momentum of the Harlemites' movement. Wirth goes so far as to say that what was perhaps the movement's primary source of propulsion, Hughes's artistic credo, enjoyed concrete manifestation in *Fire!!* Hughes's statement had appeared in *The Nation* only five months before *Fire!!* itself appeared. Hughes had insisted that

> we younger Negro artists who create now intend to express our individual dark-skinned selves without fear or shame. If white people are pleased we

are glad. If they are not, it doesn't matter. We know we are beautiful. And ugly too. The tom-tom cries and the tom-tom laughs. If colored people are pleased we are glad. If they are not, their displeasure doesn't matter either. We build temples for tomorrow, strong as we know how, and we stand on top of the mountain, free within ourselves (quoted in Wirth 1982).

That these young artists stood at or very near a cultural apex cannot be denied. But whether they stood free within themselves, as Hughes has contended, is dubious at best.

With the New Negro—first- or second-generation—seeking to define and express a black identity within a cultural context circumscribed by white Americans, it comes as no surprise that black artists jointly did not arrive at a consensus about what mode of creative expression would best bespeak the black "essence." Generally speaking, two different intellectual forces seemed at odds during the brief decade in which the New Negro thrived. Comprising the first of these "camps" were the old patron guards—James Weldon Johnson, Charles S. Johnson, W.E.B. Du Bois, and George Schuyler—whose primary aspirations included promoting and converting black folk materials to the level of "high" culture. The new order, the younger black artists—among them Hughes, Thurman, Hurston, Douglas, Countee Cullen, Sterling Brown, and Carl Van Vechten, whose sympathies (though not his skin) were black—tended to abandon genteel traditions in favor of exploring and articulating art forms from their African heritage. This group intended to utilize the fruits of their past and present to produce black art that was fit to hold its own—stereotypical notions of the "black character" and European standards for "high art" aside.

Nugent aptly compares the persona of the younger group with that of "the Beats of the 50's and the flower children of the 60's." He shares with us an anecdote representative of relations between the two groups:

After *Fire!!* appeared, Du Bois asked him "Why don't you write about Negroes?" To which Bruce Nugent responded, "I write about myself, and I am a Negro, aren't I?" (Nugent 1982 [3]).

These were indeed adventurous attitudes at work. In their quest for new, less confining standards for measuring artistic excellence, the younger group seems to have defied principles upheld by the old guard.

The Harlem Renaissance seemed to hold a great deal for black individuals. On the face of it, the Renaissance promised change for the better, respect, and socioeconomic justice for blacks. Yet the movement did much in the way of serving the white community's needs, slaking its enormous thirst for entertainment. Whites, too, longed to go to Harlem where, in the words of Langston Hughes, "the long-headed jazzers play" (Wirth 1982 [1]). In some clubs both communities could enjoy "frenetic dancing, bathtub gin and devil-may-care fun" (Tarrant and Tarrant 1986, 94). The white community enjoyed the best of both black and white worlds to a greater extent than did members of the black community—a topic too lengthy to be treated here. Suffice it to say that for every white dancer with a devil-may-care attitude on the floor of a given club, there was a black musician possessed of a mixed bag of musical traditions on which to draw.

The word "Harlem" meant literally "where the tom-toms beat." As long as black singers and dancers remained entertainers embodying some exotic, seemingly primitive simplicity, white America would give them acceptance. In fact, the white-American consciousness during the Roaring Twenties was such that it would have been hard-pressed to survive without the various forms of exotica that the black artist was expected to provide. American and European whites, hungry for a break from a fast-paced, increasingly industrialized world, overran theaters, cabarets, and honky-tonks. Uptown, meanwhile, the Apollo Theater, Savoy Ballroom, Small's Paradise, the Red Rooster, the Cotton Club, and the Renaissance Ball Room were enjoying unprecedented popularity.

For the most part, black musicians had to sing a song of primitive imagery in order to survive. More often than not, black singers had both to live and sing according to stereotypical frameworks designed for them by white as well as black Americans. A handful of the New Negro artists did, however, resist. During the mid-1920s, theaters like the Frolic, Blasco, Comedy, Imperial, Provincetown Playhouse, Sixty-Third Street, the Guild, and Liberty began producing and supporting a new Negro theater with serious drama. Many new playwrights refused to imitate popular minstrelsy and vaudeville shows, offering instead what appeared to be serious alternatives for many ambitious black singers and actors. Here, several black artists enjoyed performing—among them, Paul Robeson in *Black Boy* (1926), Charlotte Murray and Jules Bledsoe in *Deep River* (1926), Abbie Mitchell and Bledsoe in *In Abraham's Bosom* (1926), and Bledsoe again in *Show Boat* (1928) (Johnson [1930] 1972, 202–12).

With the conclusion of World War I, blacks continued fleeing from the South to the northern ghettos. Harlem had become no less than a giant magnet attracting unfulfilled blacks into a temporary, indeed delusive, promised land. As more than one critic has suggested, Harlem was falling short of the kingdom-come that people had hoped for:

This was a Harlem desperately seeking pleasure as an antidote for the blues. There is no real joy here, only a pathetic grasping for transitory delights (Dickinson 1967, 36–37).

The younger Renaissance leaders' dream of bringing African and Afro-American art forms to the fore was becoming increasingly less tangible. By the late twenties the image of race pride as a potential rallying point for all interested Harlemites had dimmed, and in spite of some artists' striking perseverance and diversification—like that of Jules Bledsoe and Paul Robeson, who worked in both theater and concerts—the power of music as a general humanizing force for the "cultural advancement of the race" (Dannett 1968, 149) had weakened considerably. Those black performers who were renowned by the late twenties tended to be blues and jazz musicians, not the least of whom were W. C. Handy, Duke Ellington, Eubie Blake, Bob Cole, James P. Johnson, Noble Sissle, and Fletcher Henderson.

One folk form, the sorrow song or spiritual, had in the recent past been revived from its relatively simple solo or congregational form. The Fisk Jubilee Singers were largely responsible for its revival and development into dignified choral expression as early as 1871 (Marsh 1880; Pike 1873). Their travels and fund-raising performances across America and Europe helped to erase some of the stigma that had been attached to black folk music. Though the activity of the Fisk Jubilee Singers was by no means unproblematical, the fact of their rather wide exposure enlightened some listening audiences about the significance of the sorrow song as an art form and as an index of its creators' heritage.

Orin Clayton Suthern, II (1952, 22–23), attributes black composers' accomplishments to the spiritual, which he calls the "head waters" for all of the genres of black music to follow: jazz, gospel song, rock and roll, and the blues. Of particular interest to the present study is Suthern's address on black composers whose efforts toward elevating the spiritual into arranged art songs are notable: Clarence Cameron White, William Dawson, R. Nathaniel Dett, William Grant Still, Ulysses Kay, Margaret Bonds, and Harry T. Burleigh are among these.

Burleigh's contributions are especially illustrious. As Suthern suggests (1952, 22–23), he was "a very fine baritone singer who did not aspire to the concert stage, but as a composer and arranger has over 300 songs and spirituals to his credit." Alain Locke, too, gives credit to several black composers he considers responsible for "turning the tide," elevating the spiritual into an arranged art song. Locke claims that

> The credit for turning this tide goes principally to a convinced group of Negro musicians in New York City, all of them with formal conservatory background, but a deep faith in the dignity of Negro Folk Music. Two of them, J. Rosamond Johnson and Will Marion Cook, projected a Negro Conservatory of Music and another, Harry T. Burleigh, was destined to dignify and popularize the spiritual by winning a place for them [sic] in the general repertory of the concert stage (Locke [1936] 1969, 119–20).

This marriage of singer and composer proved highly significant to the basic tenets of the Harlem Renaissance, in which various mergers were taking place with varying degrees of success. Black composers not only had learned to use spirituals as a harmonizing and theoretical basis for developing their compositional skills for choral arrangement, but also had expanded spirituals into a means for composing entirely new art songs. Burleigh himself had afforded the concert singer both opportunities: to sing his arranged spirituals as well as his composed art songs on the concert stage. Other black composers followed his example.

Lawrence Brown and William Lawrence, accompanists for Hayes during his early career, proved themselves excellent composers and arrangers of spirituals. In 1925 Brown joined Paul Robeson for a memorable concert made up completely of Negro music. Here, we find,

> was the beginning of another unique partnership. [One night at a rehearsal] Lawrence Brown came in as the second voice on some refrains (call and response). "It was completely spontaneous," says Brown, "and history was made" (Robinson 1972).

Here, indeed, was history in the making: spirituals, like jazz, had gone from being considered an unacceptable music to being quite widely received as bona fide art songs.

Some Harlem Renaissance leaders with considerable clout chronicled the events and accomplishments of black composers and concert singers. To be sure, for many writers and critics—Du Bois, Johnson, Locke, Hughes, and others—artists such as Burleigh and Hayes represented ideal models of black individuals seemingly at new heights of upward artistic mobility. But it is to the dedication and inspiration of black music critics that we owe particular thanks for having kept record, on both yearly and seasonal bases, of the development and careers of black concert artists during and after the Harlem Renaissance. Two leading examples of such critics were Nora Douglas Holt, who wrote for the *Chicago Defender* and the *New York Amsterdam News* (Spearman 1984), and H. Lawrence Freeman, who wrote for the *Afro-American* and the *New York Afro-American* (Davidson 1984, IV–2). The *Cleveland Gazette*, the *New York Age*, the *Norfolk Journal and Guide*, the *Pittsburgh Courier*, and the *Washington Bee* were other papers that fostered music criticism and reviews by black music critics during the 1920s (McGuire 1984, V–2).

Many of the new black critics possessed outstanding musical qualifications. Most had conservatory training as performers or composers and possessed strong backgrounds in music history. Their attitude toward their responsibilities as music critics is exemplified by Nora Holt's statement in the Saturday, September 14, 1946, *New York Amsterdam News:* "Criticism must be given not only in the spirit of service, but as a result of expert preparation and a fundamental background sufficient for the job."

Clearly, black music critics considered it their role not only to chart and analyze trends in the presentation of black music-making, but also to evaluate regularly the musical events in their communities. Their announcements informed the community of musical events, and the musically competent critics also judged performances. Further, black music critics sometimes took on managerial roles for singers like Hayes, Robeson, and Anderson, since white managers—often still concentrating on minstrel shows—did not usually have the performers' best interests in mind. Given the importance of the black music critic, it comes as a bit of a surprise that in many of the black newspapers, music criticism during the twenties was nonexistent. Most black newspapers printed announcements rather than appraisals and criticism of classical performances (Spearman 1984, IX–5).

For the black singer with professional aspirations, the time of the New Negro presented a number of challenges. The black singer faced the choice of either shunning or spotlighting traditional Afro-American art forms. Many black singers had been classically trained before the decade of the twenties. Entrenched in traditional singing discipline and techniques, these musicians identified with modes of European vocal study: operatic training, foreign-language study, and concentration on the art song. So, on one hand, the black musician had to sift through Afro-American music with an eye toward merging its most significant features with European parallels; on the other hand, advocates of full-scale promotion and undiluted expression of traditional Afro-American art forms abounded. For better or worse, the spiritual provided a point of intersection for singers on both sides, as we will see.

For the most part, however, black concert singers distinguished themselves not by performing the spiritual, but by having learned the standard European repertoire. Black music students received their training from limited sources, often in some of the private studios of an earlier generation of singers; some musical training was available to them at black colleges and universities; other students were trained in such well-known centers as the Oberlin Conservatory, the Chicago Musical College, and the New England Conservatory in Boston. These conservatories remained among the few "centers liberal enough to accept black music students" (Locke [1936] 1969, 119).

Scores of older, often retired, singers came to Harlem to teach, finding refuge in either private studios or black musical institutions. Mme. Marie Selika (ca. 1849–1937), after retiring from the concert stage, returned to Harlem to teach voice in the Martin-Smith School of Music (Johnson [1930] 1972, 99). Abbie Mitchell, Charlotte Murray, Florence

Cole Talbert, Caterina Jarboro, Lillian Evanti, Todd Duncan, and other retired singers have continued that tradition (Allen 1986).

While it is perhaps laudable that even some white voice teachers at conservatories and private studios in America took it upon themselves to teach black students, one doubts whether these instructors were familiar with black art songs or spirituals. In all likelihood, then, these teachers did not encourage their students to sing them. A review of the music criticisms of concerts by Sissieretta Jones, dramatic soprano (1869–1933), reveals that she and many other black singers of her generation did not include spirituals on their concert programs (Southern and Wright 1976, 191; Southern 1979, 95).[1]

As a traditional Afro-American musical form, however, the spirituals suffered comparatively little derision from whites. Secular songs derived from slavery, minstrelsy, and the emerging blues, ragtime, and jazz, on the other hand, were early perceived as vulgar, erotic, primitive, and lowbrow. These primarily white perceptions greatly influenced the kinds of songs programmed by black concert singers. The kind of cultural statement and artistic vision they wished to set forth in the texts of the songs also had to be considered. Speaking to this point, Roland Hayes, in an interview with Laura Haddock, insisted that "The song I sing is nothing. But what I give through the song is everything" (Carter 1977, 189).

The spiritual has remained the best-suited folk form to be included on concert programs of black singers. White and black audiences around the world began receiving the spiritual favorably. Locke points up the suitability of this genre of folk music:

> With technical skill added to such natural equipment, and the discipline of classical music added to the powerful originality of folk music, an almost unmatched combination is made that appeals both to the musical layman and the musical expert (Locke [1936] 1969, 42).

Experts in their own right, classically trained black singers had long hoped for an audience that would appreciate and respect their accomplishments. It was a courageous step for them to have begun including the spiritual in their programs in an attempt to garner support—long overdue—for the form. Hayes and a few other dedicated singers thus saw fit to persist in their singing of the spiritual. Hayes underscores the form's importance:

> My people have been very shy about singing their crude little songs before white folks. They thought they would be laughed at—and they were! And so they came to despise their own heritage. . . . If, as I truly believe, there is purpose and plan in my life, it is this: that I shall have my share in

rediscovering the qualities we have almost let slip away from us; and that we shall make our special contribution—only a humble one perhaps, but our very own—to human experience (Southern 1983, 402).

Hayes and his trend-setting career can serve as an exemplar of black concert singers of the period. Having entered Fisk University at a rather late age, he had to work to overcome a late start in his musical education. His determination and ability to concentrate with a "single eye" (Helm [1942] 1969, 125) helped him to gain a sense of identity, to accept the fact that he was a black singer, and to enjoy some assurance of his talent. These largely self-definitional concerns behind him, Hayes turned his attention to training his voice.

Hayes studied under Arthur J. Hubbard, a voice teacher in Boston, from 1911 to 1920. In addition to this he gained a good deal of experience singing community concerts as well as performing as church soloist. He took private lessons in German and French, and he enjoyed an abundance of individualized attention from the likes of Harry T. Burleigh, William Lawrence, Lawrence Brown, and William Richardson, who shared with Hayes their arrangements of art songs and spirituals. His first recital was presented in Jordan Hall on November 11, 1912. He continued to perform there and in Symphony Hall until he departed for Europe in 1920 (Hackett 1923).

The years 1915 through 1920 found Hayes starting to expand his repertoire. His programs would now include both art songs by black composers, such as Burleigh, J. Rosamond Johnson, William S. Lawrence, and Will Marion Cook, and European art songs by Mozart, Beethoven, Schubert, and others. Meanwhile, his continued study of French and German increased his proficiency to such an extent that he would be able to draw upon this knowledge later in his career (Helm [1942] 1969, 110). Yet Hayes found himself—in his zeal to become proficient in European art song classics—neglecting his own heritage:

> I had still to be taught that I, Roland Hayes, a Negro, had first to measure my racial inheritance and then to put it to use. It remained for me to learn, humbly at first, and then with mounting confidence, that my way to artistry was a Negro way (Helm [1942] 1969, 111).

Hayes may well have been on his way within this five-year period of musical expansion. But the year 1918 seems to mark the point at which he began to sing less like his white colleagues and to program one or two spirituals on his concerts. From both black and white audiences he began to appreciate the "fury of applause after singing spirituals" on his programs, especially "My Soul Is a Witness for My Lord" (Helm [1942] 1969, 121). During the next two years Hayes developed a model concert program, distinguished by its inclusion of the Negro spiritual, that was to become the standard for black concert artists. In April 1920, Hayes arrived in England. During the next three years, he programmed African as well as Afro-American songs on his concerts. Jeffrey P. Green (1982, 41) discussed why Hayes's repertoire might have so expanded:

> How much his association with African and Caribbean blacks increased his awareness of the black folk culture remains speculation, but it would seem reasonable to assume that this talented black American was encouraged to take a closer look at his own folk roots by his black and white friends in London.

It was regrettable, yet imperative, that so many of the great black singers had to travel abroad as a result of American racism or, as Locke describes this tragedy, "compete in a double contest . . . first to gain the respect of musicians and at the same time win the public ear. For only in terms of overwhelming public interest was it possible to compel the attention of managers and critics" (Locke [1936] 1969, 41). But approval is indeed what Hayes enjoyed once he made his British debut.

In a 1921 letter to Nora Holt written from London, Hayes gives a vivid account of his acceptance as a black artist living abroad. He would have liked for Holt to have

> witnessed the occasion of my singing "The Star Spangled Banner" before this assemblage of dukes, earls, counts, and countesses, Indies, etc., and the elite of America. . . . I sang two other songs "Oh, My Love," by Burleigh, and "Noon," by Montague Ring. There was prolongued applause. The one thing I am happiest over is the fact that I am established in London as an artist and my work is accepted without any provisos (Holt 1921, 7).

The implication here is that the black concert singer had not enjoyed unconditional acceptance in the United States, even as late as 1921.

During the three years Hayes was in London, he combined study with performances in much the same manner as when he was in America, the difference being that he was now performing his English and continental concerts as a mature artist, with Lawrence Brown as his accompanist. On April 23, 1921, two days after his Wigmore Hall concert, Hayes was commanded to sing before the king and queen of England. Other European audiences, meantime, heard Hayes sing their native art songs; in addition, these audiences began hearing a new American song, the spiritual.

Hayes returned to America in 1923, only to travel frequently between Europe and America during the next eight years and ultimately to accept Europe as his home. His critical reception in major cultural centers such as Boston, New York, and Chicago proved highly favorable. Some excerpts from his critical announcements are illustrative:

> Roland Hayes was recalled times without number after the last spiritual (Downes 1923).
>
> • • • • •
>
> I am sure that I was not tilted from my just balance by surprise that a negro should have such powers, and therefore gave him more than his due. It was beautiful singing (Hackett 1923).

Hayes was to find himself earning still more honors in the summer of 1924, when he received the Spingarn Medal. Members of the awards committee included Theodore Roosevelt, Dorothy Canfield Fisher, and W.E.B. Du Bois. Harry T. Burleigh accepted the medal for Hayes, since the latter was solidly booked abroad that summer.

Though himself often absent from the American musical scene in the mid-1920s through the early 1930s, Hayes's concert programs were fast falling into the hands of many black concert singers. Examination of seven of Hayes's programs, spanning the years 1923 to 1932, reveals them to be well worth absorption. They show, among other things, a consistent chronological order of the songs that Hayes had prepared for his audiences. Broadly speaking, the repertoire that was heard on these seven concerts was divided into four major groups. The concerts usually began with a group of songs by Baroque and Early Classical composers, among them works by Torelli, Bach, Handel, Purcell, and Beethoven. The second group included songs of German Lieder composers: works by Schubert, Brahms, Schumann, and Wolf, for example. The third group of songs, most often from the pens of romantic composers, tended to be an eclectic group of songs usually sung in English or French. This group offered the opportunity to sing art songs by composers of almost any nationality: Rachmaninoff, Fauré, Burleigh, Debussy, Julia Perry, and even songs by Hayes himself. Last but far from least, the fourth group was composed of Negro spirituals. Hayes saw fit to introduce this genre with an introduction; to contemporary eyes his words seem tragically optimistic:

> "Spirituals" are the spontaneous outbursts of intense religious fervor, and had their origin chiefly in camp meetings, revivals, and other religious exercises. It is a serious misconception of their meaning and value to treat them as "comic songs," for through all these songs there breathes a hope, a faith in the ultimate justice and brotherhood of man ("Roland Hayes" 1924).

Would that this expression of faith had given rise to a class of Americans equally magnanimous. To Hayes, the appearance of spirituals on a concert program no doubt symbolized a new age in which distinctions between black and white, "high" and "low," would be of little import.

But events at the end of the 1920s and continuing into the early 1930s were to prove otherwise. The collapse of the stock market, Harlem race riots, and the end of prohibition, among other conditions, left white managers (and club owners) in little need of—if not hostile to—black performers. By the 1920s, in fact, black singers had already been stereotyped as entertainers, and singing and dancing were viewed as the Negro's only two claims to fame. Alain Locke details this racist profile:

> For this reason the serious Negro musician was driven away from a good deal of his folk music by the prejudiced insistence that this represented his particular musical province. The sensitive, ambitious, and well trained artist saw in this, with some warrant, the threat of a musical Ghetto. Often he reached too violently the extreme of ignoring his own folk music and renounced its rich heritage. So for a painful period there was a feud in the ranks of Negro musicians between those who championed the "classics" and those who defended the folk-forms. And the latter were for a long while in the great minority (Locke [1936] 1969, 118).

Renaissance leaders of all ages, then, sought to break free of the entertainer stereotype. The younger leaders, to a greater extent than the old guard, had as a primary goal to defend folk forms, if not to legitimize them as works of art in their own right. To this end the group searched for a credo that would encourage composers and writers to develop a cultural nationalism firmly rooted in Negro folk experience. As goals for a new master Renaissance plan, they anticipated combinations of skills intended to produce changes in music, literature, and theater. These changes would then "show off the Negro as an American, motivate pride, and inspire the New Negro generation to challenge the injustices which prevent human freedom" (Spear 1968, vi–vii). The young black artist tended not, however, to work toward these goals with blinding zeal. The New Negro artist valued acceptance. To be accepted by audiences—black and white—and represented by managers remained the dream of many black concert singers. And they expected this dream to come to fruition since they had immersed themselves in European opera and art song classics. No doubt these musicians possessed sufficient talent. But despite their training, the most they could attain for a long while was a part on the roster of an all-black vaudeville or musical theater.

The Harlem Renaissance as a movement thus came to a premature halt, and Hayes and other Harlemites were left unable fully to express the materials of their Afro-American nativity. The Renaissance, however, did set in motion an inspiration for young, talented artists to follow—an inspiration and promise that would begin to be fulfilled by artists and composers by mid-century.

NOTE

1. Jones later became known as "The Black Patti," because her voice "compared in richness and musicality to that of the reigning prima donna of the period, Adelina Patti" (Southern 1983, 242).

REFERENCES

Allen, William Duncan. 1986. Interview with the author. San Francisco, California, August 20.

Carter, Marva Griffin. 1977. In retrospect: Roland Hayes—Expressor of the soul in song (1887–1977). *The Black Perspective in Music* 5, no. 2:188–220.

Dannett, Sylvia G. L. 1968. Nora Douglas Holt. In *Profiles of Negro Womanhood*. Yonkers, N.Y.: American Book—Stratford Press.

Davidson, Celia E. 1984. Articles in the Afro-American newspapers by Harry L. Freeman, composer-critic, 1936–1937. Typescript prepared for the NEH Summer Seminar for College Teachers, Howard University:IV–1—IV–30.

Dickinson, Donald C. 1967. *A bio-bibliography of Langston Hughes, 1902–1967.* Hamden, Conn.: Archon Books.

Downes, Olin. 1923. Review quoted in *Boston Symphony Orchestra Programme Book,* November 16–17, edited by Philip Hale.

Green, Jeffrey P. 1982. Roland Hayes in London, 1921. *The Black Perspective in Music* 10, no. 1:29–42.

Hackett, Carlton. 1923. Review quoted in *Boston Symphony Orchestra Programme Book,* November 16–17, edited by Philip Hale.

Helm, MacKinley. [1942] 1969. *Angel Mo' and her son, Roland Hayes.* Reprint. Westport, Conn.: Greenwood Press.

Holt, Nora Douglas. 1921. News and the world of music. In *Music and Poetry.* Chicago: Holt Publishing Co.

———. 1946. The role of the music critic. *New York Amsterdam News* September 14:4.

Johnson, James Weldon. [1930] 1972. *Black Manhattan.* Studies in American Negro Life. New York: Atheneum.

Locke, Alain. [1936] 1969. *The Negro and his music.* Reprint. New York: Arno Press and the New York Times.

Marsh, J.B.T. 1880. *The story of the Jubilee Singers; With their songs.* Rev. ed. Boston: Houghton Mifflin and Co.

McGuire, Phillip. 1984. Black music critics and classic blues in the 20s. Typescript prepared for the NEH Summer Seminar for College Teachers, Howard University:V–1—V–33.

Nugent, Richard Bruce. 1982. Lighting FIRE!! Inserted preface to *FIRE!!* Reprint. Metuchen, N.J.: The Fire Press. (Original publication date of *FIRE!!*, 1926)

Pike, Gustavus D. 1873. *The Jubilee Singers and their campaign for twenty thousand dollars.* Boston: Lee and Shepard.

Robinson, Frances. 1972. Liner notes to *Songs of my people.* RCA–LM 3292.

Roland Hayes concert program. 1924. Academy of Music, Philadelphia, January 29.

Southern, Eileen, comp. 1979. Black prima donnas of the nineteenth century. *The Black Perspective in Music* 7, no. 1:95–106.

———. 1983. *The music of black Americans: A history.* 2d ed. New York: W. W. Norton.

Southern, Eileen, and Josephine Wright, comps. 1976. Sissieretta Jones (1868–1933). *The Black Perspective in Music* 4, no. 2:191–201.

Spear, Allan H. 1968. Preface to the Atheneum edition. In *Black Manhattan*, James Weldon Johnson, v–xv. Studies in American Negro Life. New York: Atheneum.

Spearman, Rawn W. 1984. Music criticism by Nora Douglas Holt in the *New York Amsterdam News:* Saturday edition (1944–1952). Typescript prepared for the NEH Summer Seminar for College Teachers, Howard University:IX–1—IX–61.

Suthern, Orin Clayton, II. 1952. *The case of the Negro composer.* Lincoln, Penn.: Lincoln University—American Studies Institute.

Tarrant, Dorothy, and John Tarrant. 1986. *John Held, Jr., inventor of the jazz age.* Washington, D.C.: Smithsonian Associates.

Wirth, Thomas M. 1982. FIRE!! in retrospect. Inserted preface to *FIRE!!* Reprint. Metuchen, N.J.: The Fire Press. (Original publication date of *Fire!!,* 1926)

CHAPTER 4

Harlem Renaissance Ideals in the Music of Robert Nathaniel Dett

Georgia A. Ryder

In his lifetime, Robert Nathaniel Dett (1882–1943) was known as a consummate musician, being active as a composer, pianist, choral conductor, essayist, and teacher and gaining fame in various of these pursuits not only in America but in Europe as well. His precocity as a pianist was evident, by his own account, while he was "still in little dresses" (Dett 1934, 79). He was only eighteen at the time his first published composition, *After the Cake Walk* for solo piano, appeared.

Between 1912 and 1938 his published works included five piano suites, numerous anthems, motets, spiritual arrangements, folk-song collections, and essays. During the remaining five years of his life, he created or set additional works for piano, chorus, solo voice, and one for orchestra, but among the whole of his prolific output, most of which was choral, only two extended works, each for chorus and orchestra, were composed: *The Chariot Jubilee* (1919) and *The Ordering of Moses* (1932).

It is significant that these two works span the peak period of activity during the Harlem Renaissance (Southern 1971, 413). In explaining the character and uniqueness of the first composition, Dett remarked:

> The "Chariot Jubilee" for tenor solo, eight-part chorus of mixed voices and orchestra, which I wrote for the Syracuse Festival Chorus, and which was performed by them and the Cleveland Symphony Orchestra, with Mr. Lambert Murphy soloist, Keith's Theatre, Syracuse, May 4, 1921, marks, so far as I know, the first attempt to develop the spiritual into an oratorio form (Dett 1936b, 4).

With this statement Dett revealed fruition of his oft-expressed beliefs and ambitions which clearly showed his kinship to the intellectuals and artists who gave impetus to the Harlem Renaissance movement. In tracing "The Development of the Negro Spiritual," he cited Harry T. Burleigh, Clarence Cameron White, the brothers James Weldon and J. Rosamond Johnson, William Dawson, and William Grant Still for their contributions; and Florence Price, Edward Boatner, John Work, Jr., and Noah Ryder as "ones more recent on the list of those who would advance the cause of their native idiom" (Dett 1936b, 4).

Along the path of his professional career, Dett did not heed the call to come to New York, nor did he reside there as did some of those he cited. However, it is important to view this circumstance in light of the observation by Southern that while Harlem was the center of the Renaissance movement, the movement itself was national in its scope (Southern 1971, 436).

After his graduation from Oberlin in 1908, Dett taught at Lane College in Jackson, Tennessee, then from 1911 to 1913 at the Lincoln Institute (now University) in Jefferson City, Missouri, and from 1913 until 1931 at Hampton Institute (now University) in Virginia. His sojourns away from these colleges, except for touring, were for the purpose of further music study: Oberlin Conservatory (summer 1913); Columbia University and the American Conservatory of Music (summer 1929); and the Eastman School of Music (1931–1933) from which he received a master's degree. He maintained his residence in Rochester, New York, teaching music privately before returning south to Bennett College (Greensboro, North Carolina), where he served as Director of Music from 1937 until his untimely death in 1943.

The impact of continuous academic experience on Dett cannot be minimized as a factor in the formation of his mature musicianship by the 1930s; and being a traveler as well as a scholar, he would have been well informed about many important activities of the "New Negro Movement" as they happened during the twenties. Nevertheless, McBrier advises, "there can be no doubt that his emotional attitude, his spiritual understanding and awareness, and his sincere personal appreciation of the spiritual served as a most significant influence and motivating factor in determining his decision to cast the Negro spiritual into art-forms" (McBrier 1967, 6).

Dett was well along the way in this regard by the 1920s, and during that decade his active affiliation with the National Association of Negro Musicians, organized in 1919, added another dimension to the furtherance of his ideas as he shared the organization's purposes "to mold taste" and "to advocate racial expression" (Southern 1971, 414).[1] Dett continued to compose settings of spirituals as well as other works, and he met with stunning success on the presentation of *The Ordering of Moses* in its premiere performance.

The importance attributed to *The Ordering of Moses* by its publisher,

J. Fisher & Bro., is evident in a broadsheet issued by that house following the premiere of the work in the concluding concert of the Cincinnati
May Festival, 1937. The broadsheet is devoted entirely to reprints of one
preview, an editorial, and four reviews of that event. The editorial,
which originally appeared in the Cincinnati *Times-Star*, put forth the
view that, in choosing the oratorio as the representative American work
for the 1937 May Festival, conductor Eugene Goosens "paid deserved
honor to a musical leader of a musically gifted race." It observed that
"Dr. Dett has looked into the heart of his people and composed what he
saw there," and, it concluded, "as a result he has added something important to American culture" (Smith 1937).

Critic Dwight Bicknell, who dwelt on the event more than the musical
technicalities, noted that the composition "is said to be the most important contribution to music yet made by a member of the Negro race."
He went on to describe the ovation Dr. Dett received from a "wildly
enthusiastic audience" (Bicknell 1937).

Writing for the *Cincinnati Enquirer* on May 8, 1937, Frederick Yeiser
focused on the composition, which he regarded as "naive" and reminis-
cent of *The Green Pastures*. He advanced the theory that

> Dett's music . . . has that quality which has come to be agreed upon as
> being characteristic of the American Negro—a strong racial flavor plus the
> influence of hymn tunes of the Protestant sects as they flourished during
> the Moody-Sankey period. These ultimately took form in what has become
> known as the Negro Spiritual.

On examination of the reviews, much is revealed about the writers as
well as the oratorio and its composer. While Yeiser seized the opportunity to posit a theory espoused—and soundly refuted—by earlier writers,[2] the *New York Times* critic Olin Downes (who was in Cincinnati for
the Festival) observed that Dett had reason to congratulate himself upon
the effect of his music. But he continued with his opinion that the appearance of the score "led the reader to believe that a wilder and more
emotional treatment could have been given certain of the solos and reci-
tatives, done in the pale white fashion" (Downes 1937).

Undoubtedly, Dett appreciated the recognition accorded him by
J. Fisher and Bro. on issuance of the reprints. From Bennett College on
May 18, 1937, he wrote in a letter to Mr. and Mrs. Noah Walker Ryder
(Dett 1937b): "My publisher got out a special edition, a copy of which I
enclose." He did not indicate in the letter what he thought of the re-
views or of the viewpoints.

From time to time, as we shall see later, his own statements had di-
vulged an ambivalence in regard to his deep feeling for the music of his
race and his desire to identify with intellectual attitudes that were inhos-

pitable to these folk expressions in their purer forms. This trait fit him precisely into the mode of thought that generated and sustained the Harlem Renaissance.[3]

Though records do not show that he associated directly with leaders in that movement, he is cited by Johnson ([1922] 1959) and Locke (1925) as being among the promising composers of the time. The latter felt that "the proper idiom" of Negro spirituals calls for choral treatment and observed that

> Musically speaking, only the superficial resources in this direction have been touched as yet; just as soon as the traditional conventions of four-part harmony and the oratorio style and form are broken through, we may expect a choral development of Negro folk song that may equal or even outstrip the phenomenal choral music of Russia (Locke 1925, 208).

Dett himself referred to the spirituals as "quaint" or "crude," and so did Locke, who also characterized their "childish imagery" as naive (Locke 1925, 200). It does not seem risky to assume, therefore, that Dett would have reacted to critics' views from the level of his own ambivalence and in the spirit of the times, making such pronouncements (as came out of Cincinnati) secondary to the sure knowledge of his enormous, unprecedented success with the premiere performance of *The Ordering of Moses*.

Nearly ten years later, an unsigned preface appearing in a collection of solo spiritual settings by Dett might hardly be thought noteworthy for its inclusion. Indeed, singers or scholars wishing to get on with the music might skim it or skip it altogether in order to experience the five songs (with etude-like accompaniments) that bear the inscription "especially arranged at the request of Miss Dorothy Maynor" (Dett 1946).[4]

On closer inspection, however, the preface is worth the study of its tone and chronological context. Amid biographical details about the composer, there is the statement that "R. Nathaniel Dett's name is synonymous with the development of the Spiritual *from the beginning of the 20th Century*" (italics mine).

The author explained, further, that Dett had given form and a piano accompaniment to many spirituals for the first time, thereby doing much to make the spiritual an art song while retaining its spontaneity and intensity. The composer would have agreed, very likely, but the publication appeared three years after his death.

One may wrestle with interpretation of the author's chronology, "from the beginning of the 20th Century," in terms of whether it was meant to apply to the development of the spiritual or to Dett. If the latter, a question arises as to when Dett's name became "synonymous" with this development.

It is interesting to note that as early as 1908 Dett arranged "Nobody Knows the Trouble I've Seen" for violin and piano, presenting it as one of four original compositions on his senior recital at Oberlin.[5] He identified his second piano suite, *In the Bottoms* (1913), as a characteristic suite, but it does not rely on folk tunes for its idiomatic expression. In 1915, however, he revealed in a letter to Natalie Curtis-Burlin that he had written a slow movement for string quartet on an old Negro spiritual (McBrier 1967, 43). He noted further that he was surprised to find strong prejudice at [G.] Schirmer's against the higher development of Negro music. "As for me," he continued, "I cannot see why the same principles . . . making English folk music a success should not do so for Negro music. . . . [F]olk music is folk music and development is development."

By this time Dett had become a well-respected composer, known especially for *In the Bottoms*, which was premiered and performed in concerts by distinguished pianists. In 1918 he articulated his views in an article, "Negro Music," written for *Musical America*.

> We have this wonderful folk music—the melodies of an enslaved people, who poured out their longings, their griefs and their aspirations in one great universal language. But this store will be of no value unless we utilize it, unless we treat it in such manner that it can be presented in choral form, in lyric and operatic works, in concert suites and salon music (Dett 1918).

At a later time he further explicated his idea to put Negro music on a "truly dignified" basis: "As the spirituals stand, they are not suitable for any church service" (Dett 1928).

These aims, to which Dett gave voice, were later echoed by composer William Grant Still, a participant in New York City music activities (Haas 1975, 5–7; Huggins 1971, 134).[6] They addressed precisely the hopes and expectations of the Harlem Renaissance leaders as expressed confidently by James Weldon Johnson: "There will yet come great Negro composers who will take this music and voice through it not only the soul of their race, but the soul of America" (Johnson [1922] 1959, preface).

Thus, it is not surprising that Dett set about creating his first extended choral work, *The Chariot Jubilee*, which was published in 1919 as a Motet for Tenor Solo, Chorus, and Orchestra. Perhaps it is pedantic to argue the acceptance of "motet" or the composer's other description, "an oratorio form" (Dett 1936b, 4), as applied to *The Chariot Jubilee*. The composition conforms to the broad description of a motet as a choral work with or without accompaniment, generally of sacred character and intended for religious or festive occasions.

The motet has undergone great changes during its long existence and "it is almost impossible to give a general definition which would cover all the various phases of its development" (Apel 1967, 457). Moreover, English motets are called anthems and have a history of their own, including the innovation of a multi-sectional structure resembling a cantata, the diminutive form of oratorio. On consideration of these points, an understanding of the probable relatedness of Dett's thoughts emerges. More important than the title he gave the work, however, is his concept of it as an art form incorporating Negro folk music, specifically the spiritual.

THE CHARIOT JUBILEE

The Chariot Jubilee, though multi-sectional, is not designed to have independent choruses and solos but, rather, it is organized in such a way that choral passages are interwoven with brief and generally declamatory passages for the tenor soloist.

The spiritual "Swing Low, Sweet Chariot" is the basic reference for *The Chariot Jubilee*, and it provides the overriding thematic and textual material throughout. As the composition unfolds, both chorus and soloist are given phrases of the spiritual. Eventually, near the end, it is sung in its entirety (see example 4.1), thereby unifying and confirming all of its parts as previously exposed and becoming the final focal point before the triumphant conclusion. Yet, the overall character of the work is determined by the manner in which the composer treats the traditional music and by his original material, with which it is combined. It is clear that styles of formal sacred music prevail.

Example 4.1. *The Chariot Jubilee*, R. Nathaniel Dett, mm. 158–163

The first reference to the spiritual comes early in the orchestral introduction, where a literal quotation from the traditional melody's first phrase establishes the motive for that section (see example 4.2). The motive is altered by inverted thirds as the tenor enters in recitative style, the chorus joins the solo, and all approach the setting of the spiritual shown in example 4.3—a bitextual, the simplest form of polytextuality. The latter feature, found in early motets, has been described as a kind of

Example 4.2. *The Chariot Jubilee*, R. Nathaniel Dett, mm. 5–6

Example 4.3. *The Chariot Jubilee*, R. Nathaniel Dett, mm. 68–69

counterpoint of ideas paralleling a counterpoint of tones (Grout 1980, 105). This device is only one among those discussed here that set the character of *The Chariot Jubilee* during its opening portion.

The spiritual tune is presented, emerging through motivic development before occurring in a straightforward melodic line as part of a structure that relies equally upon the composer's own material. Dett retains the characteristic features of syncopation and leader-response effect, as found in "Swing Low, Sweet Chariot," while he employs harmonic, rhythmic, and textual devices in the nature of a motet or anthem as he would have encountered and understood those forms during his academic training.

As the work continues, there are revealed other compositional techniques related to motets and other forms representative of various historical periods in music. Among the techniques employed are contrapuntal treatment and cross-rhythms (see example 4.4). He also set a recurring text, "God made a covenant," in chorale style initially and presented it finally in a climactic passage with an *ostinato*, as example 4.5 shows. An outstanding feature of the work is a concluding Hallelujah chorus in fugal style, a characteristic of the Restoration anthem (Apel 1967, 40).

In many passages of *The Chariot Jubilee* there may be a perception that folk-like spontaneity has been supplanted by formality in structure and

Example 4.4. *The Chariot Jubilee*, R. Nathaniel Dett, mm. 90–100

Example 4.5. *The Chariot Jubilee*, R. Nathaniel Dett, mm. 148–149

mood; yet, the composer never abandons the prime subject with which he is concerned. There is no question of the composer's sincere love of his folk material, in this case the spiritual from which *The Chariot Jubilee* derives its name. It was he who chose it, but in simultaneously choosing characteristics of a motet, he related it to the formal church service for which he had said spirituals in their native state were "too crude" (Mc-Brier 1967, 66). The work commingles formal and idiomatic material in various ways throughout.

Some idioms are easily recognizable and reflect not only song sources but also performance practice, as in the leader-response presentations of "Swing Low, Sweet Chariot." In another instance, a reference to the spiritual "Ride Up in the Chariot" is punctuated with a two-note rhythmic figure, "Tell it" (see example 4.6, m. 125). The latter motive appears in H. T. Burleigh's arrangement of "Father Abraham" (Krehbiel 1914, 90), but here it is altered to provide the effect, between the bass and

Example 4.6. *The Chariot Jubilee*, R. Nathaniel Dett, mm. 124–126

tenor, of alternating foot-patting and hand-clapping. The frequent use of syncopation in the work creates an ongoing rather than isolated idiomatic reference.

On the whole, the composition exemplifies the concept of "high art" as the justifying framework which, supporting the elaboration of folk idioms on the one hand, is made self-evident on the other hand.

The Chariot Jubilee, while having characteristics of nineteenth-century oratorio, is obviously not a dramatic narrative. Its Biblical quotations and allusions are not knit together with characters, chronology, or dialogue. Rather than soli, there is the tenor solo—given a declamatory role but not a character identification.

The composer's hallmarks are there: skillful development of idiomatic material; superb choral effects; the use of triplets; two-against-three (cross-rhythms); well-crafted fugal treatments; sensitivity to the human voice; and as aptly stated in the anonymous preface previously cited, "the epic intensity and religious emotion of the chorale." There is also what this writer senses as a "metrical insistence"—a sometimes subtle, yet surging, on-the-beat pulse prevalent in his choral pieces, especially the motets.

THE ORDERING OF MOSES

Many of these same characteristics are developed in *The Ordering of Moses*, which is set for chorus, orchestra, and five soloists representing Miriam (soprano), Moses (tenor), The Voice of God (baritone), The Voice of Israel (alto), and The Word (baritone). Dett called this work a "Biblical Folk Scene," thereby indicating succinctly his textual source, the context for his treatment of it, and its potential for dramatic realization. The "scene" concerns the Old Testament story of Moses leading the Israelites out of the bondage of Egypt, the exultant song of Miriam, and the rejoicing of the liberated people.

In correspondence excerpted in the *Cincinnati Enquirer*, Dett offered to the Cincinnati Festival Management Committee the following explanation of his new composition:

> Although the text is very free in form, and embraces a number of styles, blank verse, and rhyme . . . the story is continuous, very understandable, and absolutely fits the music. . . . The similarity of folk text to the words of the scripture is striking, and the fusion of the two seems natural; moreover, the light which is thrown subsequently on the true meaning of the spiritual is very revealing (Dett 1937a).

In this description, the composer touched upon some of the most identifiable features of oratorio that apply to *The Ordering of Moses*. In addition to the dramatic continuity and scriptural reference to which he alluded in his comments, the work displays characteristics of oratorio in its use of chorus and narrator as important elements; and it is obviously of greater extension than a motet or a cantata. The singular distinction from these general features, however, is Dett's clear intention to "fuse" scripture and folklore in a work of such scope.

In much the same manner as we have seen in *The Chariot Jubilee*, he has used a spiritual as the source of principal unifying ideas in the oratorio. From that spiritual, "Go Down, Moses," he draws thematic material, organizational devices, and the subject of his title, again in similarity to the earlier composition; but different here is a well-developed narrative elaborated by full-length choruses, soli, and several instrumental interludes. All of the latter features indicate the overall concept of an art work to which Dett adheres in the matter of form. At the same time, he sets out immediately to invest the form with folk music idioms. For instance, the work begins with a motive consisting of a characteristic melodic pattern, 5–4–3♭–1, in a syncopated rhythm (see example 4.7). It is derived from the refrain "Go Down, Moses" (see Example 4.8, m. 4) and recurs throughout the orchestral "prelude" and interludes.

Choruses are given idiomatic character through responsorial techniques either based directly on "Go Down, Moses," as in "All Israel's

Example 4.7. *The Ordering of Moses*, R. Nathaniel Dett, mm. 1–2

Example 4.8. "Go Down, Moses," from *The Ordering of Moses*, R. Nathaniel Dett, mm. 259–262

Example 4.9. *The Ordering of Moses*, R. Nathaniel Dett, mm. 56–58

Children Sorely Sighed" (see example 4.9), or reflective of it. Other prevalent features of black folk music are revealed in configurations of rhythmic patterns and melodic patterns such as the 5–6–1 progression or repeated minor thirds.

Dett also gives an integral role to the spiritual "He Is King of Kings." As noted in discussion of *The Chariot Jubilee*, passing reference was made to a spiritual other than the title's source. The same idea was applied to *The Ordering of Moses*, but here an entire chorus is based on "He Is King of Kings," affirming that song's identity in the opening choral theme (see example 4.10) and affirming its importance by developing it into the triumphant anthem of praise that concludes the oratorio.

Example 4.10. *The Ordering of Moses*, R. Nathaniel Dett, mm. 906–910

On viewing the characteristics described above, it must be seen that they occur within or in juxtaposition to settings that are not derived from black folk music. For enhancement of the narrative, Dett has incorporated harmonic and melodic movement having the flavor of Hebraic music for the lengthy "March of the Israelites through the Red Sea," of which a few measures suffice to illustrate the effect (see example 4.11).[7] As inferred from the title, this entire section—for orchestra and wordless voices—is designed to portray the emotional intensity of the Hebrew people and the motion of water. There is nothing at all extraordinary about such a programmatic conception; but in the creation of this orato- rio, the composer's perceptions of relatedness, concerning narrative ele- ments, seem to give the conception special meaning when consideration is given to his statement that "the light which is thrown subsequently on the true meaning of the spiritual is very revealing" (Dett 1937a).

This devotion to spirituals notwithstanding, Dett's affinity for art- music styles is not diminished in his composition of *The Ordering of Moses*; rather, it is demonstrated in his command of motivic develop-

Example 4.11. *The Ordering of Moses*, R. Nathaniel Dett
    a. mm. 604–605

    b. mm. 617–618

ment, fugal and other contrapuntal treatments, orchestral coloration, and other aspects of his personal style.

According to McBrier, the composer's personal notebook records that

> the representation of the singing of primitive peoples was not so difficult as I had had many conferences with Mr. Ballanta-Taylor, an African musician, who was an enthusiast on the subject of aboriginal harmonies and scale systems (McBrier 1967, 98).

Nevertheless, the total idiomatic effect of *The Ordering of Moses* is not achieved in the sense that song style involves singing style. McBrier comments that the work is on a high academic level, being restrained musically and having "none of the primitivism or abandon that might be expected from the dramatic idea and the text" (McBrier 1967, 131). A very similar opinion was expressed by Olin Downes (1937), as we have seen, in his review of the oratorio.

Although the commentaries might be arguable, it is readily apparent that *The Ordering of Moses* is formal in its organizational and harmonic concepts and employs thematic material of Dett's own invention as well as that derived from the spiritual. By his own account (in his notebook), the composition of it took about ten years. Because it was completed in 1932, the idea to create it must have been in flower by 1922, about the time of Johnson's "prophecy" quoted above, three years before Locke enlarged upon Johnson's ideas in *The New Negro* (Locke 1925), and very shortly after the premiere of *The Chariot Jubilee* on May 4, 1921.[8]

SUMMARY

In retrospect, Dett's accomplishment may not seem to be a "breakthrough" in the sense expressed by Locke (1925). Yet, it is not superficial, and upon public emergence its impact "greatly excited the audience," according to Downes (1937) whose review stated, "The musical emblem and predominant motive of the whole work is the great thunderous Negro spiritual, 'Go Down, Moses.'"

Alain Locke considered spirituals naive though profound and of great value (1925, 200). During his time, he noted in their concert versions a tendency toward "sophisticated over-elaboration"; but he cautioned:

> In calling for the folk atmosphere and insisting upon the folk quality, we must be careful not to confine this wonderfully potential music to the narrow confines of "simple versions" and musically primitive molds (Locke 1925, 208).

As we have seen, Locke also felt that the proper idiom of Negro folk songs called for choral treatment, and he cited Dett as one of the young composers turning to the choral form. In the same essay, he observed that

> up to the present, the resources of Negro music have been tentatively exploited in only one direction at a time. . . . A genius that would organize its distinctive elements in a formal way would be the musical giant of his age (Locke 1925, 209).

The foregoing remarks are not so much incongruent as reflective of the debate that nurtured the vitality of the Harlem Renaissance. Issues were discussed in terms of practice and options; many minds were at work, whether in general agreement or not, producing thoughts that wove around a central concern for the New Negro. One wonders how many of the individual participants were, like Dett, "of two minds."

Dett's greatest output consisted of short choral compositions. Of the forty-five published between 1914 and 1942, twenty-one have their source in Negro folk music. But, not unlike some poets and artists of his day, he consciously chose styles and art forms as frameworks for many of his compositions and cast his two largest choral works, *The Chariot Jubilee* and *The Ordering of Moses*, in this way.

Compositional commonalities between the two works give credence to the sustained ideas of Dett, developed not only during the twenties but emerging well before that decade.[9] He made it clear, repeatedly, that he was committed to the worth and preservation of Negro folk idioms (Spencer 1982, 134–38), to their "development" in art forms, and to his ambition to advance the cause of his people. In this regard, it seems that he was in line with some of the dominant thought of his time.

Among the young composers who were looked to with hope by the Renaissance leaders, Dett is the one whose major works outline the period of prime activity in that movement. William Grant Still's earliest concert works for orchestra, written during the 1920s, were performed but "scrapped" or "discarded," according to Verna Arvey (Haas 1975, 145–47). While he still did not go unnoticed by his colleagues or critics, it was the performance of his *Afro-American Symphony* in 1931 that brought him real recognition, as noted by Southern (1971, 456). Clarence Cameron White was known primarily for his violin pieces. William Dawson's *Negro Folk Symphony* was not premiered until 1934.

But here it is not necessary to catalog any further the works of Dett or his contemporaries to understand that, in light of the Harlem Renaissance ideals, his music—including the motet and oratorio examined above—captured and still reflects the ambience, the ambivalence, the *zeitgeist* of that singular period of black history in America.

NOTES

1. Dett was president of the National Association of Negro Musicians from 1924 to 1926.

2. Newman White ([1928] 1965) and Guy Johnson (1930) advanced the "imitation" theory concerned with the provenance of slave songs and spirituals. The stand against white-to-Negro acculturation was maintained by James Weldon and J. Rosamond Johnson in their books of American Negro spirituals (1925; 1926) and also by Ballanta (1925). Dett disputed the Moody-Sankey theory in his article, "The Authenticity of the Spiritual" (1936a, 3). The controversy is summarized in several sources, for example, Chase (1955, 254–55).

3. See, for example, the foreword to *The New Negro* (Locke 1925).

4. Curiously, the collection includes "Hymn to Parnassus," distinctly an original art song.

5. According to McBrier (1967, 18), it was Dett's hearing of a slow movement from a Dvořák quartet (probably the Quartet in F [American]), played at Oberlin by the Kniesel Quartet, that generated his idea to use traditional folk melodies in art music—an idea about which he had been told earlier by a Dr. Hoppe from Berlin, Germany, but which made little or no impression at the time.

6. In his chapter "A Composer's Viewpoint" in *Black Music in Our Culture,* Still states that he knew Dett (Still 1970).

7. For a discussion of Jewish chants, see Apel (1967, 380–81). Dett described his own approach to the relationship between oppressed blacks and Jews at the time of Exodus (McBrier 1967, 98).

8. *The Chariot Jubilee* did not receive the recognition gained by *The Ordering of Moses.* Even McBrier (1967) gives it only passing mention, though it is discussed briefly in her book (1977).

9. One of Dett's best-known choral pieces is his setting of the spiritual "Listen to the Lambs," published in 1914.

REFERENCES

Apel, Willi. 1967. *Harvard dictionary of music.* Cambridge: Harvard University Press.

Ballanta, Nicholas George Julius. 1925. *Saint Helena Island spirituals: Recorded and transcribed at Penn Normal Industrial and Agricultural School.* New York: G. Schirmer.

Bicknell, Dwight L. 1937. Special praise given to festival chorus. *Cincinnati Enquirer* May 9.

Chase, Gilbert. 1955. *America's music from the pilgrims to the present.* New York: McGraw-Hill.

Dett, R. Nathaniel. 1913. *In the bottoms: Characteristic suite for the piano.* Chicago: Clayton F. Summy.

Dett, R. Nathaniel. 1918. Negro music. *Musical America* 28 (July):17.

———. 1919. *The chariot jubilee* (motet for tenor solo, chorus, and orchestra [or organ]). Cincinnati: John Church.

———. 1928. Majors and minors. *New York Times* April 15:sect. 10, 10.

———. 1934. From bell stand to throne room. *Etude* 52 (February):79–80.

———. 1936a. The authenticity of the spiritual. In *The Dett collection of Negro spirituals*, 3d group, 3. Chicago: Hall & McCreary.

———. 1936b. The development of the Negro spiritual. In *The Dett collection of Negro spirituals*, 4th group, 3–4. Chicago: Hall & McCreary.

———. 1937a. Another world premiere! Festival audience to hear "The Ordering of Moses." *Cincinnati Enquirer* May 7.

———. 1937b. Letter to Mr. and Mrs. Noah Walker Ryder (Cincinnati), May 18.

———. 1937c. *The ordering of Moses* (Biblical folk scene for soli, chorus, and orchestra). New York: J. Fisher & Brothers.

———. 1946. *Spirituals* (voice and piano). New York: Mills Music.

Downes, Olin. 1937. Cincinnati hears music by Berlioz; Dett piece also is heard. *New York Times* May 8:22.

Grout, Donald Jay. 1980. *A history of western music*. 3d ed. New York: W. W. Norton.

Haas, Robert Bartlett, ed. 1975. *William Grant Still and the fusion of cultures in American music*. Los Angeles: Black Sparrow Press.

Huggins, Nathan Irvin. 1971. *Harlem Renaissance*. New York: Oxford University Press.

Johnson, Guy B. 1930. *Folk culture on St. Helena Island, South Carolina*. Chapel Hill: University of North Carolina.

Johnson, James Weldon, ed. [1922] 1959. *The book of American Negro poetry*. New York: Harcourt, Brace, & World.

Johnson, James Weldon, and J. Rosamond Johnson. 1925. *The book of American Negro spirituals*. New York: Viking Press.

———. 1926. *The second book of Negro spirituals*. New York: Viking Press.

Krehbiel, Henry E. 1914. *Afro-American folksongs*. New York: G. Schirmer.

Locke, Alain. 1925. The Negro spirituals. In *The new Negro: An interpretation*, Alain Locke, ed., 199–213. New York: Albert & Charles Boni.

McBrier, Vivian Flagg. 1967. The life and works of Robert Nathaniel Dett. Ph.D. diss., The Catholic University of America, Washington, D.C.

———. 1977. *R. Nathaniel Dett: His life and works (1882–1943)*. Washington, D.C.: The Associated Publishers.

Smith, Nina Pugh. 1937. Editorial, The ordering of Moses. *Cincinnati Times-Star* May 8.

Southern, Eileen. 1971. *The music of black Americans: A history*. New York: W.W. Norton.

Spencer, Jon Michael. 1982. R. Nathaniel Dett's views on the preservation of black music. *The Black Perspective in Music* 10, no. 2:134–48.

Still, William Grant. 1970. A composer's viewpoint. In *Black music in our culture*, Dominique-René de Lerma, ed., 93–108. Kent, Ohio: Kent State University Press.

White, Newman I. [1928] 1965. *American Negro folk-songs*. Hatsboro, Penn.: Folklore Associates.

Yeiser, Frederick. 1937. Racial flavor strong to Dett's "Moses." *Cincinnati Enquirer* May 8.

CHAPTER 5

William Grant Still, Florence Price, and William Dawson: Echoes of the Harlem Renaissance

Rae Linda Brown

In critical discussions of the first orchestral music by black American composers, William Grant Still's *Afro-American Symphony*, Florence Price's *Symphony in E Minor*, and William Dawson's *Negro Folk Symphony* are often cited in the context of American musical nationalism. While these works properly fall within that context, they also represent the culmination of a black cultural awakening that emerged in metropolitan cities throughout the country in the 1920s and continued to the early 1930s. Nationalism was the backdrop from which the New Negro adapted old artistic forms into self-consciously racial idioms. This race consciousness united black intellectuals with common attitudes, ideals, and a sense of purpose.

The Negro Renaissance spawned a surge of literary, artistic, and musical creativity by America's black elite. This affirmation of the values of the black cultural heritage had a decisive impact on composers, who had as their primary goal the elevation of the Negro folk idiom—that is, spirituals, blues, and characteristic dance music—to symphonic form. This elevation could be accomplished through the fusion of elements from the neo-romantic nationalist movement in the United States with elements from their own Afro-American cultural heritage.

Although composers such as Henry Gilbert, Daniel Gregory Mason, John Powell, and William Arms Fischer earlier in the century had used Afro-American folk themes in their symphonic works, many of these composers lacked the cultural identification necessary to make the source material sound convincing out of context. In Still's *Afro-American Symphony*, Price's *Symphony in E Minor*, and Dawson's *Negro Folk Symphony*, the Afro-American nationalist elements are integral to the style.

The deceptively simple musical structure of these symphonies is inherently bound to the folk tradition in which they are rooted.

William Grant Still (1895–1978) was born in Woodville, Mississippi, and spent his youth in Little Rock, Arkansas. He attended Wilberforce College in Wilberforce, Ohio, from 1911 to 1914. Prior to his arrival in New York at the beginning of the Negro Renaissance, Still worked, during the summer of 1916, for Charles Pace's and W. C. Handy's music publishing company in Memphis. While in Memphis, Still heard the blues in the honky-tonks and dance halls, and he also played oboe and cello in and made arrangements for Handy's newly organized Memphis band.

In 1917 the Pace and Handy publishing company moved to New York, and in 1919 Still joined the staff there. Handy's office was to become important in Still's career. It was here that prominent black musicians met and made personal contacts so critical to their professional survival. In 1921, recommended by his friend Hall Johnson, Still also played oboe in Eubie Blake's orchestra for *Shuffle Along,* one of the most successful black musicals to appear on Broadway.

After touring with the show, Still returned to New York in 1923 and accepted the position of recording director for the Black Swan Phonograph Company. Established as the first recording company owned and operated by blacks, the Black Swan Company was also a gathering place for black artists. This recording company proved to be yet another stepping stone for Still. He wrote arrangements for a wide variety of recording artists, including classical, popular, and jazz singers; and he played in and directed the Black Swan Orchestra (see figure 5.1). During this time, Still also wrote popular music under the name "Willie M. Grant." Unfortunately, the Black Swan label went bankrupt in December 1923 and was purchased by Paramount Records the next year.

During the twenties and thirties Still was a successful arranger for Artie Shaw and Donald Voorhees, among others. In addition, Still had opportunities to further his musical education. He studied with George Chadwick at the New England Conservatory (1922) and with Edgar Varèse in New York (1923–1925). All the while, Still's understanding of and love for black music was growing. He always found time to attend black churches, where he continued to immerse himself in black folk music. It was the blues and the spirituals that penetrated deeply into Still's soul. With this recognition of the folk roots of black music, the *Afro-American Symphony* was born.

The *Afro-American Symphony,* composed in 1930 while Still lived in New York, was written as part of a symphonic trilogy based on a composite musical portrait of the Afro-American. When the symphony was

Figure 5.1.   William Grant Still conducting the Black Swan Orchestra, 1923

completed, the composer added program notes and appended descriptive verses from poems by Paul Laurence Dunbar to each movement. Still's intention was to write an American work that would "demonstrate how the Blues, so often considered a lowly expression, could be elevated to the highest musical level" (Still 1965). He explained further:

> Long before writing this symphony I had recognized the musical value of the Blues and had decided to use a theme in the Blues idiom as the basis for a major symphonic composition. When I was ready to launch this project, I did not want to use a theme some folk singer had already created but decided to create my own theme in the Blues idiom (quoted in Haas 1975, 11).

The formal scheme of the *Afro-American Symphony* is somewhat unorthodox in that its divisions are labeled as Part I, Part II, Part III, and Part IV, corresponding to individual movements.[1] Further, although all of the movements are in modified sonata form, Still uses the terms Division I, II, and III rather than exposition, development, and recapitulation. These designations and the nontraditional key areas used for these divisions demonstrate Still's desire to break away from established rules of musical form.

In the first movement the primary theme in A flat, often described as the blues theme, adheres to the standard twelve-bar blues pattern. Significantly, the blues melody is accompanied by a typical blues progression: I I⁷ IV I V⁷ I (see example 5.1). Variations and transformations of this theme are heard throughout the composition; although other harmonies are introduced, the underlying blues progression remains intact.

Example 5.1. *Afro-American Symphony*, William Grant Still, primary theme, first movement

The secondary theme, played by solo oboe in G major, is in the style of a spiritual and bears a relationship to the blues theme in its simple chord progression (see example 5.2). A spirited Division II (development) ensues in A-flat minor, followed by the subordinate theme at the beginning of Division III (recapitulation) in the same key. The final appearance of the blues theme, richly orchestrated, returns the movement to the parallel major.

Example 5.2. *Afro-American Symphony*, William Grant Still, secondary theme, first movement

The mood of the second movement is sorrow, but sorrow not given over to despair. Accompanied by obbligato flute and strings, the principal theme, in F major, is stated by the solo oboe. The secondary theme, in F major and minor, first given to the flute, is an alteration of the blues theme. At the close of Division I (exposition), a transformation of the principal theme "represents the fervent prayers of a burdened people rising upward to God" (Haas 1975, 25). Musically, this is depicted by slowly rolled harp arpeggios. Division III (recapitulation) ensues with the movement's two themes presented in reverse order, just as in the corresponding section of the first movement.

The mood of the third movement is jovial. Syncopated cross rhythms clearly rooted in Afro-American dance are accentuated by the extensive use of the tenor banjo throughout the movement. This movement represents the first-known use of the banjo in a symphonic work. At the same time its sacred text proclaims, "An' we'll shout ouah halleluyahs, on dat mighty reck'nin' day." The listener will readily recognize a theme in this movement that bears a striking resemblance to the Gershwin tune "I've Got Rhythm." In fact, Verna Arvey reports that W. C. Handy reminded Still that he, Still, had improvised the tune in the Broadway musical *Shuffle Along*. It appears that Gershwin later adopted the tune as his own (Arvey 1984, 62; Arvey 1987).

The culmination of the symphony, a majestic Lento movement which recapitulates most of the symphony's themes, was described by the composer as "a retrospective viewing of the earlier movements with the exception of its principal theme. It is intended to give musical expression to the lines from Paul Laurence Dunbar which appear: 'Be proud, my race, in mind and soul'" (Haas 1975, 40).

At this time Still was consciously writing in the Negro idiom. The harmonies, melodies, and orchestration employed in the *Afro-American Symphony* betray Still's desire to be true to the Afro-American folk tradition. The attainment of simplicity forces the listener to concentrate on those musical qualities that are recognizably Negro.

The influence of the Negro Renaissance upon Still's work was a subtle one. Although Still was not a conscious participant in the Negro Renaissance, his music speaks of the essence of the New Negro. Still's *Afro-American Symphony* may be considered a hallmark of the Renaissance because in its verses by Paul Laurence Dunbar, its transformation of the blues theme, and its powerfully inspiring last movement, the symphony affirms the values of the Afro-American heritage through decidedly characteristic idioms with which Still could identify. This affirmation is embodied in Dunbar's text:

> Be proud, my Race, in mind and soul.
> Thy name is writ on Glory's scroll
> In characters of fire.
> High mid the clouds of Fame's bright sky
> Thy banner's blazoned folds now fly,
> And truth shall lift them higher.

The *Afro-American Symphony* is a direct manifestation of Still's desire not only to recognize but also to celebrate "the sons of the soil."

Chicago, like New York's Harlem, had a cultural vitality in the 1920s and 1930s that was generated by the black elite located in that city. There were regular gatherings of artists where musicians, writers, and visual artists could assemble to support each other. It was here that William L. Dawson was inspired to write his *Negro Folk Symphony*.

Born in Anniston, Alabama, Dawson (b. 1899) received a Master of Music degree from the American Conservatory of Music in Chicago in 1927, and from 1926 to 1930 he played first trombone with the Chicago Civic Symphony Orchestra. In 1930 and 1931 Dawson won Wanamaker prizes for composition.

Writing a symphony had been a longtime ambition of Dawson's. He was repeatedly discouraged, however, by the faculty of the Conservatory who felt that Dawson should confine his creative energies to composing in small-scale genres or in playing jazz (Dawson 1986). Dawson disagreed, and his perseverance led to the composition of the celebrated *Negro Folk Symphony*. The symphony was begun in the late 1920s during the composer's postgraduate studies and was completed in 1932.

The *Negro Folk Symphony* was first performed by the Philadelphia Orchestra in a series of successful concerts conducted by Leopold Stokowski at the Philadelphia Academy of Music on November 14, 15, and 17, 1934, and at Carnegie Hall, New York, on November 20, 1934. Following these performances Dawson tried to interest American conductors in further performances, but he met with little success. At the same time, Dawson, who had become Director of Music at Tuskegee Institute in 1930, began to turn his attention toward choral music. During his twenty-five-year tenure at Tuskegee, Dawson raised the Tuskegee choir to international fame.

In 1952, following a visit to West Africa, Dawson revised his symphony, infusing it with African-influenced rhythms. Stokowski performed the work again and later recorded it with the American Symphony Orchestra.

In many ways Dawson's symphony is the most conventional of the three symphonies considered here. The first and third movements, based on Afro-American folk themes, are in sonata form with a clearly recognizable exposition, development, and recapitulation. Dawson scored his symphony for a romantic-era orchestra, but it includes an African clave and Adawura.

Dawson's three-movement symphony differs somewhat from Still's symphony in that it is highly programmatic; the understanding of the work depends, in part, upon the recognition of the spirituals that form the basis of the symphony. In addition, each movement has a subtitle that expresses, as Stokowski said, "The spirit of his people struggling in a new land; the ancient voice of Africa transferred to America" (quoted in Dawson 1978).

In the first movement in E-flat major, "The Bond of Africa," Dawson introduces the "missing link" motive in the horn (see example 5.3). This motive is heard in all three movements. In the composer's view, "a link was taken out of a human chain when the first African was taken from the shores of his native land, and sent to slavery" (Dawson 1978). Of the movement's two principal themes, the first is original, while the second is based on the Negro spiritual "Oh, M' Littl' Soul Gwine-a Shine."

Example 5.3. *Negro Folk Symphony*, William Levi Dawson, "missing link" motive, first movement

The dramatic second movement, "Hope in the Night," begins with the tolling of three bells. Suggesting the monotonous life of a people held in bondage, unrelenting harp chords accompany a haunting English horn solo. A contrasting, sprightly Allegretto theme is introduced, symbolizing children yet unaware of their dark future. The "missing link" motive returns, and with it, the dark theme begins to interrupt the brighter second theme of this second movement. Once again, the "missing link" motive, played by full orchestra, reclaims the solemn spirit of the movement's opening as if to recall the slaves' African heritage. The movement closes with the gradual dying away of the final chords against the tom-tom's steady beating.

Also in sonata form, the joyous third movement, "O Le' Me Shine," is based on two spirituals: "O Le' Me Shine, Lik' a Mornin' Star" and "Hallelujah, Lord I Been Down into the Sea." In the development section the two themes are intertwined. At the coda, the brasses forcefully echo "O Le' Me Shine," which transforms the expression of the entire symphony into one of fervent hope and triumph.

In November 1935, when thousands of people heard the National Broadcasting Company's performance of William Dawson's *Negro Folk Symphony* played by the Philadelphia Orchestra under Leopold Stokowski and when the radio announcer allowed the audience to hear the spontaneous applause that interrupted the symphony at the close of the second movement, the work's performance signaled a marked triumph for the Afro-American composer of concert music.

In writing about the Still, Price, and Dawson symphonies of the early 1930s, the prominent literary critic Alain Locke, an ardent spokesman of the Negro Renaissance whose theories of an Afro-American aesthetic still merit attention today, clearly favored Dawson's work. He noted:

> But with the successful presentation of the symphonies based on folk themes from each of these young composers [Still and Dawson] in the last year, the hope for symphonic music in Negro idiom has risen notably. In 1935, ten years after his enthusiastic championing of the serious possibilities of jazz, Leopold Stokowski was able to present with his great Philadelphia Orchestra William Dawson's *Negro Folk Symphony;* certainly one of America's major contributions thus far to symphonic literature (Locke [1936] 1969, 114).

For Locke, the symphonies of Still and Dawson, based on recognizable folk themes and idioms, no doubt suggested a prototypical genre for black composers.

First performed after Still's *Afro-American Symphony* and before Dawson's *Negro Folk Symphony* was Florence Price's *Symphony in E Minor,* written in 1931. Although the score is relatively unknown, Price's symphony contributes significantly to the musical legacy of the Negro Renaissance.[2]

Originally subtitled the "Negro Symphony," this work assimilates characteristic Afro-American folk idioms into classical structures. But unlike Still and Dawson, Price abandoned a title that would have suggested a programmatic work and, perhaps, would have limited the perception of the symphony's scope. Since the subtitle was almost obliterated from the score I examined, it can be concluded that Price changed her mind prior to the work's first performance; none of the reviews refer to its programmatic name.

Florence B. Price (1888–1953) was born in Little Rock, Arkansas, and educated at the New England Conservatory of Music. In 1926 Price and her family settled in Chicago, where she established firmly her career as a teacher, composer, and organist.

During the summers of 1926 and 1927, Price found opportunities for further study in composition, harmony, and orchestration at the Chicago Musical College. In 1929, through the efforts of Charles J. Haake, a member of the American Conservatory faculty, she won a scholarship to study orchestration at the Conservatory.

The late 1920s were productive years for Price, and her musical activities were varied. She became a prolific composer of piano music for teaching; she was also active as a church organist. And during this time she began to win awards for her compositions (1926 and 1927 *Opportunity* magazine prizes). In addition, Price wrote musical commercials for radio.

Like Dawson, Price found Chicago a stimulating environment in which to work. The home of Estella C. Bonds, a church organist and the mother of Margaret Bonds, the celebrated black concert pianist and composer, provided a nurturing environment for Price and the community of professional black artists in Chicago during that time. Margaret Bonds said of her mother, "A true woman of God, she lived the Sermon on the Mount. Her loaves and fish fed a multitude of pianists, singers, violinists and composers, and those who were not in need of material food came for spiritual food." Regarding the supportive professional environment that was cultivated in her mother's home, she went on to say: "During the cold winter nights in Chicago, we used to sit around a large table in our kitchen—manuscript paper strewn around, Florence [Price] and I extracting parts for some contest deadline. We were a God-loving people, and when we were pushed for time, every brown-skinned musician in Chicago who could write a note, would 'jump-to' and help Florence meet her deadline" (Bonds 1969, 192).

In 1932 the first mark of recognition as a serious composer came for Price when she won first prize in the Wanamaker Music Composition Contest. It was this contest that brought her music to the attention of Frederick Stock, who thereafter conducted the Chicago Symphony at Orchestra Hall in a performance of the award-winning *Symphony in E Minor* in 1933. Stock conducted Price's symphony again that summer at the World's Fair Century of Progress Exhibition when it was also broadcast over radio.[3] The symphony won critical acclaim and was the first symphony composed by a black woman to be played by a major American orchestra.

Like Still's and Dawson's symphonies, Price's score specifies a standard romantic-era orchestra, but it includes several "special effects" instruments in the percussion section: cathedral chimes, small and large African drums, wind whistle, and orchestral bells. The score also stipulates trumpets and clarinets in A (rather than B♭) to be used throughout the symphony.

The first movement of the symphony is structured in sonata form. Beginning with a six-measure introduction in E minor, the bassoons carry a simple four-measure melody accompanied by strings. The bassoon melody then becomes a countersubject to the principal theme of the exposition announced by solo oboe and clarinet. Significantly, the principal theme and its countermelody are built on a pentatonic scale, the most frequently used scale in Afro-American folksongs. The simple harmonization of the theme—i iv v i—grows out of the suggested harmony of the theme itself. Note that the harmonization is entirely in the minor mode (see example 5.4).

A French horn plays the four-measure secondary theme, in G major,

Example 5.4. *Symphony in E minor*, Florence Price, primary theme, first movement

with a sustained, chordal string accompaniment. This theme bears a marked relationship to the principal theme of Dvořák's *Symphony No. 9*, first movement. This "Symphony of the New World" provided a role model for many American composers in the use of Afro-American folk materials in symphonic works, and it is likely that Price used Dvořák's American works as a source of inspiration for her first symphony.

In the development section, harmonic and motivic alteration of the themes is explored, but in contrast to the exposition, the texture is primarily contrapuntal. Several moments are particularly interesting thematically. At times, the themes are restated simultaneously. Also included in the development are inversions of the secondary theme and the primary theme. A modified recapitulation follows the development.

Church music and the idiosyncrasies of organ sound and technique are doubtless the source of inspiration for the hymn-like form and texture of the second movement, Largo Maestoso. Essentially, the movement is based on a twenty-eight-measure hymn that Price composed. It is played solely by a brass choir consisting of four horns in F, two trumpets in A, three trombones, and tuba with the melody in the first trumpet part (see example 5.5). Short interludes by flutes and clarinets separate the phrases, while African drums and timpani provide a continual underlying pulse. The overall structure of the movement is ABA; its parallel is in the verse-and-refrain form common in many Afro-American spirituals and other sacred music.

Example 5.5. *Symphony in E minor*, Florence Price, second movement, mm. 1–5

Entitled "Juba Dance," the third movement of the symphony is based on the syncopated rhythms of the antebellum folk dance. For Price, the rhythmic element in Afro-American music was of "preeminent importance." "In the dance," she wrote, "it is a compelling, onward-sweeping force that tolerates no interruption" (Price 1939). Referring to her *Third Symphony* (1940), which also uses the juba as the basis for a movement, she wrote:

In all of my works which have been done in the sonata form with Negroid idiom, I have incorporated a juba as one of the several movements because it seems to me to be no more impossible to conceive of Negroid music devoid of the spiritualistic theme on the one hand than strongly syncopated rhythms of the juba on the other (Price 1940).

Price was the first composer to base a movement of a symphonic work on the rhythms of the juba, although the most famous and popular instrumental version of the juba is the fifth movement of R. Nathaniel Dett's *In the Bottoms* piano suite published in 1913, which Price surely would have known.[4] In addition to the first and third symphonies, the syncopated rhythms of this dance are also used in the third movement of the *Piano Concerto in One Movement* (1934) and the third dance from the *Suite of Dances* (1939). Several works for piano are also based on the antebellum folk dance, including "Ticklin' Toes" from the third dance from *Three Little Negro Dances* (1933) and "Silk Hat and Walking Cane" from *Dances in the Canebrakes* (1953).

Price set the juba dance movement of the E-minor symphony in rondo form. In the A section, the violins present a sprightly, syncopated eight-measure rhythmic pattern, simulating an antebellum fiddler. Against it, an "um-pah" bass is provided by a tonic-dominant pizzicato ostinato in the remaining strings and percussion (see example 5.6). The figures that form the basis of the dance are African-derived figures that entered the juba dance by way of black banjo and fiddle music with its percussive accompaniment of hand-clapping and foot-tapping.

Example 5.6. *Symphony in E minor*, Florence Price, third movement, mm. 1–4

The last movement of the symphony, marked "Finale," is the most straightforward. A Presto movement in E minor, in duple meter, its melodic and harmonic content is based on a four-measure triplet figure which ascends and descends around an E-natural-minor scale. Flutes, oboes, and violins render the unison line, and the remainder of the orchestra accompanies with sparse chords. Taken as a whole, the form of the fourth movement loosely resembles a rondo.

The absence of overt identifiable ethnic characteristics in Florence Price's *Symphony in E Minor*, namely quotations of black folk themes or the use of a blues progression, prompted criticism from Alain Locke in the essay cited above. He asserted:

> In straight classical idiom and form, Mrs. Price's work vindicates the Negro composer's right, at choice, to go up Parnassus by the broad high road of classicism rather than the narrower, more hazardous but often more rewarding path of racialism. At the pinnacle, the paths converge and the attainment becomes, in the last analysis, neither racial nor national, but universal music (Locke [1936] 1969, 115).

As a close examination of Price's *Symphony in E Minor* has revealed, by no means did she exclude cultural elements in her music. Price's symphony, like Still's, does not depend upon the quotation of folksongs for its distinctive ethnicity. R. Nathaniel Dett has explained: "As it is quite possible to describe the traits, habits, and customs of a people without using the vernacular, so it is similarly possible to musically portray racial peculiarities without the use of national tunes or folk-songs" (Dett [1913] 1973, 33).[5]

Alain Locke's approach to black music was based on the degree to which certain black musical characteristics were present in a given composition. While this approach is valuable, it limits the scope of the black music tradition. If one examines Price's symphony from the qualitative perspective, rather than from Locke's quantitative approach, it becomes evident that Price's music is reflective of her cultural heritage.

Before examining Locke's criticism of Price's work, one must be clear about those particular characteristics of Afro-American music that distinguish it from other types of music. Call-and-response organizational procedures, dominance of a percussive approach to music, and off-beat phrasing of melodic accents have been cited as typical musical characteristics in Afro-American music and have been well documented in almost every study of the music. A predilection for a percussive polyrhythmic manner of playing and the inclusion of environmental factors as integral parts of the music event, such as hand-clapping and foot-patting, are also common characteristics.

An analysis of Price's *Symphony in E Minor* reveals the presence, to a significant degree, of many of these and other underlying conceptual approaches to Afro-American music. For example, Price demonstrably transforms the polyrhythmic manner of approaching rhythm and the inclusion of environmental factors into musical entities in the juba-dance third movement. The steady accompaniment of the melody is a direct manifestation of physical body-movements that were the essence of "patting juba."

Afro-American music also has a tendency to maintain an independence of voices by means of timbral differentiation, or stratification. Nowhere in Price's symphony is this more clear than in the second movement where the tonal colors of the brass choir and woodwind ensemble are juxtaposed with large and small African drums, cathedral chimes, and orchestral bells (see example 5.5). Call-and-response patterns, also exhibited in this movement, between the brass choir and the woodwind ensemble, are another example of stratification.

Cultural characteristics are also borne out implicitly in the themes of the first movement. The first melody is based on a pentatonic scale, one of the most frequently used scales in Afro-American music (see example 5.4). The preference for duple meter with syncopated rhythms and altered tones (lowered third and seventh, the so-called "blue notes") are also specific features of Afro-American music that characterize the melodies of this movement.

A reevaluation of Price's symphony reveals that she does not abandon her Afro-American heritage. Rather, the symphony inherently incorporates many aspects of the black music tradition within a Euro-American medium—orchestral music. In a more subtle way than either Still's *Afro-American Symphony* or Dawson's *Negro Folk Symphony*, Price's compositional approach does make manifest the Afro-American heritage in music. As Samuel Floyd has stated, "When it [the music of black American composers] successfully communicates essentials of the Afro-American experience, in spite of its European basis, it becomes something more than either European or Afro-American. It becomes, to some extent, at least, black music" (Floyd 1982, 83). Following the first performance of the symphony, Edward Moore of the *Chicago Tribune* wrote:

> Mrs. Price . . . displayed high talent both in what she did and what she omitted, each one of which is a test for a composer. She has based her work on racial folk song idioms, choosing some first rate melodies and harmonizing them fully and yet with the essential simplicity that they demand. She would seem to be well acquainted with the use of orchestral instrumental color. With these merits she has another and perhaps greater one. She knows how to be concise, how to avoid overloading and elaboration. The performance made a well deserved success (Moore 1933, 1).

Black racial pride was quintessential to the Negro Renaissance. It was this attitude of black pride and consciousness that permeated many of Still's, Price's, and Dawson's early works in the 1920s and was fully developed and realized in their symphonic works in the early 1930s.

These composers were not really *of* the Negro Renaissance, but the essence of the New Negro Movement was the background against which Still, Price, and Dawson moved and developed as composers.

Within the ideals of the New Negro Movement, an understanding of the potential of Afro-Americans and a reinforcement of their dignity prevailed. Rooted in the hope for the future of black people, the New Negro no longer apologized for his musical heritage but rather celebrated his cultural uniqueness. For Dawson, Price, and Still the Negro idiom in music became a source of inspiration in serious composition, and audiences were ready to accept it.

Thus, in 1935 Shirley Graham could boast of the accomplishments of America's first three Afro-American symphonists. "Spirituals to Symphonies in less than fifty years!" she wrote in an article in which she recounts the development of black art music in America from the triumphs of the Fisk Jubilee Singers and their spiritual arrangements to the critical acclaim of William Dawson's *Negro Folk Symphony* (Graham 1936, 691). In the *Afro-American Symphony*, the *Symphony in E Minor*, and the *Negro Folk Symphony*, Still, Price, and Dawson spoke as Afro-American composers. One must accept their music not as propaganda but as an important legacy of the New Negro's contribution to America's writings.

NOTES

1. Moe (1986, 63) suggests a five-part division of the symphony.

2. Price's score has not been published or recorded. A copy of the manuscript is held in the Price Archive, University of Arkansas, and consists of 105 pages on 53 leaves.

3. Contrary to most recent articles, which refer only to the later Century of Progress performance of Price's E-minor symphony, the Chicago Symphony did in fact have both this symphony and her *Concerto for Piano and Orchestra* in their repertoire.

4. Dett's suite, published by Clayton F. Summy, was given its premiere in Chicago in 1913 by Fanny Bloomfield-Zeisler, a distinguished pianist of the day.

5. Black folk music, per se, is not national; Dett here is referring to the quotation of black folk themes in large-scale works.

REFERENCES

Arvey, Verna. 1984. *In one lifetime*. Fayetteville: The University of Arkansas Press.
———. 1987. Conversation with the author, July 28.
Bonds, Margaret. 1969. A reminiscence. In *International library of Negro life and history: The Negro in music and art*, compiled and edited by Lindsay Patterson, 191–93. New York: Publishers Co.

Dawson, William. [1932; rev. 1952] 1965. *Negro folk symphony*. Delaware Water Gap: Shawnee Music Press.

———. 1978. Liner notes, *Negro folk symphony*. Leopold Stokowski and the American Symphony Orchestra. MCA Records, VC 81056. Reissue of Decca "Gold Label Series" records, Monaural DL 10077, Stereo DL 710077.

———. 1986. Telephone conversation with the author, October 10.

Dett, R. Nathaniel. [1913] 1973. Introduction, *In the bottoms: Characteristic suite for the piano*, 33. Chicago: Clayton F. Summy.

Floyd, Samuel A., Jr. 1982. Toward a philosophy of black music scholarship. *Black Music Research Journal* 2:72–93.

Graham, Shirley. 1936. Spirituals to symphonies. *Etude* (November):691+.

Haas, Robert Bartlett, ed. 1975. *William Grant Still and the fusion of cultures in American music*. Los Angeles: Black Sparrow Press.

Locke, Alain. [1936] 1969. *The Negro and his music*. Reprint. New York: Arno Press and the New York Times.

Moe, Orin. 1986. A question of value: Black concert music and criticism. *Black Music Research Journal* 6:57–65.

Moore, Edward. 1933. City assured symphony season of 28 weeks for next winter: Negro in music given place in concert of Century of Progress series. *Chicago Tribune* June 16:sec. 1, 1.

Price, Florence. 1939. Program notes, inside cover, *Three Negro dances* (arranged for band by Erik W. G. Leidzen). Bryn Mawr, Pa.: Theodore Presser.

———. 1940. Letter to Frederick L. Schwass, Allen Park, Michigan, October 22. Held in the Price Archive, University of Arkansas, Fayetteville, Arkansas.

Still, William Grant. 1965. Liner notes, *Afro-American symphony*. Karl Krueger and the Royal Philharmonic Orchestra of London. Preservation of the American Musical Heritage MIA-118.

———. [1930] 1970. *Afro-American symphony*. London: Novello.

CHAPTER 6

Black Musical Theater and the Harlem Renaissance Movement

John Graziano

Although black musical theater flourished during the years of the Harlem Renaissance, it was treated with grudging respect by the cultural leaders of the movement. While they were aware of its popularity among both black and white audiences, spokesmen for the movement were critical that the books, music, and lyrics of black musicals did not project the appropriate intellectual image of the "New Negro" (Huggins 1971, 196). In spite of their recognition that the public and many critics were hailing the better examples of the genre and although many "hit" songs continued to be written, the fact that the music was popular in design, was commercial in intent, and was not intended to serve as "high art" kept some of the more important spokesmen of the movement from accepting it as completely as they did the poetry, novels, plays, choreography, and classical music created during the period (Butcher 1956, 33). Creative efforts in the fields of popular music, Broadway shows, and jazz were viewed as artistic forays that "evidenced qualities in the Negro character that might be converted into something important" (Huggins 1971, 198).

Perhaps the lack of enthusiasm evinced by various commentators of the period has led to the general perception that there is little of value in the songs of black musicals of the 1920s. Even a cursory inquiry into the nature and variety of the songs in these musicals challenges that assumption. I hope to document, within the limits of this chapter, the existence of a significant number of first-rate innovative songs, within this body of nearly forgotten music, that contributed to the growth and development of American musical theater in the 1920s.

BACKGROUND AND DEVELOPMENT

The development of black musical theater during the Harlem Renaissance owes little to the proclamations of those involved with the establishment of the movement. In contrast to the literary arts, which appear to have burgeoned and caught the general public's attention at the conclusion of World War I, black musical theater was already established and acclaimed by the turn of the century. Between 1895 and 1911, more than a half-dozen black musicals reached Broadway and were seen by both black and white audiences. Shows like *In Dahomey* (1902), *Abyssinia* (1906), and *The Red Moon* (1908) introduced many major black talents to the public. Performing teams like [Bert] Williams and [George] Walker and [Bob] Cole and [J. Rosamond] Johnson were perhaps the most visible and in demand, but their contributions were equaled by talents like Jesse Shipp (1869–1934), Will Marion Cook (1869–1944), and J. Leubrie Hill (1869–1916).

Regional black theater was also important to the development of the pool of talent. Several writer/performers formed stock companies that performed throughout the year. The famous team of Miller and Lyles, for example, did their earliest work for the Pekin Stock Company in Chicago (Sampson 1980, 111). The weekly shows of Billy King (1875– after 1937) were seen in various cities in the Midwest and South. From 1915 through 1923, his company played the Grand Theatre in Chicago (Sampson 1980, 96). Finally, the existence of a network of theaters that presented black attractions across the country was also important to the investors in Broadway productions. Many shows were able to repay their production costs through the road company tour even when the Broadway run was not financially successful.

Several distinct lines of development, which continued to provide a basis for popular entertainments during the twenties, are to be seen in the early black shows. The minstrel show provided one obvious model for black troupes that were faced with the task of constructing a show that would attract large audiences. One of the earliest and most successful black shows, the *Creole Show* of 1890, followed in that tradition (Johnson 1930, 95). The minstrel show model was modified to some extent in 1896, when, in *Oriental America*, the popular finale was revised to include a medley of well-known operatic and operetta arias and duets. The altered model was performed by troupes like the Black Patti Troubadours, which continued to tour the country until Sissieretta Jones's retirement in 1915.

Another model for black artists was the revue. Although revues were not new to Broadway, they were seen more frequently after the commercial success of Ziegfeld's *Follies* as the public eagerly accepted the concept. From a commercial standpoint, the revue was less risky to produce than the book musical because it did not depend on a single idea for the evening's entertainment. If an act or skit proved unpopular with audiences, it could be removed without disturbing the remainder of the show. The revue also allowed for the innumerable changes that occurred when an act left one show to join another. By featuring specialty acts, a few short comic sketches, and lots of dancing, these shows were not only able to provide entertainment to compete with vaudeville, but to surpass it through the additional use of opulent sets and costumes.

The most important model that attracted black artists around the turn of the century was the book musical. Bob Cole's *A Trip to Coontown* (1898), which has been cited as the first black show to be "organized, produced, and managed by Negroes" (Johnson 1930, 102), is possibly the first example of a full-length black musical comedy to reach Broadway. It has been noted that the scripts for *A Trip to Coontown* and the full-length shows that followed in its wake, including *In Dahomey, Abyssinia, The Red Moon,* and *Mr. Lode of Koal* (1909), represented a new direction for black musical theater because they jettisoned the stereotypes seen for so long in minstrel shows (Huggins 1971, 281). However, an examination of the extant scripts demonstrates that the changes were not all that significant. The penchant for exaggerating black stereotypes was still in evidence (Graziano 1984, 212–13).

The plots of black musical shows, both full- and skit-length, from the turn of the century through the end of the Renaissance, were almost entirely based on a limited number of subjects. Variations on the return to Africa movement were to be found in *In Dahomey, Abyssinia, An African Prince* (1920), and *Bamboula* (1921). Black concern with the relationship to white society was developed in several shows, including *The Cannibal King* (1900), *Jes' Lak White Fo'ks* (1901), and *Brown Sugar* (1927). In *Jes' Lak White Fo'ks,* for example, the plot revolves around Pompous Johnsing's attempt, after he has discovered gold, to convince his daughter, Mandy, to marry a royal suitor, Prince JuJu, in spite of her love for a common black, Wait R. Shufflehood. He ultimately accepts his daughter's choice of a mate, spurns the idea of upward mobility, and declares that he will no longer act like the white folks do.

One of the more persistent plot devices revolved around swindles perpetuated by fast-talking dandies. These swindles most often involved money, property, and oil strikes. A partial list of such shows would include *Bandana Land* (1908), *Who's Stealing?* (1918), *Africana* (1922), *Liza* (1922), *Come Along Mandy* (1924), and *Lucky Sambo* (1925). Another favored subject was gambling, as seen in *The Man from 'Bam* (1906), *They're Off* (1919), and *The Chocolate Dandies* (1924). Many shows and revues also included a cemetery or ghost scene; during the 1920s, such scenes appeared in *Alabama Bound* (1921) and *Runnin' Wild* (1923).

New subjects were also explored: rent-party scenes, in *Hot Rhythm* (1930); prohibition, in *How Come* (1923) and *Darktown Scandals* (1927); stardom on Broadway, in *North Ain't South* (1923), *Miss Bandana* (1927), *Bottomland* (1927), and *Bombolla* (1929); and the new black image, in *Over the Top* (1919), *Negro Nuances* (1924), and *Deep Harlem* (1929) (Sampson 1980, script synopses, 136–337).

Regular audiences were made comfortable by the return of characters they had seen previously. Steve Jenkins and Sam Peck, played by Miller and Lyles, appeared in *The Colored Aristocrats* (1909), *Shuffle Along* (1921), *Runnin' Wild* (1923), and *Keep Shufflin'* (1928). George Washington Bullion, played by Salem Tutt Whitney, appeared in *George Washington Bullion Abroad* (1915) and *How Newton Prepared* (1916). Whitney and his brother, J. Homer Tutt, also created the characters Abraham Dubois Washington and Gabriel Douglass; they appeared in the shows *Darkest Americans* (1919) and *The Children of the Sun* (1919).

If the subjects discussed above seem to us today to perpetuate racial stereotypes, it should be noted that the vast majority of black shows written and performed from 1890 through the 1930s were intended for black audiences and were not seen on Broadway at all. Eubie Blake, for example, relates how he complained to B. C. Whitney, the producer of *The Chocolate Dandies*, about the costumes used to open the second act. "The girls wore white dresses, with *hoop skirts*." Blake felt the scene was "too *beautiful* for a colored show." Whitney's response, according to Blake, was, "Eubie, this is *not* a colored show. This is Sissle and Blake's show for Broadway" (Kimball and Bolcom 1973, 178). Stock companies were a regional phenomenon in Chicago, Kansas City, and other communities with a large black population. A considerable number of the New York shows played only in Harlem, where they were seen during the 1920s by a few white visitors. Very successful "uptown" shows were sometimes moved to a downtown theater, where they occasionally achieved a limited success, but some successful shows skipped Broadway altogether. The first of the various "Blackbird" revues, *Lew Leslie's Blackbirds of 1926*, is an example of a show that did not play a downtown theater, although it was seen in Paris and London, for five- and six-month runs, respectively, after a six-week engagement in Harlem's Alhambra Theatre (Johnson 1930, 199).

Because a long run on the "Great White Way" would provide financial stability, it was to be hoped that white critics and audiences would respond favorably if and when a show reached Broadway. Even so, the needs of a white audience were probably seen as a secondary goal. Most shows that reached Broadway, in fact, went on extensive road tours after the run. In most cities they played for audiences that, once more, were primarily black. Thus, it can be assumed that one of the more important goals of the writers was to produce scripts that appealed to the-ater-going middle-class blacks across the country (Mitchell 1967, 70). In general, I believe that the needs of white audiences were mostly ig-nored, which may help to explain why so many of the shows reaching Broadway during the Renaissance were able to sustain only limited en-gagements there.

Reviews of the period note that, by Broadway standards, many of the shows had "thin" plots. It appears that, especially in the case of Miller and Lyles, various skits, sometimes a decade or more old, were recycled with minimal change. Since some scripts were literally "pasted" to-gether, it is not surprising to find that black shows were altered dramat-ically and musically, even during a Broadway run, when one or more of the principals dropped out of the production or when a number proved unpopular with the audience. *Keep Shufflin'* provides a good example of the kind of changes one might find. A program from the opening night performance on February 27, 1928, gives the following order of musical events:

ACT I

1. Opening chorus (Creamer and Vodery)

2. Chocolate Bar (Razaf and Waller)

3. Labor Day Parade (Razaf and Todd)

4. Give Me the Sunshine (Creamer, Johnson, and Conrad)

5. Pining (Creamer and Todd)

6. Leg It (Creamer, Todd, and Conrad)

7. Washboard Ballet (Waller)

8. Exhortation (Creamer and Conrad)

9. Sippi (Creamer, Johnson, and Conrad)

10. How Jazz Was Born (Razaf and Waller)

11. Finale (no details given)

ACT II

1. Keep Shufflin' (Razaf and Waller)

2. Ev'rybody's Happy in Jimtown (Razaf and Waller)

3. Give Me the Sunshine (Reprise)

4. Dusky Love (Creamer and Vodery)

5. Charlie, My Back Door Man (Creamer and Todd)

6. On the Levee (Creamer and Johnson)

7. Harlem Rose (Gladys Rodgers and Conrad)

8. Finale (no details given)

The program makes no mention of three additional published songs, "Willow Tree. A Musical Misery" (Razaf and Waller), "Got Myself Another Jockey Now" (Razaf and Waller), or "'Twas a Kiss in the Moonlight" (Conrad, Creamer, and Stephen Jones). These songs probably appeared in the Finales of Acts I and/or II.

By the third week (March 12, 1928), the program contains several changes: a new number, "Buck Up to Me" (no authors given), has been added after the opening chorus of Act I, and two numbers, "Pining" and "Washboard Ballet," have been dropped from the show. "Harlem Rose" is likewise dropped from Act II. The program for April 23 shows additional changes: "Buck Up to Me" has now been replaced by "Teasing Mama" (Creamer and Johnson), and "Skiddle-de-Skow" (Johnson and Bradford), which would resurface the following season as part of *Messin' Around*, is listed as the Finale to Act II.

The credits for *Keep Shufflin'* also hint at changing relationships among the principals; when the show opened, the program credits read as follows:

> *Con Conrad, Inc.* offers
> *Miller and Lyles*
> in the Musical Comedy
> *"Keep Shufflin'"*
> Book by Flourney Miller and Aubrey Lyles
> Music by Jimmy Johnson, "Fats" Waller and Clarence Todd
> Lyrics by Henry Creamer and Andy Razaf
> Dances and Ensembles staged by Clarence Robinson
> Orchestrations by Will Vodery   Musical Director, Jimmy Johnson
> Entire Production Staged by Con Conrad

By April 23, after the show had moved from Daly's on 63rd Street to the Eltinge Theatre on 42nd Street, Conrad's name was no longer listed as producer, and as noted above, one of his songs had also been dropped.

After 104 performances, *Keep Shufflin'* closed; a road company was evidently organized and played through at least September 1928. Two extant programs, from theaters in the Bronx and Brooklyn, New York, give evidence of a very different show. The changes start with the credits:

> *The Original and Only*
> *Miller and Lyles*
> —in—
> *Their Latest Jazz Riot*
> *"Keep Shufflin'"*
> —with—
> Their Own Company of 75 Dusky Singers and Dancers

—and—

The Original "Shuffle Along" Orchestra under direction of Jimmy Johnson
Book Written and Staged by Flourney Miller
Dances and Ensembles Staged by Byron Jones

The list of musical numbers documents numerous changes; three numbers, "Labor Day Parade," "Leg It," and "Exhortation," are dropped from Act I and replaced by "Brothers," "Don't Wake 'Em Up," and "Whoopem Up" (no authors given). Act II follows similarly with six new numbers: "Bugle Blues," "Deep Blue Sea," "My Old Banjo," "Pretty Soft, Pretty Sweet," "Let's Go to Town," and "You May Be a Whale in Georgia" (no authors given) replace the original songs, "Dusky Love," "Charlie, My Back Door Man," and "On the Levee." The book also appears to have been altered, although until it has been determined if the scripts are extant and until they have been examined, it will not be possible to detail the textual differences. However, a comparison of the scenes listed in the programs shows the following differences:

Original Show (2/27/1928)	Revised Show (as of 9/3/1928)
ACT I	*ACT I*
Scene 1	*Scene 1*
Exterior of Industrial School, Jimtown	Grand Hotel, Outskirts of School, Palm Beach
Scene 2	*Scene 2*
Street in Jimtown	In front of drapery
Scene 3	*Scene 3*
Front Yard of Steve Jenkins's Home	Backyard of Steve Jenkins's Home
	Scene 4
	In front of blue curtain
	Scene 5
	Backyard of Steve's home
ACT II	*ACT II*
Scene 1	*Scene 1*
Town Hall	The Levee
Scene 2	*Scene 2*
Main Street, Jimtown	A bit of lace
Scene 3	*Scene 3*
Interior of Steve Jenkin's Home	Dinnertime at Steve's home
Scene 4	*Scene 4*
Outskirts of Jimtown	Sunflower Lane

Scene 5	*Scene 5*
Back in Front Yard of Steve Jenkins's Home	A graveyard
	Scene 6
	Exterior of Steve Jenkins's Home

From a textual point of view, then, the character of black musical theater during the Harlem Renaissance did not change essentially from that which the public had known previously. Although billboards and marquees no longer carried notices like "Williams and Walker, the Two Real Coons" and "coon" songs were no longer in vogue, the premise of the plots of black musicals had not basically changed. The reasons for this apparent stagnation would seem to be the result of several independent though interrelated events.

1. The years 1911–1920 saw no full-length black musical or revue on Broadway (Johnson 1930, 170). Although shows continued to be written and produced, they were seen almost exclusively by black audiences, and most of the sketches and comedy numbers in these shows were tailored to meet the demands of a local population.

2. Very few young black writers were drawn to musical theater during the second decade. The writers whose names are most often represented by successful shows were born before 1890, with some as early as 1869. These writers had participated in the great success of black theater at the turn of the century, which had catapulted Williams and Walker, among others, to stardom. Their books during the teens and twenties attempted to prolong that success by continuing the formulas that had been so popular. Whether Miller and Lyles tried to bring in an audience by writing a new play for their well-known stage characters, Sam Peck and Steve Jenkins, or whether Frank Montgomery tried to attract attention by producing *In Ethiopiaville* (1913) with two bumbling detectives, Shylock Holmestead and Dandy Jones Pinkerton (which would remind audiences of *In Dahomey's* Shylock Homestead and Rareback Pinkerton), the result was clear: black musical theater was following a safe commercial course.

3. The force of the Harlem Renaissance movement during the years following the war might have produced a major change of direction had it not been for the phenomenal success of the first black musical to reach Broadway in almost a decade. *Shuffle Along,* with book by Miller and Lyles, featuring their popular characters, Peck and Jenkins, and recycling parts of their 1918 show,

Who's Stealing?, probably doomed any effort to advance a more serious concept (Sampson 1980, 306). Almost all the books for black musicals during the 1920s tried to equal the success of *Shuffle Along* by recycling plot devices that were almost two decades old; most shows were unsuccessful in their attempt to attract a Broadway audience for more than several months. By 1930 James Weldon Johnson had already recognized the problem: although Miller and Lyles "were as funny as ever" in *Rang Tang* (1927), "the thought arose that perhaps the traditional pattern of Negro musical comedy was a bit worn" (Johnson 1930, 209).

THE MUSIC

Musically, however, the situation was considerably different. Composers like Bob Cole (1868–1911), Will Marion Cook, J. Rosamond Johnson (1873–1954), Chris Smith (1879–1949), James Reese Europe (1881–1919), and Ford Dabney (1883–1958) had paved the way at the beginning of the century by introducing ragtime rhythms and adventurous harmonies to vaudeville and the Broadway scene. By the middle of the second decade their innovations had entered the musical mainstream and were embraced by most Tin Pan Alley composers.[1] Many popular tunes and the songs of Broadway musicals reflected this influence through the increased use of sophisticated harmonic progressions and the use of major seventh and ninth chords. Many black composers during the period continued to infuse Tin Pan Alley with music that was drawn from ethnic black culture (Butcher 1956, 35). By the 1920s another aspect of their culture, the blues, was infusing the form and substance of popular song as it had earlier with piano ragtime (Berlin 1980, 158–60). This secular genre was first popularized by Ma Rainey in the early part of the century and was brought to wider public attention through the success of W. C. Handy's "The Memphis Blues" (1913) and more particularly "St. Louis Blues" (1914), which, according to one source, was "the most important piece of popular music published in 1914" (Spaeth 1948, 390). Throughout the twenties, novel and innovative harmonic experimentation continued to be in evidence. It is regularly encountered in the music of Eubie Blake (1883–1983), James P. (Jimmy) Johnson (1894–1955), C. Luckeyth Roberts (1895–1968), and Thomas (Fats) Waller (1904–1943), who were active as composers of instrumental rags as well as songs. Their songs often reflect the influence of instrumental writing, especially in the use of more secondary dominant chords and modal borrowing.

The importance to white society of the orchestras founded by Europe, Dabney, and Cook added another sphere of influence; they played many white engagements and popularized ragtime dances that were black in origin. As early as 1913 the dancing public was introduced to a new step in Jim Burris and Chris Smith's "Ballin' the Jack"; over the next decade, other new dances were introduced. The various trots, the Grizzly Bear, the Charleston and its inevitable imitations, and the Black Bottom, among others, were all well received and became the rage of the period (Locke [1936] 1969, 65–67).

As in all periods of musical development, remnants of an earlier style of composition continued to coexist with the newer music. Sentimental ballads, usually in triple time, were still evident, although their harmonic progressions were somewhat more involved than earlier examples. Likewise, the march-like accompaniments associated with ragtime and the two-step, which were so dominant at the beginning of the century, continued to be heard from time to time, even though that style of song had gone out of vogue.

An examination of the published songs for black musicals of the 1920s gives ample evidence of the variety of music that was heard.[2] A composer like Eubie Blake not only had the option of writing in the prevalent white styles of the period, but could also compose in the several current black styles. In *Shuffle Along,* for example, commercial Tin Pan Alley songs like "Love Will Find a Way" and "I'm Just Wild about Harry" as well as a black comedy number like "If You've Never Been Vamped by a Brownskin, You Haven't Been Vamped at All," and an ethnic dance number, "African Dip," were all heard in the course of one evening.

Blue notes and the use of coloristic blue chords quickly became an identifiable signature of many composers; the mixing of major and minor modes is heard in many songs. A few black composers, however, wrote popular songs that used the blues more idiomatically. Their songs not only exhibit the more readily recognized blue notes and blues chords, but also utilize the less familiar static harmonic progressions and repetitive melodic-rhythmic formulas associated with the country blues form.

Two songs by James P. (Jimmy) Johnson demonstrate his fluent use of blues idiom. Example 6.1 presents the verse of "Love Bug," which was heard in the successful show *Runnin' Wild* (1923). Formally, Johnson has expanded the traditional twelve-measure A A′ B blues structure to sixteen measures. The harmonic progression, however, is characteristic of blues. The tonic chord, F-major/minor, is heard in the first A section (m. 1–4). The second A section does not start on the expected subdominant chord, but rather on the lowered mediant, A♭ major, borrowed from the minor mode, which resolves in measure 8 to the dominant seventh. The B section is expanded to eight measures. It starts with an abrupt shift to

Example 6.1. "Love Bug," Jimmy Johnson, verse, mm. 1–16

another borrowed chord, the ♭VI⁷, for two measures, before returning to the tonic. The closing four measures emphasize the dominant through use of a secondary dominant as Johnson prepares for the return to the F major at the beginning of the Chorus.

A blues influence is noted in the melody also. Its opening measures are modally ambiguous because of the insistent alternation of *a* with *a♭* and *c* with *c♭*. In measure 9, Johnson introduces a new pitch, *d♭*, which is supported by its seventh chord. It comes as a surprise after the static beginning and provides the impetus for the melodic descent that follows. The pitches c♭ and c return reharmonized in measures 10 and 11. The former functions as the seventh of the D♭-major chord rather than the third of an A♭-major chord, while the latter is now heard as the fifth of the tonic chord. Although ragtime rhythms can be discerned, they are not insistent; they do, however, provide a rhythmic propulsion to the music.

Another blues-inspired song, "Skiddle-De-Skow" (see example 6.2a), was heard in *Messin' Around* (1929). Although the verse is only eight measures, it suggests the basic harmonic pattern associated with the traditional blues—four measures in the tonic followed by four measures in the dominant. Johnson once again uses the ♭VI⁷; this time, however, it functions coloristically within the phrase. In measures 1 through 4 it alternates with the tonic, F minor. In measures 5 through 7 the alternation once more is heard, but this time in conjunction with the subdominant. In the final measure Johnson unexpectedly introduces an E⁷ chord, which serves as the link to the refrain, which is cast in the relative minor. Over this harmonic sequence, the singsong repetition of the melody gives the piece more than a hint of Afro-American influence. The opening of the refrain (see example 6.2b) is now in A♭ major, but tonal ambiguity is achieved through the almost continuous use of seventh chords. Johnson again uses the tonic-subdominant progression so characteristic of blues progressions. One other point of interest is his use of a secondary dominant ninth chord (m. 7) at the half cadence, which prolongs the pitch c/c♭ through the first seven measures of the period.

Similarly, several identified conventions of the blues style are interpolated by Fats Waller in many of his pieces. In *Keep Shufflin'* (1928), the chorus of "Got Myself Another Jockey Now" joins the newer blues idiom with the older two-step style in a convincing way (see example 6.3). Measures 1 through 4 introduce a typical tonic-subdominant blues accompaniment; although this type of accompaniment is heard in many blues, its appearance in a show tune is unusual. The harmonic ambivalence that one hears because of the opening measure's F-major seventh chord is not resolved in measures 3 and 4, which are harmonized by a B♭-major ninth chord. By measure 5 Waller has returned to the tonic; simultaneously, he changes the style of his accompaniment by falling back on the old two-step march cliche, while a traditional cadential I V⁷ I progression is heard. Measures 7 and 8, however, reintroduce the blues style through the use of lowered VII and VI chords. The second period proceeds identically to the first, except for the final two measures, in which the lowered third is heard melodically for the first time.

Example 6.4, an excerpt from the song "Rhythm Man," which was

Example 6.2. "Skiddle-de-skow," Jimmy Johnson
a. verse, mm. 1–8

b. refrain, mm. 1–8

heard in *Connie's Hot Chocolates* (1929), demonstrates Waller's use of melodic blue notes in the vocal part (in m. 5 and 6). The harmonic progression is notable for its limited use of the tonic (m. 5 and 7) and its effective use of consecutive seventh chords.

Example 6.3. "Got Myself Another Jockey Now," Thomas Waller, chorus, mm. 1–16

Example 6.4. "Rhythm Man," Thomas Waller, chorus, mm. 1–8

After four measures of alternating G-major^7/C-major^7 chords, Waller briefly lands on the tonic. A sophisticated, somewhat jazzy cadential progression follows: ($\flat$VI^7 V^7) V^7 German Aug.^{6} V^7 I$^{(added\ 6)}$.

Other examples of songs with blues influence can be found in Donald Heywood's score for *Africana* (1927), in the songs "Clorinda" and

"Smile," and in "Give Me the Sunshine" (Henry Creamer, Jimmy Johnson, and Con Conrad) from *Keep Shufflin'*.

While blue notes and blue chords are an important aspect of the musical language of the 1920s, they do not constitute the only means by which black composers achieved musical novelty in their songs. Their experiments with harmonic progressions constitute an important addition to the musical language of the twenties. One such example is seen in "Jungle Rose" by Ford Dabney, heard in *Rang Tang* (1927). The text of the chorus, with its occasionally forced rhymes, is a paean to the charms of the lady in question; it brings to mind the lyrics of a song like "My Dahomian Queen," which was heard almost three decades earlier in *In Dahomey*.

> Arrayed in all her jungle splendor
> The peacocks stared amazed in wonder;
> The crocodiles and lions wild
> Crouch like a naughty child
> Begging for one of her smiles.
> The voice of spring is in her laughter
> For all the birds to copy after;
> And when she sings
> All living things
> Fall in love with Jungle Rose.

Dabney has set this text as a march. Example 6.5 presents the first sixteen measures of the chorus. The musical rhythm of the accompaniment

is decidedly old-fashioned. Dabney has barely disguised the two-step alternation on which it is based and which, by 1927, was hardly being used as the basis for an entire song. Once again, much of the interest here centers on the harmonic progression. Although the basic progression, I IV V⁷ I V, is not, in itself, unusual, Dabney's use of secondary chords in measures 2, 6, and 9 and delayed resolutions in measures 3 and 7 gives it a new life.

According to his biography, Luckeyth Roberts learned to read and write music late in life; he played by ear and often improvised (Southern 1983, 322). His use of harmony, therefore, was not so much learned as it was intuited; it is probably safe to assume that much of his notated music, including the songs, consists of transcriptions of some of the improvisatory bits he played. In 1923 Roberts teamed up with Alex Rogers to provide the score for *Go-Go*. The show had a brief run, but eight

Example 6.5. "Jungle Rose," Ford Dabney, chorus, mm. 1–16

numbers were published. They show Roberts to be a first-rate and innovative composer for the musical theater, although he never had a commercial success on Broadway.

Example 6.6 presents the verse from "Isabel." Traces of ragtime
rhythm infuse the opening measures, and the vocal part, which encom-
passes a minor tenth, has an instrumental flavor to it. But Roberts's
most important contribution in this song is his use of unusual harmonic
progressions. "Isabel" utilizes a sequence of ninth chords that, to my
knowledge, is unique in a song in the 1920s. Although the song is in F

Example 6.6. "Isabel," C. Luckeyth Roberts, verse, mm. 1–12

major, the tonic appears unequivocally only once (in m. 4); by measure 6, the progression has moved to A minor. Roberts leads one to believe that he will cadence in the new key; instead, in measure 7, he moves deceptively to an F-major ninth chord (the submediant in A minor) and then, in parallel motion, through nine more ninth chords until, finally, he prepares the cadence for his C-seventh dominant chord. Roberts's use of parallel fifths in the bass is most likely another indication of the improvisatory origin of this passage. A similar passage constructed from descending diminished seventh chords appears in "Mo' 'Lasses," which was also heard in *Go-Go*.

"Mo' 'Lasses" is also of interest because of the unusual form of its chorus, A, A (transposed), B, A, A (transposed), C, and the subtlety of its harmonic progression. The C section (which, along with the last four bars of the transposed A, is presented in example 6.7) toys with the listener's expectations. After seven static ragtime-influenced measures of F major, the music comes to a sudden stop in measure 40 on what mo-

Example 6.7. "Mo' 'Lasses," C. Luckeyth Roberts, chorus, mm. 38–49

mentarily appears to be an incomplete F♯-diminished chord. It is quickly converted to a German augmented sixth chord by the addition of a♭. The C section opens with a respelled chord (e♭ becomes d♯) which resolves to a C-major chord. It changes to a seventh chord through the addition of b (measure 42). The progression continues through seventh chords on b♭ and a. This last chord begins a cycle of dominant seventh chords that eventually leads us back to the tonic.

Thus far, this chapter has focused on ethnic-derived innovations of several black composers to musical theater; although many non-ethnic songs were written by black composers during this period, no examples of a standard commercial song have been discussed. It should be emphasized that much of the music by songwriters like Shelton Brooks, Eubie Blake, Fats Waller, and Spencer and Clarence Williams was indeed a part of the popular Tin Pan Alley style discussed by Hamm, Wilder, and others. Most black composers could write equally well in both the ethnic black and non-ethnic white styles. Blake's 1930 song, "You're Lucky to Me," written for *Lew Leslie's Blackbirds of 1930*, is an example of his mastery of the non-ethnic white song. While some music historians might consider this song imitative of the white style rather than original, I believe it not only exemplifies Blake's familiarity with the conventions of a downtown commercial song, but demonstrates his instinct for setting a conventional tune unconventionally (see example 6.8). The tune, which starts on step 5 of the scale, moves conjunctly through a major ninth before settling back on c. It then skips to the highest point of the contour with the introduction of a dissonance, e♭.

Example 6.8. "You're Lucky to Me," Eubie Blake, chorus, mm. 1–8

Once resolved, the tune stays within the diatonic scale of the tonic, F major. Although the chord progression (as presented in figure 6.1) is essentially diatonic, the listener's attention is caught by the music's attractive surface, created by Blake's unexpected harmonizations of the melody (in measure 3, for example, the underpinning of *c* with an A-half diminished seventh chord rather than the expected F-major chord), his use of secondary chords in the harmonic progression (measures 1, 3, and 4), and passing tones, upper and lower neighbors, and appoggiaturas.

Figure 6.1. "You're Lucky to Me," Eubie Blake, harmonic analysis, mm. 1–8

THE LYRICS

As might be expected, the lyrics for the songs written during the Renaissance are as varied as the music. Lyricists like Henry Creamer (1879–1930) and Andy Razaf (1895–1973), and composers like Alex Rogers (1876–1930) and Noble Sissle (1892–1954), were able to turn out lyrics in both the non-ethnic and ethnic styles, from mainstream white ("You're Lucky to Me" and "Isabel"), to colloquial, nonsense, and slang ("Charleston" and "Skiddle-de-Skow"), to black comedy or dialect ("If

You've Never Been Vamped by a Brownskin" and "Mo' 'Lasses"). I have chosen the texts to three songs to represent the various styles outlined above, though I realize that this brief survey cannot hope to document thoroughly the vitality and variety of the lyrics written during the Renaissance.

One of the most successful and brilliant lyricists of this period was Andy Razaf. Whether he was writing *double entendre* lyrics like "My Handy Man Ain't Handy No More" (with Blake) or "Got Myself Another Jockey Now" (with Waller), or a "New Negro" lyric like "We're Americans Too" (with Blake), or poetically eloquent verse in "Roll, Jordan" (with Blake) and "Weary" (composed in 1940 with Blake), or a sophisticated, colloquial lyric like "Ain't-cha Glad?" (with Waller), his work was well crafted. In "Ain't-cha Glad?" Razaf plays with internal rhyme structure ("Folks declare, 'What a pair!'"), varied phrase lengths (lines 1 through 4 of the Chorus), and unrhymed couplets (lines 7–8 and 15–16).

Verse

Folks look in surprise,
Hearin' us sing our happy song,
They can't b'lieve their eyes;
Seein' the way we get along.

Chorus

Ain't-cha glad, we were mated for each other?
Ain't-cha glad, that we waited for each other?
We agree constantly.
Life is just a symphony of perfect harmony.
Ain't-cha glad, how we get along together?
Ain't-cha glad, we can laugh at "stormy weather"?
Folks declare, "What a pair!"
They can see we're happy, ain't-cha glad?
Just like two lovers on picture covers,
In spite of sun or rain,
We find romance,
Ev'ry street we meet is lover's lane,
Ain't-cha glad, that our kisses keep their flavor?
Ain't-cha glad, ev'rything is in our favor?
Ev'ry day, we can say,
Ev'rything is rosy, ain't-cha glad?

Although he is not as well known today as Razaf, Alex Rogers, whose career as a lyricist and composer reached back to the beginning of the century, was also a versatile professional. His lyrics in the 1920s for several C. Luckeyth Roberts scores give continuing evidence of his wide abilities. Standard texts like "Rosetime and You" and "Heartbeats" contrast dramatically with his nonsense dialect lyric for "Mo' 'Lasses" (which surely is not concerned with the syrup). Rogers's repeating rhyme scheme (aaab) in the Chorus, which is matched by Roberts's static musical setting, gives way in the B section (lines 9 through 12) to rhymed couplets (ccdd). After a return to the opening, the final *three* lines (all utilizing the b rhyme) unite the Chorus with the Verse by breaking the symmetry that has preceded them.

Verse

Down in New Orleans
There's a dance that cleans
Right up, I mean
(It's a bear, I declare, Its class is)
Way out there alone
That dance done shown
A class its own
(At the ball they call it 'Lasses)
Got me so each night that passes
I just got to have mo' 'Lasses
Oh! it seems to me
Done got to be
Necessitee
(Oh! mo' 'Lasses good to me)
When they want some more
They sing this encore
And they sing it loud:

Chorus

I want some mo' 'Lasses
Gimme some mo' 'Lasses
 Must have some mo' 'Lasses
Like dem 'Lasses I just had.
Don't b'lieve there's mo' 'Lasses
There can't be no 'Lasses
But if there's mo' 'Lasses
Like dem 'Lasses den I'm glad.
Oh! so sweet and oh! so bendable
I'll say that they're recommendable
Music starts dem 'Lasses tricklin'
Den they start to ticklin',
[Repeat lines 1–8 of chorus]
An' I want to add
Want 'em mighty bad
Mo' 'Lasses like I had.

While it is true that black musical theater during the 1920s took little note of the "New Negro," isolated examples of awareness on the part of various lyricists are sometimes seen. Razaf's "What Did I Do to Be So Black and Blue" is one example; another, heard in *Rang Tang,* is the lyric "Brown" by Jo' Trent (1892–1954), which expresses optimistically the hopes and aspirations of the "New Negro" during the Renaissance.

Verse

Never crave for riches,
But I know where bliss is,
Sunshine just lives in my smile,
Some folks criticize me,
Others idolize me,
I know what makes life worthwhile.

Chorus

I'm brown, my hair is curly,
Jes' brown with teeth so pearly,
In style I'm neat, my color won't fade,
Tho' folks try to copy my delicate shade;
My skin is smooth as velvet,
And all you see is real.
Jolly eyes, sunny smiles,
Trail behind me for miles,
I'm satisfied I'm brown.

SUMMARY

The relationship of the black musical to the philosophical underpinnings of the Harlem Renaissance is a tenuous one. The genre never rose to the "high art" expectations that spokesmen envisioned; it was, therefore, not truly accepted by them. But the success of *Shuffle Along* in 1921 could not be ignored; it almost single-handedly brought black musical theater back to Broadway and provided the impetus during the following decade for a renewed interest among whites in black popular art and artists. Although any intellectual interaction between the movement and the shows of the 1920s would appear to have been minimal, in the public's mind, some linkage was probably perceived. Thus, the Renaissance as a movement probably benefited from the success of the black musicals on Broadway.

In this chapter I have attempted to show that many of the songs to these shows, even if they are forgotten today, were innovative rather than imitative and were an integral part of the development of musical theater during the 1920s. They contributed to the musical developments of the mainstream style through the introduction of new ethnic elements and through harmonic experimentation. Because a mere handful are currently available to performers, most of these songs rest quietly in research libraries. Publication of an anthology of representative songs would be a most welcome addition to musical theater literature; such a source would reintroduce the public to a body of works that deserve to be heard once again.

NOTES

1. The mutual interaction and influence of black and white composers during the first two decades of this century is a subject that has generated much controversy. Charles Hamm, in *Yesterdays* (1979), discounts the argument posited by Alec Wilder in *American Popular Song. The Great Innovators, 1900–1950* (1972, 28) that "the early anonymous Negroes . . . had managed to create the beginning of an entirely new music." Hamm sees that "only several quite superficial aspects of 'negro' music were skimmed off by [white] songwriters." He concludes that "the chief stylistic features of the songs . . . came from an earlier generation of American songwriters and from the music of Central and Eastern Europe" (1979, 309–10). More recently, Bruce Kellner, in *Harlem Renaissance: A Historical Dictionary* (1984, xix), summarizes the music of the period as "essentially imitative of the white tunes downtown." He is also critical of the fact that the "enormous popularity" of *Shuffle Along* "made it a model for most of the shows which followed, many of them with equally invidiously racist titles: *Alabama Bound, Bandana Land, Black Bottom Revue, Black Scandals,* and of course *Blackbirds.*" I believe that Kellner has missed completely the essence of black musical theater during the period. Certainly, shows like *Darktown Scandals* and *Black Scandals* were an attempt on the part of their authors to imitate the success of the various editions of *George White's Scandals,* and shows like *Black Bottom Revue* can be seen as an effort to attract audiences smitten by the latest dance craze (see Spaeth 1948, 451–52). I hope the ensuing discussion of the music will respond to Kellner's dismissal of it as imitative; as to his criticism that many of the songs (by which I assume he means the lyrics) are as racist as the show titles, I have already pointed out that a large percentage of the total number of shows written during the period were not necessarily meant to be seen by white theatergoers. Many of the lyrics deemed by Kellner to be racist may be seen in a satirical light when viewed in the context of their intended audience.

2. Songs from black musicals were generally published only when their shows played a Broadway theater. Thus, they represent only a small percentage of all the black music heard during the 1920s. It is a welcome surprise to sometimes find published songs from a musical that only had a brief run. *Strut Miss Lizzie* (1922) is such a show. Al-

though it closed after a run of four weeks, six songs, including "Way Down Yonder in New Orleans," were published. Another song, "I Love You Sweet Angeline," was recorded by Ted Lewis and his band (Columbia A3676). When a successful musical, black or white, played Broadway, there was no guarantee that all its numbers would be published. Of the twenty or more numbers written for *Keep Shufflin'*, for example, I have been able to trace publication of only ten. Published lists are sometimes helpful in finding "lost" songs; however, they do not always reflect accurate data. For example, even though Waller and Razaf are credited in the program of *Keep Shufflin'* as the authors of the songs "Keep Shufflin'" and "Everybody's Happy in Jimtown," neither appears in the "complete" listing of Waller's published and unpublished compositions in Maurice Waller and Anthony Calabrese's *Fats Waller* (1977).

REFERENCES

Berlin, Edward A. 1980. *Ragtime: A musical and cultural history*. Berkeley and Los Angeles: University of California Press.

―――. 1983. Cole and Johnson Brothers' *The Evolution of "Ragtime." Current Musicology* 36:21–39.

Bordman, Gerald. 1978. *American musical theatre: A chronicle*. New York: Oxford University Press.

Butcher, Margaret Just. 1956. *The Negro in American culture*. New York: Mentor Books.

Graziano, John. 1984. Sentimental songs, rags, and transformations: The emergence of the black musical, 1895–1910. In *Musical theatre in America*, edited by Glenn Loney, 211–32. Westport, Conn.: Greenwood Press.

Hamm, Charles. 1979. *Yesterdays: Popular song in America*. New York: W. W. Norton.

Huggins, Nathan Irvin. 1971. *Harlem Renaissance*. New York: Oxford University Press.

Johnson, James Weldon. 1930. *Black Manhattan*. New York: Alfred A. Knopf.

Kellner, Bruce. 1984. *The Harlem Renaissance: A historical dictionary for the era*. Westport, Conn.: Greenwood Press.

Kimball, Robert, and William Bolcom. 1973. *Reminiscing with Sissle and Blake*. New York: The Viking Press.

Locke, Alain. [1936] 1969. *The Negro and his music*. New York: Arno Press and the New York Times.

Mitchell, Loften. 1967. *Black drama*. New York: Hawthorn Books.

Sampson, Henry T. 1980. *Blacks in blackface: A source book on early black musical shows*. Metuchen, N.J.: The Scarecrow Press.

Southern, Eileen. 1982. *Biographical dictionary of Afro-American and African musicians*. Westport, Conn.: Greenwood Press.

―――. 1983. *The music of black Americans: A history*. 2d ed. New York: W. W. Norton.

Spaeth, Sigmund. 1948. *A history of popular music in America*. New York: Random House.

Waller, Maurice, and Anthony Calabrese. 1977. *Fats Waller*. New York: Schirmer Books.

Wilder, Alec. 1972. *American popular song: The great innovators, 1900–1950*. New York: Oxford University Press.

CHAPTER 7

The Renaissance Education of Duke Ellington

Mark Tucker

Harlem was home to Duke Ellington for many years. He arrived there unknown in 1923, a ragtime pianist and aspiring songwriter seeking his way in a world both faster and more competitive than the one he had known growing up in the District of Columbia. Yet like the heroes of the Horatio Alger stories he had admired as a child, Ellington slowly scaled the ladder of success. His ascent took him from the basement obscurity of the Hollywood Cafe to the elevated grandeur of Harlem's Cotton Club, where he began leading a ten-piece orchestra late in 1927. By the early thirties he was famous as the composer of "Mood Indigo" and "Sophisticated Lady" and was living high on Sugar Hill, Harlem's most prestigious neighborhood. Even when touring took him away from home—which, from the mid-thirties on, was often—Ellington continued to celebrate Harlem in music. His compositions described its echoes and air shafts, boys and blue belles. His songs advised people to drop off there and to slap their soles on Seventh Avenue. His signature piece even told them which train to take. And he paid tribute to his adopted community in "Beige," from the extended work *Black, Brown, and Beige* (1943), and in *A Tone Parallel to Harlem* (1950), a joyous evocation of Harlem's sounds, street-life, and citizens.

Ellington's initial rise to fame in New York during the 1920s coincided with the flowering of black creative expression that has come to be called the Harlem Renaissance. While Ellington honed his skills as a bandleader, Alain Locke was proclaiming the arrival of the New Negro, Countee Cullen and Langston Hughes were publishing their first volumes of poetry, Jessie Fauset and Charles S. Johnson were energetically editing *The Crisis* and *Opportunity*, and Aaron Douglas was placing his drawings in magazines like *Harlem* and *Fire!!* It is tempting, in retrospect, to view Ellington's arrival as part of that cultural explosion and to see his career as fulfilling the dreams of Renaissance theoreticians. For after the 1920s Ellington came to embody the ideals of the New Negro artist in his dignified manner and cultivated persona, his social consciousness, his use of vernacular sources as the basis for original compositions, and his deep pride in the Afro-American heritage. More than a glamorous show-business celebrity like Cab Calloway or a popular dance-band leader like Jimmie Lunceford or Count Basie, Ellington became a crusader who took on what Nathan Huggins has described as the New Negro's mission: "to discover and define his culture and his contribution to what had been thought a white civilization" (Huggins 1971, 59).

Harlem may have strengthened Ellington's resolve to carry out this mission. In the mid-twenties it was rich in black talent and ripe with possibilities for the many young writers, painters, and musicians who made their pilgrimage to this Negro mecca. But like most of the major Renaissance figures, Ellington came to Harlem after being trained for his mission elsewhere. Long before he had glimpsed the Tree of Hope or set foot on Seventh Avenue, Ellington had received the basic framework of a Renaissance education in a place over two hundred miles to the south: the black community of Washington, D.C. It was there that he spent his early years, gained experience as a pianist and bandleader, and met musicians who guided and inspired him. And it was there that he first formed ideas about who he was, what he might achieve, and how he could succeed as a black composer in a profession and a society dominated by whites.

The city into which Edward Kennedy Ellington was born in 1899 had the nation's largest urban black population; at the turn of the century it was, according to Constance Green, Washington's chief historian, the "undisputed center of American Negro civilization" (Green 1963, viii). Support for such a claim rested on the educational and economic opportunities available to Washington's black residents; on the high number of black professionals, especially teachers, doctors, and lawyers; on institutions such as Howard University, the M Street High School (later Dunbar High), the Howard Theater, and the Washington Conservatory; and on the social cultivation and intellectual distinction of the black upper class. This was the city that produced writer Jean Toomer, poet Sterling Brown, scientist Charles H. Drew, scholar and diplomat Mercer Cook, physician and teacher W. Montague Cobb, and lawyer Charles Hamilton Houston. It boasted strong civic organizations and independent churches. It was a place that fired black ambition, fostered black pride, and honored black achievement.

Although his family did not belong to the top stratum of black Washington society, Ellington grew up in a secure, middle-class home and was exposed early to people who were successful. His maternal grandfather, James William Kennedy, was one of the city's few black police officers.[1] His father, James Edward Ellington, earned enough as a butler and part-time caterer to buy a house in 1920 at 1212 T Street NW, a good neighborhood near fashionable LeDroit Park. Both parents taught their two children to aim high in their goals, assuring them they could "do anything anyone else can do" (Boatwright 1983). They encouraged Edward when he showed talent in drawing and continued their support when his attention turned to music.

The Ellington family's high expectations seem to have been common among Washington's middle- and upper-class blacks. Pianist and educator Billy Taylor (b. 1921), a Dunbar High alumnus, has described the advantages of a Washington upbringing:

> I had much reinforcement in terms of who I was, what I was about, and the tremendous contributions that black people have made to science, music, art, government. Black accomplishment was very visible in Washington, what with the judges, lawyers, and other over-achievers. . . . I was led to believe that any field that I wanted to go into, I had the possibility of success (Clarke 1982, 182).

A. Barry Rand, another Washington native, and in 1987 one of the top black executives in America (corporate vice president at Xerox), has echoed Taylor's words:

> I have always wanted to show that blacks can perform as well as or better than their white counterparts. . . . If you're raised in an environment where you have developed a lot of confidence in yourself, you view the racism you encounter as their problem and not your own (Hicks 1987, 4).

Like Taylor and Rand, Ellington inherited a drive to excel and a resilient optimism from Washington's black community. Wherever he was—in nightclubs or recording studios, on the road or behind a deadline—he somehow always managed to turn difficult circumstances to his advantage. His philosophy held that "every problem is an opportunity" and "gray skies are just clouds passing over" (Ellington 1973, 468). He never lost his Washingtonian worldview; late in life it was there when he recalled his initial motivation as a composer: "The driving power was a matter of wanting to be—and to be heard—at the same level as the best" (Ellington 1973, 457).

Together with ambition and optimism, another trait Ellington exhibited throughout his long public career was self-confidence—the solid core of belief in one's ability and potential that makes possible the highest aspirations. Ellington traced the origins of this attitude to Washington. He felt provided for by a father who "raised his family as though he were a millionaire" (Ellington 1973, 10), whose speech was elegant and manners impeccable. He experienced "a wonderful feeling of security" from attending church, and from hearing his mother Daisy Kennedy Ellington tell him, "Edward, you are blessed. You don't have anything to worry about" (Ellington 1973, 15). And he credited Miss R. A. Boston, his eighth-grade English teacher (also the principal of Garrison Junior High School), with promoting proper speech and deportment, as well as pride in self:

> I think she spent as much time in preaching race pride as she did in teaching English, which, ironically and very strangely, improved your English—she would explain that everywhere you go, if you were sitting in a theater next to a white lady . . . or you were on a stage . . . your responsibility is to command respect for the race (West 1969, 10).

Although Ellington grew up in a community that encouraged, even pressured, its residents to succeed, as a young man he did not seem destined to become one of black Washington's "over-achievers." He showed more interest in playing the piano and frequenting Frank Holliday's pool room next to the Howard Theater than in his studies. He attended not Dunbar High but the Armstrong Manual Training School, where he took courses in freehand and mechanical drawing (perhaps anticipating a career in commercial art) and which he left in the winter of 1917, several months before graduating.[2] During this time, and after, he does not appear to have been involved with any of the black community's numerous civic, fraternal, religious, or literary organizations. Instead he found work as a soda jerk, messenger boy, sign-painter, and dance-band musician.

Nevertheless, Washington exposed Ellington to various influences that would shape the course of his extraordinary musical career. Three of these came from professional black musicians he encountered there; from the community's emphasis on black history; and from the example of others raised in Washington who went on to compose, lead orchestras, and champion the cause of black music.

WASHINGTON'S BLACK PROFESSIONAL MUSICIANS

The community that produced Duke Ellington was distinguished by the quality and diversity of its professional musical life. In his memoirs Ellington dwells primarily on one facet of the scene: the popular music played by pianists and small instrumental ensembles. But black Washington also spawned choral societies and glee clubs, military bands, a symphony orchestra, chamber music groups, and one of the nation's earliest black opera companies, the Original Colored America Opera

Troupe. Young black musicians could receive instruction at the Washington Conservatory founded by Harriet Marshall Gibbs (see McGinty 1979), at Wellington Adams's Columbia Conservatory, and from many private instructors, among them Marietta (Mrs. Harvey) Clinkscales, Ellington's first piano teacher. Recitals, concerts, and other musical events were regularly reviewed in the *Bee*, the city's main black newspaper.[3] Several periodicals—*The Negro Journal of Music* (which in 1903 became the official organ of the Washington Conservatory), Wellington Adams's *The Music Master*, and *The Negro Musician*—covered local as well as national activity in black music.

Ellington seems to have kept a distance from the formal world of black music in Washington. His piano lessons with Mrs. Clinkscales did not last long or mean much; later he said they "all slipped away from me" (Ulanov [1946] 1975, 6) and "had nothing to do with the thing that followed when I became fourteen" ("CBC Interview" 1965). His experiences as a fledgling ragtime pianist took him to informal "hops" and teen dances, then, as leader of a small group, the Duke's Serenaders, to embassy receptions and Virginia hunt balls. But Ellington did meet up with musicians who combined formal training with an interest in popular music—Ellington called them the "conservatory boys," as opposed to the self-taught "ear cats" (Ellington 1973, 26).

One of these was Oliver "Doc" Perry (1885?–1961), a pianist who may have had conservatory training and who was a popular black bandleader in Washington during the 1910s and early 1920s.[4] Perry's musical versatility and personal refinement put him in demand at fancy functions. Ellington began visiting Perry at his home on U Street, occasionally filling in for the older man at dances when Perry had to play downtown at the Ebbitt House (Ellington 1973, 33). From his "piano parent," as he called Perry, Ellington developed elementary reading skills and a professional attitude toward performing. Perry later claimed that he "trained Duke for public work" (Perry 1983). And when Ellington depicted Perry in *Music Is My Mistress* as a man who spoke "with a sort of semi-continental finesse," who was "extremely gifted, dignified, clean, neat," and who was "respected by musicians, show people, and the laymen as well" (Ellington 1973, 26), he hinted at traits the piano parent may have passed on to his young protégé.

In Louis N. Brown (ca. 1889–1974), another schooled pianist, Ellington met a musician active in many different sectors of the black community. Brown played ragtime and popular piano for dances, dance classes, and parties, also organ at the Lincoln Theater on U Street. He directed church choirs and appeared as piano soloist on concert programs (Tucker 1986, 94–95). Besides admiring Brown's technical facility and engaging personality, Ellington may have perceived how Brown moved fluidly from one performing situation to the next, as did other black professional musicians in Washington.[5] Even after he had become a seasoned concert-hall artist, Ellington kept an open mind about where and what he played, and resisted drawing lines between high and low, art and entertainment. His orchestra might turn up Friday in a concert hall, Saturday in a high school gym. As he told Stanley Dance, "I like going from one extreme to another. Sometimes we play for the Elks club and it's *Melancholy Baby* all night, but I love it" (Dance [1970] 1981, 11).

A third professional black musician who influenced young Ellington was Henry Lee Grant. Son of the singer Henry Fleet Grant, he was educated at Livingston College and New York University and received an Artist's Diploma in piano from the Washington Conservatory in 1910. Grant was a major figure in Washington's black musical life. Like Louis Brown, he was a many-sided musician: composer, conductor, director of choirs and glee clubs, concert pianist, and teacher at Dunbar High. He assisted Will Marion Cook in leading the Afro-American Folk-Song Singers, played in a trio with violinist Felix Weir and cellist Leonard Jeter, and in 1919 helped found the National Association of Negro Musicians.

When Ellington was about seventeen, Grant apparently invited the young piano "plunker" to become his pupil (Ellington 1973, 28). No written record survives of what Ellington later called his "hidden course in harmony that lighted the direction to more highly developed composition." But this colorful description may disguise the fact that Grant's student simply needed some basic instruction. Ellington implies as much when he writes of his lessons, "We moved along very quickly, until I was learning the difference between G-flat and F-sharp" (Ellington 1973, 33). Grant, too, seems to have realized that, despite a certain experimental bent, "Duke was anxious to learn the fundamentals" (Ulanov [1946] 1975, 9).

In addition to teaching theory, Grant represented musical ideals different from those Ellington would have encountered in the workaday world of society gigs, dances, and "hops." Grant not only proselytized for the cause of Negro music, but believed that popular music could show seriousness of purpose and meet standards of excellence. In 1921, while serving as editor of *The Negro Musician*, he announced his intention to interview "successful Negro composers, organizers, leaders, and performers" in the popular music field, listing the names of Ford Dabney, John Turner Layton, Jr., and Will Vodery (Grant 1921a, 9). That same year he enthusiastically reviewed Noble Sissle and Eubie Blake's *Shuffle Along* and revealed that Blake was one of his ex-pupils (Grant 1921b, 13). Grant's broad musical background, his solid musicianship, his belief in the "genuine art possibilities" of popular music, and his active work on behalf of black music and musicians may have impressed a young bandleader. Grant offered Ellington not just keys to commercial success—"I had to study music seriously to protect [my reputation]" (Ellington 1973, 33)—but values he would later embrace, and embody, as a black artist.[6]

A PEOPLE PROUD OF THEIR PAST

In his 1944 *New Yorker* profile of Ellington, "The Hot Bach," Richard O. Boyer wrote that the bandleader thought it "good business to conceal his interest in American Negro history," since Duke doubted it would help "his popularity in Arkansas, say, to have it known that in books he has read about Negro slave revolts he has heavily underlined paragraphs about the exploits of Nat Turner and Denmark Vesey" (Gammond [1958] 1977, 49). But if Ellington kept his reading habits private, his music made public a passion for black history. The year before, in 1943, he had premiered at Carnegie Hall his massive "tone parallel to the history of the American Negro," *Black, Brown, and Beige*. Earlier he had celebrated the emancipation of black entertainers from racial stereotypes in *Jump for Joy* (1941), and explored the Afro-American heritage in *Symphony in Black* (1934) and *Creole Rhapsody* (1931).

Stimulating awareness of the Negro's past was a goal pursued by various Harlem Renaissance figures in the 1920s, among them Countee Cullen, Alain Locke, James Weldon Johnson, Aaron Douglas, Richmond Barthé, and Marcus Garvey. Yet Ellington's hometown was filled with people equally dedicated to preserving and promoting black culture. In 1915 Howard University professor Carter Woodson founded the Association for the Study of Negro Life and History, which soon began publishing the *Journal of Negro History*. The Bethel Literary and Historical Association and the Mus-So-Lit Club provided forums for discussing black politics, social issues, and literature. And in the schools, Ellington recalled, "Negro history was crammed into the curriculum, so that we would know our people all the way back" (Ellington 1973, 17).

Another source that focused attention on black history was the pageants put on by church, school, and civic groups. The most extravagant one during Ellington's youth was "The Star of Ethiopia," presented in October 1915 at the American League Ball Park. In 1913 it had been produced in New York for the National Emancipation Exposition by W.E.B. Du Bois ("The Star of Ethiopia" 1913; Du Bois 1915; "Review of 'The Star'" 1915). The program for the Washington production gave the following description:

> The Story of the Pageant covers 10,000 years of the history of the Negro race and its work and suffering and triumphs in the world. The Pageant

combines historic accuracy and symbolic truth. All the costumes of the thousand actors, the temples, the weapons, etc., have been copied from accurate models ("Program of 'The Star of Ethiopia'" 1915).

The historic drama had five scenes: "Gift of Iron," "Dream of Egypt," "Glory of Ethiopia," "Valley of Humiliation," and "Vision Everlasting." In addition to acting, "music by colored composers, lights and symbolic dancing accompany the story and emphasize and explain it." Elzie Hoffman's band took part, as did a thousand actors and a chorus of two hundred ("The Horizon Guild Pageant" 1915, [5]). The music director was J. Rosamond Johnson. A spectator would have heard his brother James Weldon Johnson's song *Walk Together, Children* and Verdi's *Celeste Aida*. We don't know if the sixteen-year-old Ellington attended. (He did work at the ball park as a youngster, and some rehearsals for the pageant were held at his high school.) But surely he heard about it; the pageant seems to have been a major community event, and nearly seventy years later, Dr. W. Montague Cobb spoke of it as "very impressive" (Cobb 1984).

Other musical-dramatic treatments of black history themes were produced in Washington. In 1921 horn player and bandleader Russell Wooding—one of Ellington's first employers—put on his opera "Halcyon Days in Dixie," an "attempt at music drama based on themes of Negro life and music" ("Review of 'Halcyon Days in Dixie'" 1921, 18). The work featured Wooding's Jubilee Quintet and violinist Joseph Douglass (grandson of Frederick Douglass). An earlier production was "The Evolution of the Negro in Picture, Song, and Story," put on at the Howard Theater in 1911; Henry Grant directed the L'Allegro Glee Club accompanied by Mary Europe (sister of James Reese Europe, later a colleague of Grant at Dunbar High). The program drew upon American texts (William Dean Howells and Paul Laurence Dunbar) and European music (von Suppé, Chaminade, and Brahms). But perhaps most intriguing was the structure of the presentation:

> Overture
> Night of Slavery—Sorrow Songs
> Dawn of Freedom
> Day of Opportunity ("Program of 'The Evolution'" 1911).

Like "The Star of Ethiopia," this event brought together music and stories to dramatize the history of black Americans. Such endeavors could strengthen the pride of Washington's black community and may have left their mark on Ellington. In time he would compose works that treated similar themes using similar forms. His *Symphony in Black*, written for a Paramount music short, has an overture, a section titled "The Laborers," and a "Hymn of Sorrow." *Black, Brown, and Beige* moves from past to present and again features work songs and a hymn, *Come Sunday.*

WASHINGTON'S BLACK COMPOSER-BANDLEADERS

In describing qualities that made Ellington and some of his associates different from other musicians, Barry Ulanov has identified a "Washington pattern" that

> involved a certain bearing, a respect for education, for the broad principles of the art of music; a desire for order, for design in their professional lives. . . . [It gave them], from the very beginning, a line of development, a sense of growth toward a larger and more meaningful expression (Ulanov [1946] 1975, 13).

Ellington himself alludes to the "pattern" in describing Doc Perry, Louis Brown, Henry Grant, and two of his Washington-reared band members, trumpeters Arthur Whetsol and Rex Stewart:

> A great organization man, [Whetsol] would speak up in a minute on the subject of propriety, clean appearance, and reliability. If and when any member of our band made an error in grammar, he was quick to correct him. He was aware of all the Negro individuals who were contributing to the cause by *commanding respect.* He knew about all the Negro colleges, and he also knew all the principal scholastic and athletic leaders personally (Ellington 1973, 54).
>
> . . . . .
>
> [Stewart] came out of the same Washington school system that I did, and his intellectual ambitions were typical of the Washingtonian of that time, when people believed that if you were going to be something, you ought to learn something and know something. . . . [He] had been taught the responsibility of commanding respect for his race and to this end he maintained . . . a dignified, decent-sort-of-chap image, and he never strayed from it (Ellington 1973, 124–25).

The "Washington pattern," however, produced not just a different breed of "jazzmen," as Ulanov notes, but three Afro-American musicians whose careers, in some respects, may have served as models for Ellington's: Will Marion Cook (1869–1944), James Reese Europe (1881–1919), and Ford Dabney (1883–1958). All three combined roles that Ellington himself later assumed: composer, songwriter, successful bandleader, and performer who earned the respect of both black and white audiences. Like Ellington, they were champions of black musical traditions—syncopated jazz, ragtime, show tunes, Negro folk songs, arrangements of spirituals—and drew upon black vernacular idioms for their original compositions.[7]

Did Ellington encounter these men, or hear their orchestras, before heading to Harlem? Europe, Cook, and Dabney brought their large instrumental ensembles to Washington in the period 1917–1922, when Ellington was actively pursuing his musical career. Ellington lists Dabney and Europe as two of the "great talents" in New York he had "heard of" while in Washington (Ellington 1973, 36). But he may have actually seen Europe at the Howard Theater in 1913—Ellington later claimed that as a boy he went there "almost every day to hear the good music" (Ellington 1973, 104). And Ford Dabney's local appearances between 1920 and 1922 were well publicized, especially an October 1921 concert in Convention Hall (where Ellington heard James P. Johnson that same year).

Ellington's connections with Will Marion Cook were closer. He may have seen Cook's Southern Syncopated Orchestra, featuring Sidney Bechet, as early as 1919 (Cook 1983). His main contact with the older man, however, came a few years later in New York. There he would follow "Dad" Cook as he made the rounds of music publishers around Times Square, then take a cab with him back to Harlem. In this taxi classroom, Cook gave advice to the young Washingtonian. He suggested that Ellington pursue formal training at a conservatory, to which Ellington answered, "Dad, I don't want to go to the conservatory because they're not teaching what I want to learn" (West 1969, 9). Cook also may have passed along some general points of compositional method, or perhaps some ideas for a programmatic work; in 1944 Ellington said that "some of the things he used to tell me I never got a chance to use until . . . I wrote the tone poem *Black, Brown and Beige*" (Gammond [1958] 1977, 54).

Beyond any direct contact Ellington may have had with Cook, Europe, and Dabney, however, he shared with them, as a mature musician, several traits that bore the outlines of a common "Washington pattern." One was a public persona that commanded respect by its inherent dignity and decorum. Cultivating these qualities was essential for blacks working in popular music who wanted to be taken seriously—not only by whites, but by those blacks who considered popular songs and dance music lower artistic forms. Lawrence Gushee has described the dilemma faced by the Afro-American who "considered himself (and *was*) a civilized musician," but who "almost necessarily survived by working in show or dance music as leader, arranger, or musical director, often with a seriousness or dignity that seems out of place" (Gushee 1978, [2]). Ellington seems to have reconciled his image as an artist and function as an entertainer more gracefully than his predecessors.[8] Even so, his polished manner and aristocratic bearing were characteristic of Cook, Europe, and other black professional musicians who belonged to New York's Clef and Tempo Clubs. Noble Sissle recognized these qualities when he called James Reese Europe "the Duke Ellington of his time" (Anderson 1982, 76).

A second trait linking Ellington to Cook and Europe was a distaste for labels that might limit the scope of his achievements in the public eye. Ellington's lifelong battle to do away with categories is well known. His objections to the term "jazz" mirror Europe's to "ragtime"; perhaps this attitude reflected their origins in "a section of the black middle class that strove to gain the highest standing for black cultural endeavors" (Anderson 1982, 78). Will Marion Cook could even show resentment at being labeled as an Afro-American musician. In a well-known anecdote, Cook responded to a critic who called him "the world's greatest Negro violinist" by smashing his violin and crying out, "I am not the greatest Negro violinist. . . . I am the greatest violinist in the world!" (Ellington 1973, 97). When Ellington relates this story, he seems to identify and sympathize with Cook's indignation.

Yet while demanding to be judged by artistic—not racial—criteria, Ellington and his Washington forerunners still dedicated themselves to expressing in music the feelings, aspirations, and ideals of black Americans. In pursuit of this goal, these musicians discarded the conventions of minstrelsy and vaudeville and refused to emulate white performers. Cook, according to James Weldon Johnson,

> believed that the Negro in music and on the stage ought to be a Negro, a genuine Negro; he declared that the Negro should eschew "white" patterns, and not employ his efforts in doing what "the white artist could always do as well, generally better" (Anderson 1982, 34).

Europe agreed. In 1912, after his orchestra's first concert at Carnegie Hall, he took credit for developing "a kind of symphony music that . . . is different and distinctive, and that lends itself to the playing of the peculiar compositions of our race" (Southern 1983, 288). When he returned from abroad in 1919 with his 369th Infantry ("Hellfighters") Band, he proclaimed:

> I have come back from France more firmly convinced than ever that negroes should write negro music. We have our own racial feeling and if we try to copy whites we will make bad copies. . . . Will Marion Cook, William Tires [Tyers], even Harry Burleigh and Coleridge-Taylor are [only] truly themselves in the music which expresses their race (Southern 1983, 289).

Ellington endorsed these black nationalist aims in word and deed. Later he would characterize himself not as an entertainer working in a commercial field, but as a composer for his people: "I don't write jazz, I write Negro folk music" (Gammond [1958] 1977, 26). In 1937 he called for the founding of a "Conservatory of Negro Music which would teach principally the melodies and harmonies and teachings of our ancestors" (Ellington 1937). Steeped in the black consciousness of Washington, D.C., he composed works that celebrated Afro-American culture and its outstanding contributors, from Florence Mills to Martin Luther King. He sought to educate audiences in works like *Black, Brown, and Beige* and *My People* (1963), rouse them with social commentary in *Jump for Joy*, and instill hope for the Negro's future in *New World A-Coming* (1943).

Ellington's crusade for the cause of Afro-American music rested on a conviction that it deserved a place of importance next to the greatest products of the European musical tradition. This belief was manifest in the programs offered by Europe and his Clef Club orchestra at Carnegie Hall in 1912–1913 and in concerts featuring Cook and his Afro-American Folk Song Singers, in which Negro spirituals, folk songs, and Cook's original compositions might appear side by side with European classics ("In Retrospect" 1978; "Afro-American Folk Song Singers" 1913).[9] When Ellington took his orchestra into Carnegie Hall in the 1940s, he presented his own extended compositions, together with original dance pieces, concertos, songs, and blues—all derived from the rich loam of Afro-American traditions. But he rejected the view of those who claimed he had been influenced by Europeans. In his most forceful statement on the subject, written in 1944 for the classical-record magazine *Listen*, he attempted to set the critics straight:

> Jazz, swing, jive, and every other musical phenomenon of American musical life are as much an art medium as are the most profound works of the famous classical composers. . . . [To] attempt to elevate the status of the jazz musician by forcing the level of his best work into comparisons with classical music is to deny him his rightful share of originality. . . . Music, like any other art form, reflects the mood, temperament, and environment of its creators (Ellington 1944, 6).

Such words would have made Henry Grant and Will Marion Cook beam with pride. They show a man sure of himself, true to his traditions, and proud of his place in history. And they reveal a composer stamped with the imprint of the "Washington pattern"—someone with "a respect for education, for the broad principles of the art of music," who was moving, ever moving, "toward a larger and more meaningful expression."

Mercer Ellington has claimed, with some justification, that his father's "early training in Washington had really been slight and rudimentary" (Ellington and Dance [1978] 1979, 19). It was in New York that Ellington stepped up his ability to read music, learned to write it down, advanced his pianistic skills through listening to Harlem stride pianists, developed an orchestra with a distinctive style and sound, and emerged as a major composer. The performers he worked with at Barron's, the Kentucky Club, and especially the Cotton Club, were probably of a higher caliber than those he had encountered in Washington. And New York—especially Harlem—stimulated Ellington to accomplish some of his best work.

At the same time, Ellington admitted that Washington "was a very good climate for me to come up in, musically" (West 1969, 1). There he found a supportive network of pianists and an environment in which "[e]verybody seemed to get something out of the other's playing" (Ellington 1973, 26). He developed aural skills that he would rely on throughout his career. He got his start in the band business. He gained performing experience in cabarets and theaters, in fancy ballrooms and funky dance-halls.

But Washington's most important gift to Ellington may have been a set of attitudes and beliefs that allowed him to realize his artistic ambitions in a way that no other Afro-American composer had been able to do. Growing up black in Washington trained Ellington to overcome the destructive effects of racism with patience, an iron will, and the sure conviction that any goal was within his grasp. It made him aware of the rich traditions of Afro-Americans, respectful of their past, and confident of their future. Perhaps most significant for a black composer seeking his vocation in the field of popular music, it gave him a sense of being part of a historical procession. By 1931, when he wrote in the British periodical *Rhythm*, that sense had been sharpened by Harlem's Black Renaissance:

> I am proud of that part my race is playing in the artistic life of the world. Paul Robeson, Roland Hayes, your own Coleridge-Taylor, are names already high in the lists of serious music; that from the welter of negro dance musicians now before the public will come something lasting and noble I am convinced (Ellington 1931, 22).

In the same article, Ellington voiced his concern that "what is being done by Countee Cullen and others in literature is overdue in our music." The thirty-one-year-old bandleader vowed to take up the cause himself by writing a rhapsody that will

> portray the experience of the coloured races in America in the syncopated idiom. . . . I am putting all I have learned into it in the hope that I shall have achieved something really worth while in the literature of music, and that an authentic record of my race *written by a member of it* shall be placed on record (Ellington 1931, 22).

The "rhapsody," of course, appeared twelve years later as the "tone parallel" *Black, Brown, and Beige.* But the desire to leave "an authentic record of my race" became, in a way, Ellington's life's work. Few American musicians have brought to their work such fervor, determination, and uncompromisingly high standards. Few were as well qualified to succeed as this resident of Harlem, who received his early education in the proud, privileged black community of Washington, D.C.

NOTES

1. In 1910, when there were nearly 95,000 blacks in Washington, only forty were policemen (Henri 1975, 167).

2. His Armstrong transcript, available from the District of Columbia Public Schools, shows grades that were good to excellent in drawing, average in English, history, and math, and poor in the sciences. The only grade for a music course on his transcript, which he received in his first year at the school (1913–1914), is a "D" (i.e., deficient).

3. During the period 1914–1917, the *Bee* reports several recitals and programs of Mrs. Clinkscales's students. This was after Ellington's study with the teacher, however.

4. Many advertisements for Perry's band appear between 1917 and 1922 in the *Bee* and the Chicago *Defender* (in J. Le C. Chestnut's column, "Under the Capitol Dome"). No recordings by Perry—or by any other Washington pianist mentioned by Ellington in *Music Is My Mistress*—are known to exist.

5. This versatility was partly a by-product of discrimination. Since formally trained black musicians could be faced with severely limited job opportunities, they may have undertaken work in theaters, public schools, cabarets, and restaurants as a matter of economic survival. The presence of someone like Henry Grant on the Dunbar High faculty attests to the plight of the black concert musician who could not sustain a career outside the black community. The problem was not unique to musicians; before she began her work as literary editor for *The Crisis*, Jessie Fauset (B.A. Cornell, M.A. University of Pennsylvania) taught at M Street/Dunbar High from 1906 to 1919. As Billy Taylor has said about Dunbar, "There were five teachers [there] with doctorates; they were in high schools simply because there was no room for them at colleges" (Clarke 1982, 181).

6. Grant's respect for popular music was tempered by a belief that its "potential for art possibilities" was limited by its "restricted form and transitory appeal." Next to his glowing review of *Shuffle Along*, he offered a warning about ragtime: "Therefore, embrace, study, improve and utilize its values. Teach its source, history and influence, but point to its limitations and instruct of its harm as a lone medium of expres-

sion" (Grant 1921b, 13). Despite the cautionary tone, such a statement coming from a black classical music advocate could seem enlightened next to the view of a critic like Wellington Adams, who, in reviewing a Clef Club orchestra concert a few years before, had asserted that "there is as great a difference between the music of the 'jazz' and the art of Beethoven as there is between the sounds by which lower animals express their feelings and the language of Goethe" (Adams 1919, [6]).

7. Cook's works include the musicals *Clorindy; Or, the Origin of the Cakewalk* (1898), *In Dahomey* (1903), *Bandana Land* (1908), and *Darkeydom* (1915), and the songs "Darktown Is Out Tonight," "Swing Along," "Exhortation," and "Rain Song." He led and toured abroad with the Southern Syncopated Orchestra for several years, beginning in 1918 (Carter 1988; Riis 1981).

Among James Reese Europe's instrumental pieces are "Castlehouse Rag," "Castle Walk," and "Too Much Mustard." After moving from Washington to New York ca. 1905, Europe worked in musical theater, conducted orchestras, and founded the Clef Club, a protective association for professional black musicians. Around 1914 he left the Clef Club and organized the Tempo Club with Ford Dabney. His society orchestra was associated with Vernon and Irene Castle from 1914 to 1917. During World War I his 369th Infantry Band gained fame abroad (Charters and Kunstadt [1962] 1981; "James Reese Europe" 1955).

Ford Dabney was court pianist to the president of Haiti from 1904 to 1907. In New York his orchestra played for Ziegfeld's Midnight Frolic Show at the New Amsterdam Theater from 1913 to 1921. His works include the musicals *The King's Quest* (1909) and *Rang Tang* (1927), the instrumental piece *The Pensacola Mootch* (1910), and the song "That's Why They Call Me Shine" (1910) (Southern 1982; "Ford Dabney" 1955). More is known about Europe and Cook than about Dabney; accordingly, my discussion focuses more on the former two figures.

8. This may have been a matter of temperament, not just the different conditions under which Ellington worked, or the later time. Also, manager Irving Mills's successful efforts to present Ellington as an artist and composer helped pave the way for his public acceptance under these terms.

9. This concert, given November 21, 1913, at the Metropolitan A.M.E. Church, featured songs by Cook, a choral piece by Coleridge-Taylor, folk-song arrangements by Tchaikovsky and Dvorák, and Mendelssohn's *Rondo Capriccioso*, performed by Henry Grant.

REFERENCES

Adams, Wellington A. 1919. The musical world. *The Bee* May 31:[6].
Afro-American Folk-Song Singers program. 1913. Vertical files, November 21. Moorland-Spingarn Research Center, Howard University, Washington, D.C.

Anderson, Jervis. 1982. *This was Harlem: A cultural portrait, 1900–1950*. New York: Farrar Straus Giroux.

Boatwright, Ruth Ellington. 1983. Interview with the author, October 21.

Carter, Marva Griffin. 1988. Will Marion Cook: Afro-American violinist, composer, and conductor. Ph.D. diss., University of Illinois, Urbana.

CBC interview #177. April 1965. Ellington clipping file. Institute of Jazz Studies, Rutgers University, Newark, New Jersey.

Charters, Samuel, and Leonard Kunstadt. [1962] 1981. *Jazz: A history of the New York scene*. New York: Da Capo.

Clarke, Catherine K. 1982. Conversation with William ("Billy") Taylor. *The Black Perspective in Music* 10, no. 2:179–88.

Cobb, W. Montague. 1984. Telephone conversation with the author, May 29.

Cook, Mercer. 1983. Interview with the author, August 19.

Dance, Stanley. [1970] 1981. *The world of Duke Ellington*. New York: Da Capo.

Du Bois, W.E.B. 1915. The star of Ethiopia. *Crisis* 11 (December):90–94.

Ellington, Duke. 1931. The Duke steps out. *Rhythm* March:20–22.

———. 1937. Interview in *The Call*, December 31. Vertical file ("Ellington, 1930s"), Moorland-Spingarn Research Center, Howard University, Washington, D.C.

———. 1944. Certainly it's music! *Listen* October 1944:5–6.

———. 1973. *Music is my mistress*. Garden City, N.Y.: Doubleday.

Ellington, Mercer, with Stanley Dance. [1978] 1979. *Duke Ellington in person: An intimate memoir*. New York: Da Capo.

Ford Dabney. 1955. *Record Research* 1, no. 2:7–8 [includes discography].

Gammond, Peter, ed. [1958] 1977. *Duke Ellington: His life and music*. New York: Da Capo.

Grant, Henry. 1921a. The theatrical and popular music world. *The Negro Musician* 1, no. 2 (February):9.

———. 1921b. In the field of popular music. *The Negro Musician* (June):13.

Green, Constance McLaughlin. 1963. *Washington: Capital city, 1879–1950*. Princeton, N.J.: Princeton University Press.

Gushee, Lawrence. 1978. Liner essay, *Duke Ellington 1940*, Smithsonian Collection R 013.

Henri, Florette. 1975. *Black migration: Movement north, 1900–1920*. Garden City, N.Y.: Anchor Press/Doubleday.

Hicks, Jonathan P. 1987. A black's climb to executive heights. *New York Times* May 22:sec. D, 1, 4.

The Horizon Guild pageant. 1915. *The Bee* October 9:[5].

Huggins, Nathan Irvin. 1971. *Harlem Renaissance*. New York: Oxford University Press.

In retrospect: Black music concerts in Carnegie Hall, 1912–1915. 1978. *The Black Perspective in Music* 6, no. 1:71–88.

James Reese Europe. 1955. *Record Research* 1, no. 6:3–5 [includes discography].

McGinty, Doris. 1979. The Washington Conservatory of Music and school of expression. *The Black Perspective in Music* 7, no. 1:59–74.

The Music Master. 1919–1920. Held at Moorland- Spingarn Research Center, Howard University, Washington, D.C.

The Negro Journal of Music. [1902–1903] 1970. Westport, Conn.: Negro Universities Press.

The Negro Musician. 1920–1921. Held at Moorland-Spingarn Research Center, Howard University, Washington, D.C.

Perry, Mrs. Delia. 1983. Telephone conversation with the author, November 17.

Program of "The evolution of the Negro in picture, song, and story." 1911. Vertical file, Washington, D.C., programs, box 4. Moorland-Spingarn Research Center, Howard University, Washington, D.C.

Program of "The star of Ethiopia." 1915. Vertical file, Washington, D.C., programs, box 1. Moorland-Spingarn Research Center, Howard University, Washington, D.C.

Review of "Halcyon days in Dixie." 1921. In *The Negro Musician* 1, no. 2 (February):18.

Review of "The star of Ethiopia." 1915. *The Bee* October 16:4.

Riis, Thomas L. 1981. Black musical theatre in New York, 1890–1915. Ph.D. diss., University of Michigan, Ann Arbor.

Southern, Eileen. 1982. *Biographical dictionary of Afro-American and African musicians*. Westport, Conn.: Greenwood Press.

———. 1983. *The music of black Americans: A history*. 2d ed. New York: W. W. Norton.

The star of Ethiopia. 1913. *Crisis* 7 (November):339–41.

Tucker, Mark. 1986. The early years of Edward Kennedy "Duke" Ellington, 1899–1927. Ph.D. diss., University of Michigan, Ann Arbor.

Ulanov, Barry. [1946] 1975. *Duke Ellington*. New York: Da Capo.

West, Hollie I. 1969. The Duke at 70. *Washington Post*, April 27:sec. K, 1, 9–10.

CHAPTER 8

Interactions between Writers and Music during the Harlem Renaissance

Richard A. Long

The Harlem Renaissance was a period characterized by interactions—between white and black (Long 1974), between an older and a younger generation of black American writers and thinkers, between the optimism of "movement" in Afro-American life as expressed by Johnson and Johnson (1925) and Locke ([1925] 1968) and the deadly factors conditioning despair. Equally, it was a period of intense interaction between music and the writers engaged in interpreting Afro-American life. Indeed, at no previous period in Afro-American writing was there such consciousness of music among writers.

There are a number of reasons for the heightened consciousness of music among the black writers of the Harlem Renaissance. First and foremost is probably the availability of publications that intentionally encompassed a large dimension of Afro-American life; the national magazines *Crisis* and *Opportunity* are chief among these. But the widespread network of the black press encouraged this activity at the local level as well. Second, though, and in part independent of the mere availability of these means of expression, was an intensification and amplification of musical activity brought about by the development of jazz, the spread of the dance hall, the continual growth of vaudeville (later to be checked by the talking film), and the exploitation of black music by the recording industry.

Writers of the Harlem Renaissance show interest in black composers and performers, in the art of performing, and in traditional black musical genres, including spirituals and blues. Among the writers active in the 1920s who show a high degree of interest are W.E.B. Du Bois, James Weldon Johnson, Walter White, Alain Locke, Langston Hughes, Zora Neale Hurston, and a number of poets.

Two musical artists came to embody for Afro-Americans generally, and for many writers particularly, the spirit of Afro-American life. These were Roland Hayes and Paul Robeson:

> In December 1923, Roland Hayes appeared in concert at New York's Town Hall and created an uproar. He was already in his mid-thirties and had made a long and arduous progress from rural poverty in Georgia to a widely applauded European concert tour. The Town Hall recital brought him dramatically to the attention of the American public. Hayes was a lyric tenor who excelled in the art song in Italian, German, and French. But he became an instant hero of Black America for the artistry and tenderness of his singing of spirituals.
>
> Hayes had been born into the still lingering world of the Folk-Rural Culture, of which the spiritual was a vital and vibrant part. His affection for the songs sung by his mother and her generation, who had first heard and sung them in slavery, was reflected in his life-long devotion to them. The spiritual had first been brought to the concert stage in the 1870s by the Fisk Jubilee Singers. At the beginning of the twentieth century, Harry T. Burleigh had begun to arrange spirituals for solo voice and in 1919 accompanied Hayes in a recital that included them. Following the Town Hall recital of 1923, Hayes always sang spirituals as part of his programs. Thereafter these traditional songs became a permanent addition to the general recital repertory. Roland Hayes continued to perform into the early 1960s when he gave a 75th birthday recital at Carnegie Hall.
>
> Paul Robeson, already known as an actor, gave a concert of spirituals and other Afro-American folk songs in New York in 1925. He was a dramatic basso with a magnificent stage presence. Born in Princeton, New Jersey, Robeson represented the Folk-Urban tradition of the spiritual as it developed in the churches of the cities following the Civil War. His interest always was more in folk songs—of Europe and Asia as well as the Americas—rather than in art songs (Long 1985, 79–80).

Du Bois first refers to Roland Hayes in the March 1915 issue of *Crisis*. His earliest reference to Marian Anderson is even more striking. He mentions her to his readers in October 1916, when she was in her second year of high school. In the May 1920 issue of *Crisis*, Du Bois reports on a Roland Hayes concert, as well as on the career of Clarence Cameron White as a violinist. (Nowhere in *Crisis*, however, even during the high days of the jazz age, do we find Du Bois mentioning Armstrong, or Ellington, or despite the Atlanta University connection, Fletcher Henderson. W. C. Handy, however, had been mentioned favorably by Du Bois as early as 1915.)

Among other Euro-classical performers or composers mentioned by Du Bois in *Crisis* are Ethel L. Johnson (1920) and J. Turner Layton and Henry S. Creamer (1920); he pays considerable tribute to Maud Cuney Hare, who organized an exhibit at Wanamaker's Department store in Philadelphia (1924), to Harry F. Burleigh (1924), and to John W. Work,

Jr. (1926). In 1925 Du Bois published his review of *The Book of American Negro Spirituals* by James Weldon Johnson and J. Rosamond Johnson in *Crisis* and a review of Dorothy Scarborough's *On the Trail of Negro Folk Songs* in *Book Review*. Both reviews were favorable, though he had some reservations about the latter.

There is a sense in which a number of writers might be considered to fall into a group because of their affiliation with the NAACP. The group would include Du Bois, James Weldon Johnson, Walter White, and Jessie Fauset. All were perceived as, and were in fact, fervent devotees of music and musicians. Du Bois's association with Afro-American music is coeval with his emphatic entrance upon the American scene with the publication of *The Souls of Black Folk* in 1903. After preceding each of thirteen chapters with a musical superscript derived from the spiritual repertory, Du Bois devotes the final essay, "Of the Sorrow Songs," to the spiritual itself (Du Bois [1903] 1973). In 1903 he also published the brief *A Bibliography of Negro Folk Songs*.

The association of James Weldon Johnson with music before the Harlem Renaissance, both individually and in collaboration with his brother, J. Rosamond Johnson, is well known. The important study of James Weldon Johnson's theories of Afro-American music performance by Wendell Whalum (1971), invaluable for its analysis, provides a map of Johnson's writing up to and including the Harlem Renaissance. Not mentioned by Whalum is the "Preface" to the first edition of Johnson's *The Book of American Negro Poetry*, reprinted in the second edition (1931), in which Johnson provides a discussion treating black dance, ragtime, the early black musical, the blues, and the spiritual. Johnson's "Preface" to *The Book of American Negro Spirituals* is, as Whalum notes, "filled with necessary and important ideas and conclusions about the peculiarities of the music" (Whalum 1971, 395).

In his 1925 essay "Harlem: The Culture Capital," published in *The New Negro*, Johnson describes the onset of jazz in New York City around 1900:

> The West Fifty-third Street settlement deserves some special mention because it ushered in a new phase of life among colored New Yorkers. Three rather well-appointed hotels were opened in the street and they quickly became the centers of a sort of fashionable life that hitherto had not existed. On Sunday evenings these hotels served dinner to music and attracted crowds of well-dressed diners. One of these hotels, The Marshall, became famous as the headquarters of Negro talent. There gathered the actors, the musicians, the composers, the writers, the singers, dancers and vaudevillians. There one went to get a close-up of Williams and Walker, Cole and Johnson, Ernest Hogan, Will Marion Cook, Jim Europe, Aida Overton, and of others equally and less known. Paul Laurence Dunbar was frequently there whenever he was in New York. Numbers of those

who loved to shine by the light reflected from celebrities were always to be found. The first modern jazz band ever heard in New York, or, perhaps anywhere, was organized at The Marshall. It was a playing-singing-dancing orchestra, making the first dominant use of banjos, saxophones, clarinets and trap drums in combination, and was called the Memphis Students. Jim Europe was a member of that band, and out of it grew the famous Clef Club, of which he was the noted leader, and which for a long time monopolized the business of "entertaining" private parties and furnishing music for the new dance craze. Also in the Clef Club was "Buddy" Gilmore who originated trap drumming as it is now practised, and set hundreds of white men to juggling their sticks and doing acrobatic stunts while they manipulated a dozen other noise-making devices aside from their drums. A good many well-known white performers frequented The Marshall and for seven or eight years the place was one of the sights of New York (Locke [1925] 1968, 302–3).

The interaction between Walter White and a host of artists in various media is ably chronicled by Edward E. Waldron. White's fascination with Roland Hayes extended to a plan to write a biography of the singer and even to toying with the idea of leaving the NAACP to become Hayes's manager (Waldron 1978, 162). In his novel *Flight* (1926) White's heroine, a tragic mulatto engulfed in the "passing" syndrome, is brought back to appreciation of her own people through listening to the voice of Roland Hayes. This conclusion to the novel was attacked by Frank Horne in his *Opportunity* review of the novel, a review bitterly resented by White (Waldron 1978, 101). (The reader will remember with some interest that Frank Horne is the uncle and mentor of Lena Horne.) Walter White was an inveterate letter writer, and his letters, when published, will certainly reflect the nexus he established during the Harlem Renaissance and maintained subsequently with Afro-American music and musicians.

Precisely because of his towering importance as a mentor, interpreter, and analyst in all domains of Afro-American artistic expression, Alain Locke's interactions with music and musicians lie outside of a general survey and should be the subject of an essay devoted primarily to him. His briefer pieces dealing exclusively with music are reprinted in *The Critical Temper of Alain Locke*, edited by Jeffrey Stewart (Locke 1983). A comprehensive bibliography by John E. Tidwell and John Wright, published in *Callaloo* (1981), provides an overview of Locke's intense involvement with music, and Locke's own book *The Negro and His Music* (1936) expands on concepts and insights first articulated during the twenties. In *The New Negro* there is a section devoted to music, comprising Locke's own essay on the spirituals (Locke [1925] 1968, 198–227), an essay by J. A. Rogers, "Jazz at Home," and poems by Claude McKay, Gwendolyn B. Bennett, and Langston Hughes. Locke compiled much of the extensive bibliographical supplement to *The New Negro*, including "Negro Music: A Bibliography" (Locke [1925] 1968, 434–38) and "A Selected List of Modern Music, Influenced by American Negro Themes or Idioms" (Locke [1925] 1968, 439–41).

Langston Hughes occupied a unique position during the Harlem Renaissance, one which his subsequent career served to enhance. In the first of his autobiographical volumes, *The Big Sea* (1963, written in 1940), Hughes covers his life in the twenties in a series of vignettes which do not really reveal a great deal about his intense preoccupation with the musical life of the period. He mentions popular singers such as Ada "Bricktop" Smith, whom he met in Paris at the nightclub at which they both worked, and also Florence Mills and Josephine Baker. We know from other sources that he was a devotee of black musical theater in the early twenties. However, the quintessential association of Hughes during the Harlem Renaissance was with the blues.

The creation of a body of "blues poems" by Langston Hughes is a very important part of his overall achievement as a writer. His blues poems, at once evocations of the life of the folk and a reflection of a musical form as well as of a musical ethos, provided him a degree of distinction as a poet shared by no other of his contemporaries. One of the most unusual applications of his talent for blues poetry was his composition of a number of song "fragments" for Carl Van Vechten's novel *Nigger Heaven*. Some of these are rather strained, such as the following poem.

> What does it matter that
> I want you?
> What does it matter that
> You want me?
> Like a sweet lump of sugar
> In a hot cup of tea . . . (Van Vechten 1926, 35).

However, of approximately fourteen such pieces, a few reflect the blues poetry Hughes was developing at the time:

> Doan never let yo' woman have her way;
> Keep you in trouble all duh time,
> Doan never let yo' woman have her way;
> Keep you in trouble all yo' day (Van Vechten 1926, 280).

The best reflection of Hughes's involvement with Afro-American music is the role that music plays in the warp and woof of his novel *Not Without Laughter* (1969, written in 1930). He reveals this element only fleetingly in discussing the novel in *The Big Sea:*

For purposes of the novel . . . I created around myself what seemed to me

a family more typical of Negro life in Kansas than my own had been. . . .
And I added dances and songs I remembered (Hughes 1963, 304).

In this novel, the two characters most intimately associated with
music are the young hero's father, the itinerant banjo player Jimboy
Rogers, and his aunt, Harrietta Williams, who at the novel's end is being
billed in Chicago as "The Princess of the Blues." The fifth chapter of the
novel, "Guitar," is a masterly evocation of domestic blues performance
and of the blues ethos:

> On and on the song complained, man-verses and woman-verses, to the
> evening air in stanzas that Jimboy had heard in the pine-woods of Arkan-
> sas from the lumber-camp workers; in other stanzas that were desperate
> and dirty like weary roads where they were sung; and in still others that
> the singer created spontaneously in his own mouth then and there:
>
>> O, I done made ma bed
>> Says, I done made ma bed.
>> Down in some lonesome grove
>> I done made ma bed (Hughes [1930] 1969, 52).

In the eighth chapter, "Dance," Hughes evokes the dance band of the
earlier part of the century as it functioned for the relaxation of the hard-
working black proletariat:

> These mean old weary blues coming from a little orchestra of four men
> who needed no written music because they couldn't have read it. Four
> men and a leader . . . from Galveston; . . . the drummer, from Houston; his
> banjoist from Birmingham; his cornetist from Atlanta; and the pianist . . .
> from New Orleans who had brought with him an exaggerated ragtime
> which he called jazz (Hughes [1930] 1969, 94).

The lyrics of songs evocative of the folk church, of the dance hall, of
the blues recital, as well as the presentation of their contexts are an outstanding feature of *Not Without Laughter*. In the final chapter, "Princess
of the Blues," Hughes depicts both "a typical Black Belt audience, laugh-
ing uproariously, stamping its feet to the music" (Hughes [1930] 1969,
295) and "a little Southern church in a side street. . . . They were singing:

> By and by when de mawnin' comes,
> Saints an' sinners all are gathered home" (Hughes [1930] 1969, 303).

Zora Neale Hurston, whose association with Hughes included collaboration on an abortive folk-play, *Mule Bone,* shared with him a commitment to the music of the folk. In her brief essay "Spirituals and Neo-
spirituals," she provides much practical good sense on the spirituals,

material curiously lacking in nearly all of the musical discussion of this form which had preceded her and absent from much of what followed (Hurston 1983, 79–84; originally published in Cunard 1934). Her essay deserves an honored place in the bibliography and the historiography of the spiritual. It should be noted that it is referred to in John Lovell's compendium on the spiritual, *Black Song* (1972, 465–66).

In Hurston's fiction, anchored as most of it is in the folk experience, the texture that music gives to black life is consistently represented. In "Sweat," one of the few pieces of fiction she actually published in the twenties, Delia, her tortured heroine, finds solace at the "church house." At a crucial point in the action, before a climactic discovery of the dia-bolical nature of her husband, Delia returns from a "love feast":

> In the emotional winds her domestic trials were borne far and wide so that she sang as she drove homeward,
>
>> Jurden water, black an' col'
>> Chills de body, not de soul
>> An' Ah wantah cross Jurden in uh calm time (Hurston [1926] 1985, 399).

Hurston consistently made use of music in weaving her depiction of the folk, and her success in this and other respects has been undergoing a continuing re-evaluation over the last decade.

It can be asserted that Afro-American writers during the Harlem Ren-aissance reacted to and included in their work references to the whole range of Afro-American music as well as to black participation in Euro-classical music. There are, of course, grounds for assuming that certain of the older figures, products of the genteel tradition, believed that the Afro-American musical genres would achieve their full importance when they were properly assimilated into the music of the concert hall. Indeed, in his essay "The Negro Spirituals" in *The New Negro*, Locke says:

> Indeed one wonders why something vitally new has not already been con-tributed by Negro folk song to modern choral and orchestral musical de-velopment. And if it be objected that it is too far a cry from the simple folk spiritual to the larger forms and idioms of modern music, let us recall the folk song origins of the very tradition which is now classic in European music. Up to the present, the resources of Negro music have been tenta-tively exploited in only one direction at a time—melodically here, rhyth-mically there, harmonically in a third direction. A genius that would or-ganize its distinctive elements in a formal way would be the musical giant of his age.
>
> · · · · ·
>
> In view of this very imminent possibility, it is in the interest of musical development itself that we insist upon a broader conception and a more

serious appreciation of Negro folk song, and of the Spiritual which is the very kernel of this distinctive folk art. We cannot accept the attitude that would merely preserve this music, but must cultivate that which would also develop it. Equally with treasuring and appreciating it as music of the past, we must nurture and welcome its contribution to the music of tomorrow (Locke [1925] 1968, 209, 210).

It is doubtful that Locke ever abandoned the position stated in the foregoing quotations. On the other hand, it is clear that Hughes and Hurston regarded the music of the folk and the proletariat as autonomous. The post-Renaissance association of Hughes with gospel music, notably the gospel play *Black Nativity*, and his jazz and poetry readings in the sixties attest to his continuing involvement with indigenous Afro-American music.

The examination of the nexus between music, so central to the Afro-American experience, and those who reflected that experience in critical and creative writings provides the student of the Harlem Renaissance with insights that a view slighting this feature will surely miss.

REFERENCES

Cunard, Nancy, comp. 1934. *Negro: Anthology*. London: Wishart & Co.

Du Bois, W.E.B. 1903. *A bibliography of Negro folk songs*. Atlanta: Atlanta University Press.

———. [1903] 1973. *The souls of black folk*. Millwood, N.Y.: Kraus-Thomson.

Hughes, Langston. 1963. *The big sea*. New York: Hill and Wang.

———. [1930] 1969. *Not without laughter*. New York and London: Collier-Macmillan.

Hurston, Zora Neale. 1983. *The sanctified church*. Berkeley, Calif.: Turtle Island.

———. [1926] 1985. Sweat. In *Afro-American Writing*, by Richard A. Long and Eugenia Collier, 392–402. University Park: Pennsylvania State University Press. (Originally published in *Fire!!* 40–45.)

Johnson, James Weldon. [1922] 1931. *The book of American Negro poetry*. New York: Harcourt, Brace & Co.

———. [1925] 1968. Harlem: The culture capital. In *The new Negro*, edited by Alain Locke, 301–11. New York: Atheneum.

Johnson, James Weldon, and J. Rosamond Johnson. 1925. *The book of American Negro spirituals*. New York: The Viking Press.

Locke, Alain. 1936. *The Negro and his music*. Washington, D.C.: Associates in Negro Folk Education.

———. [1925] 1968. *The new Negro*. New York: Atheneum.

———. 1983. *The critical temper of Alain Locke*, edited by Jeffrey C. Stewart. New York and London: Garland.

Long, Richard A. 1974. The outer reaches: The white writer and blacks in the twenties. *Studies in the Literary Imagination* 7, no. 2:65–71. (The Harlem Renaissance Issue, edited by Victor A. Kamer.)

———. 1985. *Black Americana*. Secaucus, N.J.: Chartwell.

Long, Richard A., and Eugenia Collier. [1972] 1985. *Afro-American writing*. University Park: Pennsylvania State University Press.

Lovell, John, Jr. 1972. *Black song: The forge and the flame*. New York: Macmillan.

Tidwell, John E., and John Wright. 1981. Alain Locke: A comprehensive bibliography. *Callaloo* 4:1–3, 175–92.

Van Vechten, Carl. 1926. *Nigger heaven*. New York: Alfred A. Knopf.

Waldron, Edward E. 1978. *Walter White and the Harlem Renaissance*. Port Washington, N.Y.: Kennikat Press.

Whalum, Wendell P. 1971. James Weldon Johnson's theories and performance practices of Afro-American folksong. *Phylon* 32 (1971):383–95.

White, Walter. [1926] 1969. *Flight*. New York: Negro Universities Press.

CHAPTER 9

Interactions between Art and Music during the Harlem Renaissance

Allan M. Gordon

During the era known as the Harlem Renaissance, music, literature, and the visual arts created by black Americans began to coalesce into an experience in which form and content were increasingly being shaped by the cultural imperatives of the black experience. The emphasis placed on the validity, relevancy, and immediacy of the experience became the common point of reference for all of the arts produced by black artists, many of whom were attempting to assert and legitimize the manner in which their reality as black people differed from that of other Americans.

The difference was especially emphasized because the perception of reality for most black Americans had been shaped by the imposition of restrictive and discriminatory social and political conditions that caused them to view their condition as outsiders with a psychic "double-consciousness." For the artists, including the musicians, this forced segregation inadvertently caused the development of a unique point of view from which to comment on the world and the human condition.

The musicians were clear about both the value and the source of their creation, and these were clearly recognized by observers of and participants in the activities of the era. Carl Van Vechten, for example, who had witnessed one of Bessie Smith's performances, found that her singing was so devoid of pretense that it was like watching a woman cutting her heart open with a knife until it was exposed for all to see (Berendt 1975, 62). Van Vechten's comment may have been melodramatic, but there is no denying that whether music was viewed as entertainment or as a means of transmitting and preserving folklore, it had the power to move and to heal.

At this period the painting of the moment could neither move nor heal since it was conceptually more difficult for the visual artist to create comparable potent imagery. Unlike music, with its legacy of folk music in the form of blues, spirituals, and ragtime, the Afro-American visual arts had no viable folk tradition, their models having been garnered from the Euro-American academic tradition. Both Langston Hughes and Alain Locke tried to counter this deficiency by prescribing a set of guidelines that would direct the artists to African sources or to Afro-American folk sources, the art of the "common element" that constituted the majority of Afro-Americans.

Locke aligned himself with the Africanists because African art had exerted such a tremendous influence on European artists in the early part of the century—Picasso, Modigliani, and others. He reasoned that black artists who were blood descendants of Africans, bound by a direct cultural kinship, could not afford to be less influenced than the European artists. He hoped that Afro-American artists, instead of creating pale imitations of African art like those of the European artists, could return to an expression that was as rigid, controlled, disciplined, abstract, and heavily conventionalized as African art. But Locke's assessment of African art solely in terms of structure and formal analysis was problematic, esoteric, and confusingly ambiguous to those whom it was intended to assist (Locke [1925] 1968a).

Hughes's proposed artistic guidelines were more accessible to artists than Locke's program, since what Hughes proposed had direct implications for subject matter. The Afro-American artistic traits that Locke disdained—naiveté, sentimentalism, exuberance, improvisation, and spontaneity—were, ironically, some of the qualities that Hughes admired, extolling the distinctive virtues of Afro-Americans. His racial chauvinism, to the extent that it could be transformed into theme or content, offered a monumental challenge to the artists, and there was in his prescription an underlying militant tone and racial pride that seemed appropriate for the New Negro (Hughes 1926). Thus, the central issue for the artists was how to translate the philosophy of the New Negro into a viable, relevant aesthetic credo.

In music, the 1920s saw the ascendancy of jazz, the refinement of extemporaneous expression, and the creation of new means of expressing the black experience. In literature, Hughes was writing about the life he knew and attempting to grasp and hold some of the meaning and rhythms of jazz in his poems. However, the visual artists were, for the most part, still observing and privately experimenting, less conceptually prepared to initiate in their art the aesthetic that was being established and controlled by the lives of Ellington, Henderson, and others.

The older black artists who were acclaimed for their successful assimilation of the academic Euro-American artistic traditions dominated the scene but could not provide the artistic leadership required for transformation. Unfortunately, they were hopelessly committed to a dated aesthetic stance that had been successfully challenged by European artists and was being abandoned by their more progressive white American counterparts.

Henry O. Tanner (1859–1936) is a case in point. His stature as the most critically acclaimed black artist of his generation would have placed him in the forefront of any developing Afro-American revolution in painting—if, that is, he had been inclined to accept such a position. But his exile in France effectively removed him from the formative issues during the 1920s, and he also abhorred the idea of a "racial" school of art. His biographer, Marcia Mathews, writes that he avoided racial entanglements and was careful to deny that there was a distinction between white and black artists (Mathews 1969, 132).

Meta Warrick Fuller (1877–1968) was a sculptor who was active during the Harlem Renaissance. She has been considered "one of the most important precursors of the [Harlem] Renaissance" (Campbell et al., 1987, 25). This assessment was primarily based on a work Fuller created for the New York State Centennial in 1914 titled "Ethiopia Awakening," an allegorical statue of an African woman emerging from swaddling clothes. But Fuller was never an artistic leader of the era. Locke correctly placed her stylistically alongside such artists as Tanner and William E. Scott, all pioneers who had European academic credentials and who were responsible, as Locke contended, for black artists achieving some international recognition between approximately 1890 and 1914 (Locke [1936] 1969, 32–33). Locke thought that Fuller's contemporary, May Howard Jackson (1877–1931), also a sculptor, was more suited as a role model for younger artists since she was the "first to break away from the academic cosmopolitanism to frank and deliberate racialism" (Locke [1936] 1969, 30).

Tanner, Fuller, and others may have provided the spiritual inspiration for younger artists in the past, but during the 1920s they offered little direction on how to make art for the changing times. They were not among Locke's New Negro artists as were Aaron Douglas, Palmer Hayden, and Archibald Motley, Jr., to name a few.

For black Americans the times demanded a new image of urban life, with its corollary of risk, peril, and complexity, that emphasized self-expression, revealed and interpreted the black psyche, challenged white standards of art, and celebrated and validated personal experiences. These points represent the unwritten agenda that the musicians and writers were creating. Among the painters, however, there was little of the thematic or stylistic change that would indicate their comprehension of the ethos. Consequently, the visual art works that are most often presented as examples of the Harlem Renaissance are not from the 1920s. They would come only with the onset of the 1930s.

It was Archibald John Motley, Jr. (1891–1980), who showed the way with an exhibit in 1928. One of the most influential artists of the Harlem Renaissance, he was the first to capture in his paintings the feeling of the period, the sense of urgency and immediacy, of experimentation and exploration. But most important, he portrayed the New Negroes as contemporary, urban black people who were self-confident and assertive, who defined their own identities and expressed a certain *élan vital*. Although Motley was from New Orleans, he studied painting at the Chicago Art Institute. He had the distinction of being one of the few black artists to have had a solo exhibition at the downtown New York New Galleries during the 1920s.

The New Galleries catalog stated:

> The first one-man exhibition in a New York art gallery of the work of a Negro artist is, no doubt, an event of decided interest in the annals of the American school of painting. It seems, however, worthwhile to record the fact that the invitation to Mr. Motley to show his paintings at the New Gallery was extended prior to any personal knowledge concerning him or his lineage and *solely because of his distinction as an artist* [italics added] ("New Galleries Catalog" 1928).

The series on African tribal activities in the exhibition were described by Locke as "fantastic compositions of African tribal voodoo ceremonials" (Locke [1936] 1969, 69). Cedric Dover's assessment of the same group of paintings caused him to conclude that Motley was the first of his generation to take Africanism seriously. Dover felt that Motley demonstrated this seriousness by eschewing African motifs and design for the more challenging notion of transforming various African tribal myths in his own manner (Dover 1969, 35).

The other paintings in the exhibition were of black nightlife, and certain of them were as close to visual equivalents of the jazz idiom as those of any artist. Each medium, of course, dictates its own limitations and possibilities, but considering and accounting for the differences between the temporal and spatial modes, Motley was painting in a jazz mode.

The non-exotic paintings in Motley's exhibit were of "a broad, higher-keyed, and somewhat lurid color scheme with an emphasis on the grotesque and genre side of modern Negro life" (Locke [1936] 1969, 69). It was this side of modern black life that was to become the theme and variation of Motley's *oeuvre*. Dover thought that no other black artist "reflected the preoccupations of the 'twenties and their aftermath more typically and interestingly" than Motley. He also wrote that Motley's paintings were "evocative impressions of [black] and Parisian night life which belong to the history of the age," especially as social commentary (Dover 1969, 35). There should be little doubt that Motley's acceptance of a Guggenheim Fellowship took him to Paris between 1929 and 1931, so one of the key players of the Harlem Renaissance art world was freed to absorb the sophistication of the Parisian art world, to experiment and to transcribe a provincial, racial art into a non-provincial, racy art.

Before he went to Paris, Motley made experimental paintings in three categories: (1) "The Black Portrait," (2) "Black Night-Life (Having a Good Time)," and (3) "Black Africa." In an attempt to make a statement about developing new attitudes about the New Negro and other cultural and racial issues, Motley painted a series of portraits of black females that became symbols of pride of race, reverence for age and wisdom, and the importance of traditional values and family. These paintings were also a response to the vagaries and arbitrariness of racism. Such symbols are found in *Portrait of My Grandmother* (1923–1924) and *The Old Snuff Dipper* (1928).[1]

The paintings in the "Black Night-Life (Having a Good Time)" category carry titles such as *Syncopation* (1925), *Stomp* (1927), *Picnic in the Grove* (1928), *Blues* (1929), *Black and Tan Cabaret, Carnival*, and others. These were metaphors for the emergence of the New Negro who could only escape the harsh, existential realities in the artificial world of a perpetual Saturday Night where one could "play awhile. Sing awhile. O, let's dance!" (Hughes 1926).

In the "Black Africa" category, there were *Devil-Devils, Spell of the Voodoo, Kikuyu God of Fire, Waganda Charm-Makers*, and others, all of 1928. These paintings can be viewed as Motley's response to Locke's "Legacy of the Ancestral Arts," an article of 1925 in which Locke admonished black American artists for not using the lessons from classical African art. Motley's African series predates Palmer Hayden's *African Dancers* (1932) and his *Fetiche et Fleurs* (1932–1933) by four years.[2]

Mending Socks (1924) is typical of Motley's pre-Paris work in the "Black Portrait" category (see figure 9.1). It is a portrait of his eighty-two-year-old paternal grandmother who is mending socks and is surrounded by the things of importance to her: the hand-painted brooch of her only daughter, the Bible, the crucifix, and a portrait of her mistress during the days of slavery. More important, she is rendered by Motley with care and affection, and her stoic countenance is the summation of an era of unsung black women who became the point of reference for the black Everyman world created by several other artists such as Palmer Hayden and, later, Charles White.

In thematic treatment and content *The Old Snuff Dipper* could be a companion piece to *Mending Socks*. Both are paintings of elderly black

Figure 9.1. *Mending Socks*, Archibald Motley

women who are treated with a sense of dignity and reverence. He imparts to them a transcendental resolve, an inner strength, a resiliency—qualities upon which black Americans have drawn in order to endure. Both of the women in these early paintings by Motley are symbols from a world of the past, the "old black world" of Paul Laurence Dunbar, but not of Langston Hughes; of the Fisk Jubilee Singers, but not *Shuffle Along*. It was Motley's world before he went to Paris.

His sojourn in Paris served to underline the validity of his approach. On his return to the United States, he refined his compositions of black life, endowing them with "dingies loitering before the doors of dubious pleasure haunts, with 'sweet backs,' gamblers, streetwalkers, and the variegated population of that world in a staccato pattern of interwoven silhouettes" (Porter [1943] 1969, 116).

It was as if Motley were attempting to capture something of the quality of revolt against the restraints of the traditional past and to emphasize instead spontaneity, lack of inhibition, and sexual liberation. The milieu of jazz music was the source for Motley's paintings: the sportin' houses, honky-tonks, gambling joints, dance halls, and "other regions where the devil works."

Like jazz, Motley's paintings were a "revolt from convention, custom, authority, boredom, even sorrow" (Locke [1925] 1968a, 217) that symbolized the restlessness and displacement of the times. He shared with the musicians a common point of reference that emphasized the immediacy of the experience and the relevancy and validity of the black culture. Motley demonstrated that the academic tradition, which encouraged the artist to disdain aspects of the present, real world with its immutable imperfections, could be replaced by choosing subject matter and content that reflected the artist's most direct and immediate experience—the experience of self.

The changes in Motley's paintings, the dates of these changes, and his critical acclaim reveal clearly that he was the seminal figure in the development of the "New Horizons" in the visual arts (Porter [1943] 1969, 115–16). Most of Motley's contemporaries—artists associated with the Harlem Renaissance, such as Richmond Barthé, Aaron Douglas, Palmer Hayden, May Jackson, Malvin Johnson, William Johnson, Lois Jones, Augusta Savage, Laura Waring, and Hale Woodruff—did not employ New Negro subject matter until two or three years later than Motley. Even then, most of their works lacked the assertive verve and the bold, confident execution that characterized Motley's works. A before-and-after comparison of the style and subject matter of many of these artists would illustrate the changes that reflected the new era: Waring's development of portrait and race-type studies; Hayden's evolution from a realistic marine painter into a social-documentary artist; Barthe's portrayal of race types and rhythm groups; Douglas's allegorical scenes of the historical life and cultural background of Afro-Americans; and M. G. Johnson's symbolic, interpretive treatment of black subjects, to list a few.

Palmer Hayden, Motley's leading contemporary, was declared the most outstanding black painter in 1927 by winning the Harmon Foundation's prize in painting. He left immediately thereafter for Paris. Other than painting a few burlesques, Hayden did not treat black subject matter with any degree of seriousness until his return to the United States in 1932. In Paris Hayden was away from the Harlem scene, and he was painting marine studies and other similar works with titles such as *Schooners* (1926) and *Quai at Concarneu* (1929), while Motley was painting *Spell of the Voodoo* (1928) and *Blues* (1929). The latter is typical of the kinds of paintings for which Motley is best known (see figure 9.2). Such a composition allowed him to explore "Black Night-Life," to create a variety of black characters (which he admitted enjoying), and to paint in a frank and honest manner the Negro as he had seen him and as he had felt him.

Motley, like Langston Hughes, felt akin to the jazzmen and blues singers of the era who shared in extemporaneous expression (Huggins 1971, 222–23). In black culture the improvised statement tied together street boys, folk preachers, blues singers, jazzmen, and not so incidentally, the works of Archibald John Motley, Jr., who epitomized the new conceptual thrust of the visual arts. Thus, as Motley dispensed with the single, metaphorical portrait-figure, he began creating more complicated compositions that burst at the seams with teeming, sparkling crowds glowing from the artificial illumination of night lights. It was as close as he or any black artist of his generation would come to an expression that, in my opinion, paralleled jazz music. Titles of some of his works in the 1930s were *Playing Poker* (1933), *Saturday Night* (1934), *Chicken Shack* (1936), *Chicago* (1936), and *The Barbecue*, all of which portrayed activities on city streets or in cabarets—metaphors for the aspiration of a whole people, the New Negro who was in the process of being transformed. Motley's urban world contained the direct descendants, the immediate beneficiaries, of prevailing social and cultural changes.

The relationship among the arts of the Renaissance—literary, musical, and visual—hinged on their forceful insistence on the validity and importance of the black experience for theme and subject matter. The evolving arts were the art of the New Negro, the results of a credo that placed new emphasis on their "individual, dark-skinned selves without fear or shame" (Hughes 1926, 694). This was the common denominator that informed all the arts of the time.

The nature of the development of black music allowed it to rise to the forefront as a vehicle for expressing the existential pathos of an emerg-

Figure 9.2. *Blues*, Archibald Motley

ing New Negro while, at the same time, writers such as Langston Hughes (*The Weary Blues*, 1926), Claude McKay (*Harlem Shadow*, 1922), Countee Cullen (*Color*, 1925), and others were also exploring new racial themes in their work.

Finally, painters and sculptors, abandoning the romantic landscapes, religious themes, and other Victorian genteel themes, joined their colleagues in creating works that, sometimes self-consciously, dealt with a new awakening of the possibilities of who they were as black people. While most of their efforts were produced somewhat later than the works of the musicians and writers, Motley's works show not only that he was among the first to understand the issues involved as they related to a new black aesthetic, but that he also was able to translate this concept more successfully and sooner than most of the other artists into a modality that paralleled the expressions of black music—jazz, in particular. Therefore, his work illustrates most clearly the relationship that existed among art, music, and the concept of the New Negro.

This discussion has been an exploration of an idea that should be followed by an examination of the formal properties of the artists of the Harlem Renaissance and the comparison of these properties with those of the music of the period. Such an examination should establish the assumed relationship between Afro-American musicians and artists of the period. The ideas presented here are offered as the basis for such examination.

NOTES

1. Motley also dealt with the "Tragic Mulatto Theme" in paintings such as *A Mulatress* (1925), *The Head of a Quadroon* (1928), and *Aline, An Octoroon* (1928).

2. Some writers thought that Hayden was among the first to use African designs and subjects in his paintings (see Gordon 1988).

REFERENCES

Archibald J. Motley, Jr. 1928. *Opportunity* (April): 114–15.

Berendt, Joachim. 1975. *The jazz book: From New Orleans to rock and free jazz.* New York: Lawrence Hill and Company.

Campbell, Mary Schmidt, David Driskell, David Levering Lewis, and Deborah Willis Ryan. 1987. *Harlem Renaissance: Art of black America.* New York: Harry N. Abrams.

Dover, Cedric. 1969. *American Negro art.* New York: New York Graphic Society.

Gordon, Allan M. 1988. *Echoes of our past: The narrative artistry of Palmer C. Hayden.* Los Angeles: The Museum of African American Art.

Huggins, Nathan Irvin. 1971. *Harlem Renaissance.* New York: Oxford University Press.

Hughes, Langston. 1926. The Negro artist and the racial mountain. *The Nation* June 23: 692–94.

Locke, Alain. [1925] 1968a. *The New Negro.* New York: Atheneum.

———. [1940] 1968b. *The Negro in art: A pictorial record of the Negro artist and of the Negro theme in art.* New York: Hacker Art Books.

———. [1936] 1969. *Negro art: Past and present.* New York: Arno Press and The New York Times.

Mathews, Marcia M. 1969. *Harry Ossawa Tanner, American artist.* Chicago: University of Chicago Press.

New Galleries catalog. 1928. *Opportunity* 6, no. 4 (April):114–15.

Porter, James. [1943] 1969. *Modern Negro art.* New York: Arno Press.

CHAPTER 10

The Negro Renaissance and England

Jeffrey P. Green

The occurrence of a Harlem Renaissance in England in the 1920s seems unlikely if not absurd, but New York did not have sole possession of the ideals that led to the black artistic outflow of the Renaissance. Indeed, those who nurtured the New Negro and encouraged black artistic expression had considerable links to England; for example, W.E.B. Du Bois had traveled there and had his daughter Yolande attend school there, while Alain Locke had spent some years at Oxford University. Even those who had less or no contact with England had a wider view than many native-born Americans, for Renaissance figures such as Claude McKay, Arthur Schomburg, Casper Holstein, and Eric Walrond had links to the Caribbean.

Afro-American newspapers, those of British West Africa (Sierra Leone, Ghana, Nigeria) and of South Africa, carried details of black activities in England, as did the two London weeklies *West Africa* and *African World*. The press of the larger society, dusty files of record companies, antique shellac discs, family papers, discussions with veterans, archival material, autobiographies of contemporaries, and a handful of biographies of Afro-Americans show details of the music of the Negro Renaissance in England in the 1920s, including the activity of Ethel Waters, John Payne, Marian Anderson, Paul Robeson, Roland Hayes, Lawrence Brown, Noble Sissle, Eubie Blake, James P. Johnson, Shelton Brooks, Arthur Briggs, Turner Layton, Clarence Johnstone, Will Marion Cook, Sidney Bechet, Edmund Jenkins, Will Vodery, and Florence Mills. Renaissance figures such as Du Bois, Walter White, Jessie Fauset, Locke, and Schomburg were in London or Paris (eight hours from London), and poets McKay and Langston Hughes also crossed the Atlantic.

Although Britain's black population in the 1920s was small and dispersed, it was not as tiny as many believe. Ambitious would-be professionals went to Britain to study because the tropical empire had few facilities for college education. Some of these students settled in England, as will be seen. These African and Caribbean students, the merchants and businessmen, and vacationers unwilling to spend time in lynch-mad America formed the basis of Britain's black middle class in the 1920s. They were affected by the same sense of racial pride and national regeneration that in America led to the Harlem Renaissance. Evidence to support this can be found in a New York publication that has been ignored by most historians of the Renaissance: the *Negro World*. The very title suggests a more positive stance than *Crisis*, *Messenger*, and *Opportunity*.

A weekly, probably reaching more readers than the total touched by the three journals above, *Negro World* was the voice of Marcus Garvey's Universal Negro Improvement Association (UNIA). Garvey had left Jamaica and traveled in the Caribbean, reached England by 1913, and settled in New York in 1917. *Negro World* reflected his international outlook and carried sections in French and Spanish. Garvey's political and failed business activities are known in outline to many, but his literary and cultural efforts have been overlooked. *Negro World* published early writings of Zora Neale Hurston (her biographer was not aware of this). In 1921 it had a literary contest and reported on the Philadelphia branch of UNIA's melodrama, *The New Negro*; an editorial in 1922 welcomed the opening of Broadway to shows such as *Shuffle Along*; Garvey's UNIA was an early supporter of Marian Anderson, employing her for the women's convention at New York headquarters Liberty Hall in Harlem, where she was billed as "America's Greatest Contralto Soloist" in the August 1922 issue (Martin 1983). It is likely that the *Negro World* had readers in 1920s Britain, since this writer has a photograph of the *Crisis* being read in England during this period. What is clear is that Caribbean influences within the Renaissance in America were substantial, and that views expressed by Caribbean blacks and by Garvey and others in the *Negro World* would have been similar to those held by blacks in England.

It could be argued that, because of the acclaim throughout Britain of the music of Afro-British composer Samuel Coleridge-Taylor (1875–1912), Britain's blacks had been advanced in recognizing and promoting black culture. Certainly, in London in 1912, the Africa-born actor-turned-journalist Duse Mohamed (later Duse Mohamed Ali) established the *African Times and Orient Review*, a weekly (later a monthly) that had artistic, literary, and political content ranging all over the world of "the darker races" whose experience was not "Up From Slavery" but up from imperialism (Martin 1976, 7; McGilchrist and Green 1985, 169).

Imperialism was the offspring of British liberal concern over the Atlantic slave trade, of curiosity over the geography of Africa's great rivers, and of Christian evangelism, and from the 1880s it became the vehicle for the political and economic domination of the black world by the white. Segregation and the color line were found in Britain's colonies, and Africans and their descendants were denied many freedoms. In the struggle to assert their humanity, British blacks (by which I mean those resident in Britain and in her empire) used every facility, including the arts. Africans wrote books asserting the values of their traditions and sought to overthrow the white domination of African historiography (Jenkins 1986, 121–29). Africans, Caribbeans, and those of African descent but British birth took a keen interest in the musical and other attainments of black people generally, as the pages of the *African Times and Orient Review* and the 1912 funeral of Coleridge-Taylor demonstrate (McGilchrist and Green 1985, 170–74).

It is a little difficult, in an era when so much music is heard on tape and on disc, in cars, elevators, shopping malls, and places of recreation, to remember that for the generation that was adult in the 1920s, music was the playing of instruments or singing. An even mediocre education included instrumental instruction, and gatherings of the most refined type included recitals, soirées, and musical interludes. Members of the British black middle class owned pianos, paid for their families to study music, and expected musical skills within their circle of friends. Aspiring families in the empire had similar beliefs, and it is an unhappy result of the boom in black music that little attention has been paid to this genteel, Europeanized musical element in the colonies in the 1910s, of which examples are the existence of the music college in Ghana (colonial Gold Coast) begun in 1916 by Kwamina Abayie (a.k.a. Charles Graves) (Sampson [1937] 1969, 149–50) and the careers of concert pianists Henry Nation and Joe Derbyshire, choirmaster George Goode, and bandmaster Benjamin de Cordova Reid (all Jamaicans) (Thompson 1985).

If the New Negro in America was being prepared socially to attend the opera house, the Renaissance blacks in England already had that veneer for the large part. This very bourgeois style was part of the education system in England and her empire. Schools in Africa and in Jamaica, Trinidad, and Guyana (colonial British Guiana), although inaccessible to the majority, had a standard of education that matched those in Britain. Latin, Greek, French, and cricket, along with the works of Shakespeare, Dickens, Macaulay, and Jane Austin, were to be acquired. Choral singing was common, and church services included black singers and instrumentalists. British blacks were so English that Afro-Americans sometimes had difficulties coming to terms with them.

The sounds of the New World were known in Africa: members of the Fisk Jubilee Singers had made a lasting impact in South Africa (Willan 1984, 44–45); the band of the West India Regiment played in Sierra

Leone and Ghana (Green 1984, 107); and one Caribbean graduate of Britain's school of military music led the band in eastern Nigeria's Calabar in the 1890s (Boisragon 1897, 40–41). The absence of phonograph recordings, that later and vital method of spreading the music of black Americans around the globe, did not mean that British blacks were without contact with American music. There were also those Africans and Caribbeans who had worked and studied in the United States, where black colleges promoted choirs and instrumental music following the social and financial success of Nashville's Fisk University in the 1870s (Seroff 1986, 49–51). Aware of the global dimensions of black music, expecting to perform or attend instrumental recitals, and asserting an identity as blacks, the Negro community in England in the 1920s was, despite its numerical inferiority, a cultured and alert group of people who, as we shall see, mixed freely with Renaissance figures from America and with whites of aristocratic and financial standing.

Blacks who were not of the professional, almost elitist class to which I refer as the British black middle class did gather in locations and neighborhoods in Britain. Kinship, a feeling of being at ease, and the absence of rules made by whites made such centers important. Details are scant except when newspapers reported alleged criminal behavior or when veterans have been interviewed. In Cardiff, where Welsh coal was shipped to all the major ports of the world, there was a black ghetto in Bute Town. Sailors of all nationalities and locals on the spree frequented the cafes and illegal clubs that were found in most ports, where prostitutes, illicit alcohol, and music were available. Performers included Brylo Ford, a shoe repairer from Trinidad who played the bamboo flute, the guitar, and the quatro[1]; Victor "Narka" Parker of local birth and African descent, who sang and played the guitar; and in the 1920s, a trio of Don Johnson and Joe and Frank Deniz.

The Deniz brothers, brought up in Bute Town, were the children of a Cape Verde Island black and his Welsh wife. Johnson's father was from Barbuda and raised his family away from the ghetto to avoid the voice of that district. His death in 1924 freed young Don, who had sneaked into Bute Town some months before. Asked what it was like, he told the writer: "All those black faces and no one saying 'Nigger.'" Joining the Deniz brothers (mandolin, guitar, ukelele, and quatro), Johnson's trio played parties, often for prostitutes and their boyfriends. They played "calypso and breakdowns" from songs handed down by older songsters in the community, from records brought into Cardiff by sailors, and from varied contacts. An African lodger named Barzy had played the one-string fiddle and had impressed the youthful Johnson, who also recalled Ford's flute practicing in the back of his shop and Christmas parades that once left him asleep "on a Chinaman's couch" in Bute Town

(Green 1986; Johnson 1986). London, Liverpool, and Glasgow must have had similar musical merging. In the city of Manchester's Salford district of Greengate, the press reported black music-making and an affray in 1919 (Jenkinson 1986, 205), but British urban areas did not have the club and nightspot scene that evolved during America's prohibition years. There were places of public entertainment where black musicians played, and many were associated with jazz, for the new music was linked with public dancing. Due to the delays caused by the war years, public dancing was brought to Britain at the same time that jazz was introduced there by the white Original Dixieland Jazz Band, which recorded, toured, and settled down for months in a London dance hall, or "palais de dance" as the English called such locations (Goddard 1979, 30).

Black musicians such as Daniel Kildare from Jamaica, who later claimed American parentage, worked in quality night spots in London in the war years when shortages of musicians gave opportunities to blacks because German musicians were enemy aliens and whites were required for military service. Theater circuits gave regular employment to groups such as the Versatile Three, who were well respected in Britain in the 1910s.[2] Its drummer Gus Haston and others, such as singer Norris Smith (Paul Robeson's understudy in *Showboat* in the 1928 London production), wrote to Afro-American newspapers to tell of opportunities in England (Funk 1986, 147; Green 1982a, 48).

The blacks of England were a tiny minority compared to the number of their counterparts in New York, and even if all those of African descent who lived in London had homes in one district, these hundreds would not have had the impact of Harlem's thousands. Around the same time as Don Johnson's venture into Bute Town, Langston Hughes arrived in Harlem: "I stood there, dropped my bags, took a deep breath and felt happy again" (Hughes 1940, 81). Roland Hayes arrived in London with Lawrence Brown in 1920 (Helm 1942, 128). The pair was introduced to Mohamed, who arranged contracts and accommodation. Hughes was on his own in the big city, but Hayes and Brown, like Johnson, were welcomed because of the smallness of the black communities of Britain. No matter what origin, the newly arrived met other blacks with a broad range of experiences, and so had more reasons to aspire to represent black culture, to advance as individuals, and to grapple with the global problems facing the race. *West Africa* reported a Hayes-Brown recital on November 6, 1920, when the pair presented spirituals and Coleridge-Taylor to an audience that included John Richard Archer ("The Roland Hayes Recital" 1920). Archer presented them with a souvenir vellum address and exhorted them to "remember that Africans and their descendants can do whatever other nations are capable of

Figure 10.1.   Edmund Thornton Jenkins (left) and two
friends, probably Caribbeans, London, ca. 1921

doing, given equal opportunity." Archer was a black Englishman, born
of a Barbados father in Liverpool in 1863; a politician, Pan-Africanist,
friend of Mohamed, Coleridge-Taylor, and Ida B. Wells, he had been
mayor of the London borough of Battersea in 1913–1914. From its northern boundary the British parliament can be seen across the Thames
(Fryer 1984, 290–94, 413).

In August 1919 members of the Southern Syncopated Orchestra of
Will Marion Cook were present with their leader and business manager
George William Lattimore at a function in honor of several groups of
blacks in London that had been organized by the Coterie of Friends, a

student group of Caribbeans (and one Ghanaian) led by South Carolina-born Edmund Thornton Jenkins (see figure 10.1). Jenkins had been a student at London's Royal Academy of Music since 1914 and was currently teaching the clarinet there. Archer and Afro-American lawyer Thomas McCants Stewart mixed with South Africans and Guyanese in a room decorated with the flags of Haiti and Liberia. Jenkins, with two ladies from Cook's orchestra and vocalist Evelyn Dove, played works by Weber, Coleridge-Taylor, and himself. Dove, whose father was Francis Thomas Dove, a lawyer from Sierra Leone, was likened to Josephine Baker by Henry Champly (Green 1982a, 72–76; "A 'Many-Millioned Cry'" 1919; Champly 1936, 230).

Cook's orchestra attracted steady attention in the British press, and the group, or sections of it—for members returned to America or moved off to join white dance-jazz groups playing the new music—continued to work in Britain into late 1921 (Rye 1986, 231). Cook "was confident that a Negro Beethoven would take his proper place in the world's history of music" (M. B. 1919), but the group presented a mix of spirituals, rags, and minstrel-associated tunes. The show-business weekly *The Era* referred to "special Southern colour" in the banjos, "plantation melodies," and "camp-meeting songs" ("Southern Syncopated Orchestra" 1919). The group was listed in the daily press under "concerts and recitals," whereas the Versatile Three (which included Haston and leader Anthony 'Tony' Tuck) played at the prestigious Palladium variety theater in central London at this time. Five months later, when Jenkins and his friends produced a concert of Coleridge-Taylor's music plus a work from Jenkins's pen, Tuck and his wife were in the audience, four members of Cook's orchestra played in the otherwise white orchestra, and Jenkins conducted (Green 1982a, 79–81).

Presented by blacks as black music, this concert was not in the same category as Cook's performances, about which *The Star* commented, "It is said to be the most serious Negro band of its kind. . . . It is an excellent orchestra of its kind. . . . That it differs widely in type from other Jazz bands is less obvious to the more European" (Crescendo 1919). Cook was presented in England as a New Negro in aspirations, but his orchestra played "rhythmic swing" with "intense emotion," while humorists "are not lacking." Both the expectations of the reporter and his understanding that he was witnessing black music can be seen in his concluding remarks:

> Though it may be to confess myself still shackled by an effete civilisation, I prefer the less violent stimulus of European music to the exotic delight of corybantic agitation (Crescendo 1919).

Had this reporter attended the Coleridge-Taylor concert, he would have seen Jenkins conduct without the extravagant dancing movements of Cook. Yet *The Star*'s reporter expressed views on black music that are similar to those expressed by whites who went to Harlem in the 1920s. Blacks were expected to be different, to behave differently, and to have qualities in their music different from those of whites. That some whites liked black music might have more to do with their dislike of certain manifestations of British society than with any musical appreciation, as we shall see in the recollections of Spike Hughes. Black and white attitudes could be seen when Hayes included in his programs songs in French and German, for sympathetic commentators were surprised at his mastery. In 1921 he sang in Swahili and in Yoruba, a result of contacts with Africans in England and symbolic of the Renaissance mood (Green 1982b, 33–34, 39).

Spike Hughes, a musician, performer, and journalist, recalled Florence Mills in England in 1927, "I believe if I had shut my eyes while Florence Mills was singing I could not have told whether she was white or coloured." He said she was a song-and-dance performer who could have come from either side of the Atlantic (Hughes 1946, 305). Hughes had seen all-black shows before; in the mid-1920s in Austria, for example, he had seen and talked to Arthur Briggs whose group included a flutist from Haiti, a drummer from Senegal, and a saxophone player from the Congo (Zaire). Both Briggs and flutist Bertin Salnave had been in the Southern Syncopated Orchestra in London and had been under Jenkins's direction at the Coleridge-Taylor concert (Green 1982a, 81). But the orchestra for *Blackbirds* of 1927 was Afro-American. How did Hughes recall their sound? "Negro music played with all its characteristic colourfulness and vitality" (Hughes 1946, 307). Such understanding was rare. Britain's blacks, because of their belief in the ideas of the Renaissance, knew that this music was to be respected even if it transgressed the rules of the European schools of music. Hughes recalled how whites had raved about Florence Mills and noted, in retrospect, that "the people I have in mind were those who considered the Cotton Club to be 'genuine' Harlem—as if any place were 'genuine' Harlem that did not admit coloured guests" (Hughes 1946, 305). What Hughes wrote about British whites applied as well to American whites who were just a taxi ride from Lenox Avenue's nightspots.

The international nature of black London is seen in 1923 when Florence Mills and Sol Plaatje, the leader of the South African delegation who had attended the August 1919 gathering, met. Plaatje had first arrived in England in 1914 when he had made contact with the band of the Jenkins Orphanage of Charleston, South Carolina, playing at an international exhibition. Plaatje used postcards of the band for correspondence. Commenting on the death of Florence Mills in 1927, in the

Kimberly *Diamond Fields Advertiser* of November 14, 1927, Plaatje wrote that he had first met her in New York in 1921 when she performed in *Shuffle Along*. In London in 1923 she was in *Dover Street to Dixie*, and Plaatje was back from his trip to America and Canada. Gathering funds for his fare back to South Africa, Plaatje sought employment with George Lattimore in a London stage presentation about Africa that lasted one month (Willan 1984, 287–89) and also recorded six sides on three ten-inch records to be sold in Africa. Included, but not indicated, was almost certainly the first recording of *Nkosi Sikelele Afrika*, the anthem of black South Africans then and to this day (Willan 1984, 290). This recording of *Nkosi Sikelele Afrika* by an African author who had lived in England, met Du Bois and Garvey, and been in the front of the struggle for black rights in southern Africa, has a historical poignancy: Plaatje's career shows how Renaissance ideas were international. His singing was accompanied by Sylvia Colenso who had been a good friend of Coleridge-Taylor. The pair participated in a London concert on October 9, 1923, in which Evelyn Dove sang *Nobody Knows* (and also items by Burleigh and Coleridge-Taylor); Gwendolen Coleridge-Taylor, the composer's daughter, and Miss Mary [sic] Lawrence, "The West Indian Soprano," also performed. Accompanists included Mrs. W.E.S. Callender and Mrs. Drysdale. Callender was the English wife of an Afro-Guyanese lawyer of London (the two had lived in Canada and the Bahamas); their daughter Dorothy Grace Callender was studying at Trinity College of Music where the files note she had been awarded the Grosvenor Gooch prize in 1922. Mrs. Drysdale's husband was Jamaica-born Louis George Drysdale, a tailor and voice coach who trained Florence Mills in London and was to aid others including George Robert Garner and Ethel Waters (Green 1984, 111–12; Southern 1982, 143; Waters 1951, 198).

Drysdale had been present in December 1918 when the African Progress Union had been formed in London and when John Archer had made a stirring presidential speech. In 1921–1922 the Callenders were on its committee, as was Edmund Jenkins. Archer was replaced in July 1921 by medical practitioner John Alcindor, a Trinidad-born graduate of Edinburgh University and a London resident since 1899. From mid-1921 the African Progress Union has many mentions in the pages of *West Africa*. That weekly was read by blacks in Africa and England, and they and some of the white readers were interested in the advances made by Afro-Americans. One of the London group was Mrs. Pearson, of part African descent, whose son Alan married Marie Lawrence, a singer in one of the inexpensive restaurants in London (Thompson 1985, 42). In 1934 Lawrence was to help recruit blacks as "Africans" to support Robeson in the movie *Sanders of the River* (Green 1984, 120).

Miss Lawrence's repertoire, like that of Evelyn Dove, included spirituals. I discussed attitudes to spirituals with a London-born lady of Afro-Guyanese parentage, who also sang spirituals from the 1920s. It was the music of black people; white people couldn't sing such songs properly. She had been accompanied by a white, and as the discussion continued, my veteran informant stated that musically there was nothing so different about the Negro spiritual, but that black performers such as herself (and thus Miss Lawrence) believed it to be their music and so obtained the maximum quality from the songs. Her brother trained with Paul Robeson (Untitled article 1937).

Black theatrical performances had a long tradition in England, and recent research by Howard Rye and Rainer Lotz has uncovered something of the activities of Will Garland, who worked with W. C. Handy around 1899. Garland ran all-black shows from a London base over three decades and was to employ Evelyn Dove and other British blacks, including Africans (Lotz 1986, 136, 143). Garland worked with fellow Afro-American dancer Louis Douglas, whose career has been traced by Lotz; if nothing else, that Douglas married the daughter of Will Marion Cook and Abbie Mitchell in London shows the links in England between Americans of the Renaissance.

Following the success of *Shuffle Along* and within the spirit of "corybantic agitation," Afro-American shows became fashionable for Britons. Plaatje noted how the wife of England's ex-prime minister Asquith had seen *Shuffle Along*, and America and its shows became fashionable for certain Britons who had the time and cash to spare. Such a person was Edwina Ashley, probably the wealthiest woman in Britain. She married Louis "Dickie" Mountbatten (a godchild of Queen Victoria and related to the monarchs of both England and Germany) in 1922, and the pair went to America on a honeymoon. Her biographer noted that "they enjoyed the music hall, cabaret, jazz music, comic actors, light comedy" (Hough [1983] 1985, 90). In 1924 they returned with a party that included the heir to the British and imperial throne, Edward Prince of Wales (the late Duke of Windsor) who was attracted to America by "the freedom it offered him from protocol and formality" (Hough [1983] 1985, 102). The Mountbattens came back to England with "a stack of sheet music for the Charleston and Black Bottom" (Hough [1983] 1985, 104). She took up with blacks in England and America, and by the 1930s had compromised Paul Robeson in England through a public scandal. In 1934 she left England for Harlem (Hough [1983] 1985, 126–30). Titled, wealthy, aristocratic Britons supported black musicians in England and America, but much of their applause was not sincere, reflecting their unease with British society ("protocol and formality") more than any understanding for the ideals of the Renaissance.

The 1921 and 1923 Pan-African Congresses of Du Bois and the NAACP, which brought Walter White, Du Bois, and Jessie Fauset to England, were duly reported in the *Crisis,* but little was shown of the large gap in knowledge and vision between the Afro-Americans and their Caribbean, African, and British-born associates in London, although longer-term residents such as McCants Stewart and Jenkins and even Hayes and Brown by 1923 would have known more about Africa and African peoples than some of the intellectual Afro-Americans who controlled information outlets during the Renaissance (Green 1982a, 102, 139). The letters of Dr. John Alcindor to Du Bois in 1923 show the problems and also illustrate the bonds that linked blacks after their contacts in Britain; in that year Alcindor had a letter from Audrey Jeffers in Trinidad. She had attended the Wigmore Hall for that Coleridge-Taylor concert in December 1919.

John Alcindor could be described as one of the leaders in England's black renaissance. Certainly he had continuity of contacts with other blacks, including musical figures Burleigh, Clarence Cameron White, and Roland Hayes (McGilchrist and Green 1985, 169, 176–77). His eldest son had piano lessons from the daughter of Ira Aldridge, the American actor who had carved a career in Europe in the previous century. Alcindor's death in October 1924 deprived Britain, and British blacks, of an important and caring man.

Yet another doctor from the Caribbean was H. J. Alexander Dingwall, who was at Louis Drysdale's London home with Grenada-born pianist Leslie "Hutch" Hutchinson and *Chicago Defender* founder Robert Abbott, duly reported in the *Amsterdam News* in October 1929. Hutchinson was very popular in high society and was involved with the Mountbatten crowd (Hough [1983] 1985, 126; Kennedy 1986, 224). He had arrived in London from Paris where he had worked with Ada "Bricktop" Smith (Smith 1983, 110–29; Wilcox 1980, 11).

There are no archives with details of these pan-African gatherings but some correspondence has survived in libraries devoted to the documentation of imperialism, such as Rhodes House (Oxford). These papers, being those of colonial officials or of paternalist groups such as the Anti-Slavery Society, tend to show blacks as subservient to whites, as it is the latter's papers which have been preserved. If they have a black perspective, it is the anti-colonial one rather than that of black life in Britain. However, Alcindor's letter to the *Sunday Illustrated* in 1922 over an inaccurate scandal-mongering article on French colonial troops in occupied Germany and his work over the movie *Birth of a Nation* in England show that he was not solely concerned with the fate of African people in the empire but with black people generally. Alcindor's African Progress Union committee included blacks born in Trinidad, Guyana, Barbados,

Liberia, Sierra Leone, Ghana, and South Carolina, and was well able to take a global view of the black world in the same way that Garvey and Du Bois did.

The cosmopolitan links that were so important to the Renaissance in America also existed in England. Just using the pages of *West Africa* for a dozen weeks of 1924, we can see continuity of contact, interactions, links to high-society whites, links to white Americans, and Renaissance aspirations. "A Coaster's London Log" (1924) notes that Hayes and William Lawrence had performed at a dinner given that week by Viscountess Harcourt, graced by the Queen of England. Daughter of American banker Walter Hayes Burn (brother-in-law of J. Pierpont Morgan), the Viscountess had married Lewis Harcourt, the minister responsible for the colonies under Asquith from 1910 until 1915. Harcourt inherited his father's title in 1917. A homosexual scandal in 1921 had not ended with his sudden death, but as Carol Kennedy has commented, "The scandal did not affect Lady Harcourt's position in society" (Kennedy 1986, 205). The marrying of the daughters of wealthy Americans into Britain's titled upper class was not unusual (Hesketh Pearson has called them "the pilgrim daughters"), and research might indicate that these ladies supported black artists in England in order to deny any sympathy with American racism and segregation. Certainly Lady Simon from Alabama wrote a book on slavery in the late 1920s.

The next page of *West Africa* previews an African Progress Union reception and dance to which "The Fisk University Jubilee Singers have promised to come if their engagements permit." Marie Lawrence was to sing and the orchestra was to play works by Coleridge-Taylor and "Miss Ring (daughter of the late Ira Aldridge)," the assumption is clear that Aldridge's career would be known to those readers likely to attend the gathering ("African Progress Union Reception" 1924). Details of the radio broadcast in Yoruba made by law student Ladipo Solanke, the second African to broadcast on the fledgling radio service in London, are in the next column ("Broadcasting in Yoruba" 1924).

E. C. commented in "Gramophone Notes" (1924) that Hayes's concerts were "always crowded" and that his voice did not have a true impact in phonograph recordings. Reviewed in the same issue was the African Progress Union gathering of Dr. and Mrs. Alcindor; John Barbour-James, a Guyanese who worked in Ghana during 1902–1917; Marie Lawrence, the wife of Ghana's colonial governor Frederick Guggisberg; and "many representatives of West, South and East Africa, the West Indies, etc." ("A.P.U. Reception and Dance" 1924). On August 2, 1924, the London funeral of Kathleen Simango was reported. Born in Sierra Leone in 1893 and educated in London where, as Kathleen Easmon, she was very close to Coleridge-Taylor, she had traveled to America with her aunt Adelaide Casely Hayford, second wife of Ghanaian nationalist, author, lawyer, and politician Joseph Casely Hayford, an associate of many race leaders around the world. While there, she had married Columbus Kamba Simango, who had studied at Columbia in New York having left his native Mozambique some years before. Simango arrived in London in 1923 with Paul Robeson in *Taboo* (Johnson 1930, 192). Mrs. Simango's funeral was attended by the Alcindors, John and Edith Barbour-James, and Coleridge-Taylor's son and daughter ("The Death of Mrs. Simango" 1924).

The August 30 issue contains notice of the funeral of Nannette Boucher, the daughter of Africanus Horton, the first African doctor trained in Britain, author, nationalist, and army officer. Boucher's death shows links through music, for she had been involved distantly with Garland's Negro Operetta Company which went from London to Russia in 1913 (Lotz 1986, 136, 138), and her son James Boucher had been an important member of the Southern Syncopated Orchestra in 1921, as had Trinidad-born Cyril Blake who was with James Boucher at the cemetery (Rye 1986, 229–30). The same page reported the funeral of Grenada-born Maria Douglas, whose daughter had married an African student named L. A. Egerton-Shyngle. Present at the funeral were John Barbour-James and Gus Haston (from the Versatile Three) ("Mrs. Maria J. Douglas" 1924).

This issue also contains discussion of the career of Nicholas Ballanta-Taylor, a musician from Sierra Leone who, in 1921, had traveled to America, where he had links with philanthropist George Peabody and Tuskegee's Robert Russa Moton. He studied under Walter Damrosch in New York and visited Tuskegee, Alabama, Fort Valley, Georgia, and St. Helena Island (South Carolina) and its famous Penn school. He had worked with the late Mrs. Simango in America. His contacts with New Negroes, as well as the Gullah speakers and peasantry of the South, are not detailed, but surely many doubts over the future of the race would have been dispelled by this African musician who enthused over the culture of African peoples ("A Sierra Leone Composer's Mission" 1924). On September 13 *West Africa* reviewed his overture *Africa and the Africans* and published his photograph (A.A.C. 1924). And Africa was not unknown to black Americans who passed through London in the 1920s, for Max Yergas, who had worked for the YMCA in southern Africa, was scheduled to speak to black students in London on September 6. We must remember that it was a group of black students who had mounted the 1919 Coleridge-Taylor concert. Such were the contacts and interactions in England during the 1920s Renaissance.

Charles Cochran, the "Ziegfeld" of England, employed Jamaican multi-instrumentalist Leslie Thompson in his theater orchestras from

1931 and had brought Florence Mills to London in 1923. In 1925 he contracted to bring Eubie Blake and Noble Sissle to England, where the *Stage* of December 24 was to refer to them as "established favourites." They had three recording sessions, performed for an ex-servicemen's charity, worked in clubs and theaters, and wrote songs for Cochran before leaving via Paris and Josephine Baker in March 1926. Blake didn't like Britain or the British and never returned; Sissle loved it all and returned in 1927. In late January 1928, Sissle participated with Baker, the Four Harmony Kings, Alberta Hunter, Leon Abbey, Ike Hatch and Elliott Carpenter, "Hutch" Hutchinson, and Scott and Whaley in an "all coloured matinee" in aid of the flood relief fund of the mayor of Westminster (London) (Rye 1983, 89–91).

In December 1928, Sissle's *Camp Meetin' Day* song was promoted by a march with banners and a band, with "a large crowd of coloured folk" in central London (Rye 1983, 92). Work in France and England into 1930 included links with James Boucher at a Paris charity concert duly reported in the *Amsterdam News* of April 23, 1930, for several entertainers in Europe told the homefolk of successes in Europe through Afro-American newspapers. In London the Prince of Wales was entertained by Sissle's orchestra, according to the New York *Age* of December 17, 1930. The prince, whose attraction to American Wallis Simpson lost him the throne in 1936, had been thrilled by Blake and Sissle in a London club in 1925 (Rose 1979, 95).

Howard Rye (1983) has noted that Buddy Bradley and Billy Pierce returned to America with Sissle's orchestra in December 1930. Contacts on the ocean voyage can be overlooked in the era of jet travel. In 1926 Countee Cullen, who was to marry Yolande Du Bois, returned from France on the same boat as Schomburg and Alain Locke; the latter had just attended Edmund Jenkins's funeral in Paris, too (Ferguson 1966, 76). Bradley had been working for Cochran. His autobiography of 1932, *I Had Almost Forgotten*, refers to the pair as being responsible for training "most of the modern musical comedy dancing stars of any consequence" (Cochran 1932, 221). Spike Hughes credits Bradley with routines evolved for Fred Astaire and Jack Buchanan (Hughes 1951, 104). Choreography or jazz dance is an aspect of the Renaissance overlooked by all but the Stearnses; but Harlem's shows involved energetic dance routines on stage, and the all-black clubs had amateur dancers nightly on the dance floor. The smallness of Britain's black community and the middle-class aspirations of many British blacks who would not welcome their daughters' going on the stage led to employment for Bradley and Pierce, training white chorines. In one of Cochran's shows, Bradley was credited with the choreography, which did not happen in America (Goddard 1979, 87).

Lew Leslie brought his *Blackbirds* shows to England beginning in 1926, and among their dozens of dancers and instrumentalists, aware of the boom in opportunities since *Shuffle Along* and of the success of Josephine Baker in Europe, were some of Harlem's finest—trumpeter Johnny Dunn and conductor Will Vodery, for example. Indeed, *Dover Street to Dixie* in 1923 had included Dunn, fellow trumpeter Clifton "Pike" Davis, pianist George Rickson, and drummer Jesse Baltimore, and all returned in *Blackbirds of 1926* (Rye 1984, 134). The *Era* noted that the aristocrats of England and monarchs of Europe went to the show; by August of 1927 the Prince of Wales had seen it twenty-two times. Florence Mills and Edith Wilson were joined by Vodery in March 1927, and over two hundred performances in London were followed by provincial touring (Rye 1984, 136–37).

Spike Hughes, writing of the show, explained that Robeson had confirmed that Mills was not in the same category as Bessie Smith, who always performed to black audiences, and noted that "there was the remarkable orchestra which played in the pit." He returned to see the show mainly because of the orchestra:

> Here was a group of wind and percussion players using long-familiar instruments such as trumpets, trombones, saxophones, clarinets, piano and the rest, who played tunes with the most elementary harmonic scheme and of no great melodic originality, which yet succeeded in sounding entirely new (Hughes 1946, 257).

Soon afterwards Hughes heard a Red Nichols recording, then one by Fletcher Henderson, and so was converted to jazz, which led to some excellent 1933 New York recordings (Hughes 1951). The *Blackbirds* orchestra of 1935 England included Clifton "Pike" Davis; and Thompson's opinions of his playing and of the nature of Afro-American jazz reinforce the view of Hughes in 1927. Both Hughes and Thompson were trained musicians with open minds, and thus rare commentators (Thompson 1985, 83–85).

Just as historians of the Renaissance have largely overlooked Garvey's *Negro World,* another Caribbean element emerges from this writer's discussions with Thompson and from the researches of Howard Rye in the Public Record Office files of passenger lists, for Rye suggests that the bulk of the dancers were from the British West Indies, as American citizens were rare in the group (Rye 1984, 137). Thompson not only referred to fellow West India Regiment bandsmen working with Sissle and Blake in New York in the early 1920s, but changed an early draft of his book that suggested that it was around 1920 that blacks were getting into show business in New York, to indicate that West Indian blacks were getting into show business in New York (Thompson 1985, 53). Although most of the instrumentalists in the orchestra of *Shuffle Along* remain unidentified other than by name, it is reasonable to assume that alongside Sissle, Blake, and William Grant Still were several West India Regiment alumni who retained their British passports and worked from a New York base, as did some of the chorus girls in *Blackbirds of 1926.* The Caribbean dimension of the Renaissance was not restricted to Garvey and the *Negro World;* the owner of the *Amsterdam News* was Guyanese doctor Philip Savory, while poet Claude McKay contributed to Cunard's *Negro* (1934).

Blackbirds of 1928 was not a Lew Leslie production, and it used British pit orchestras. The suburban London weekly *Acton Gazette and Express* of September 28, 1928, noted:

> A feature is made of the dancing by individual members of the company and by the famous "Creole" beauty chorus. Although these girls are dark-skinned, it is interesting to note that a big percentage of them are British, having been born in the British West Indies ("Blackbirds" 1928).

If the Renaissance had ensured that "black is beautiful," then a major aspiration had been achieved. The patriotic element in this report may have been to avoid anti-American feelings which were endorsed by the theatrical and music unions of Britain. Garland and others employed British blacks like Mabel Mercer, James Boucher, Evelyn Dove, and those of African or Caribbean birth like Thompson, and the suggestion of Caribbean origins in this report might just be a simple way of stressing the Britishness of the troupe.

Some all-black shows in 1929 London show something of the wealth of talent available to amuse and instruct the British. In April 1929 the stage play *Porgy* opened at His Majesty's Theatre in London with the band of the Jenkins Orphanage of Charleston, South Carolina. This met with the approval of the *Melody Maker,* although difficulties in understanding the Gullah dialect led to the show closing in six weeks (Chilton 1980, 40). Cochran had ventured money to bring this play from New York to England, and two years later he recalled how the play "should have drawn all London to His Majesty's. Certainly nothing so fine in the way of realistic production has ever been seen upon the London stage." Nearly one hundred blacks crossed the Atlantic for the presentation of *Porgy* (Cochran 1932, 224).

At the beginning of 1929 an "all-black" show was arranged by John Barbour-James in West London's Acton, featuring Alyce Fraser from Guyana. Miss Fraser had been in *Blackbirds* of late 1928, and the press announcements suggest that this was the London Pavilion show, but it was not a complete show in the Lew Leslie style. She seems to have left it, for in December 1928 she was appearing as "the famous West Indian soprano" in a prologue called "Bandanna Days" [sic] with the Kentucky Revellers supporting a $10 million movie, *Uncle Tom's Cabin*, at the Shepherd's Bush Pavilion. At the nearby Empire the Afro-American duo Layton and Johnstone were top of the bill in mid-January 1929.

The all-black concert, actually entitled that in the *Acton Gazette and Express* of January 4, 1929, included a lawyer from Ghana, another lawyer named Hudson Phillips from Grenada in the Caribbean (he seems to have been present when Maria Douglas was buried back in 1924), and Alyce Fraser, who was described as:

[a] gifted linguist and expresses her songs through various languages. She has had a wide experience, not only in her native land, but also in the United States, where she became famous, and in the West Indies . . . has appeared in many places in and out of London since her arrival in the autumn ("An 'All Black' Concert" 1929).

Barbour-James, whose Freemason links may have been useful with white Britons and black Americans, stated at this concert the following: "Regarding patriotism, culture, attainments and other qualifications, there is no difference between you and my kinsmen" ("No Racial Barrier" 1929). Perhaps some of his audience were attracted by the promise of music; certainly they could see African people who were complete, skilled, and wise citizens, not a pagan, naked, or ignorant people.

Indeed, the status of black people all over the world had been one of the concerns of British blacks for decades, and some who were in England in the 1920s had considerable knowledge of the African world. For example, Dr. Theophilus Scholes had written the two-volume *Glimpses of the Ages* (1905 and 1908), made contact with Plaatje in 1915, and forged links with Schomburg and, in the 1930s, with the future president of independent Kenya. His life began in Jamaica around 1850 and included living in Scotland, Ireland, Zaire, and Nigeria (Willan 1984, 188; Geiss 1974, 110). J. Edmestone Barnes was another Jamaican author in England. He had lived in South Africa and Liberia and had visited New York before settling in London by 1920, where he was a guest at the wedding of John and Edith Barbour-James (Untitled article 1922; "An African Wedding" 1920). It seems unlikely that these writers saw anything special about black activities in England in the 1920s that deserved the Renaissance title, especially as cultural and social success for some blacks in England had been achieved years before. However, it is more certain that expressions of their ambitions for the race's future continued to be enunciated into the 1930s, encouraging that student generation which achieved political independence in tropical Africa and the Caribbean by the 1960s.

The performing arts, especially music and dance, were seen as part of the presentation of black ambitions and achievements to the larger society, and the successes of Baker, Robeson, the Mills Brothers, and Jules Bledsoe were welcomed. Black shows had two distinct levels of comment in Britain in the interwar years. The movies of Robeson and shows like *The Sun Never Sets*, as Leslie Thompson has stated, had poor supporting casts because color was the major recruiting consideration, not acting ability (Thompson 1985, 95); and the music of jazz performers such as Armstrong was wildly applauded by devotees but misunderstood and ignored by most English people (Collier 1984, 254). An exception to this was the music of Duke Ellington, which was aimed at an audience exposed to European concert traditions and had orchestral tones that Britons could comprehend. (Ellington had developed his orchestra at the whites-only Cotton Club, after all.)

By the mid-1930s, although few Europeans understood it, jazz was associated with blacks, and as restrictions on foreign bands and players reduced the numbers of visiting performers to Britain, the enthusiast for black music had to travel to America (dozens of Britons worked the Atlantic liners because they got a stop-over in New York) to listen to recordings (hence that European specialist, the discographer) or seek out black instrumentalists. And in that way the Nigerian Fela Sowande and the West Indian Swing Orchestra of Ken "Snakehips" Johnson (which, as Deniz and Thompson have pointed out, had instrumentalists of African descent but South African, Welsh, English, and Caribbean birth) obtained success presenting black music.

The 1930s were to see a summit of Negro success, as Leslie Thompson recalled (Green 1984, 120; Thompson 1985, 95). That success in Britain was not the result of a sudden fashion, however, but the accumulation of advances made over decades. The Harlem Renaissance had had an important influence, for the presence of black Americans and the news of their successes increased the efforts made by British blacks in the 1920s and broadened English comprehension of black capacities. That mother Africa was emerging was of considerable importance and certainly matched the American influence on British blacks. The cosmopolitan black community in Britain in the 1930s is seen in the range of contributors to Nancy Cunard's *Negro*, for they came from all over the African world. They continued to strive for justice, equality, uplift, and humanity, as we can see in the publications of the League of Coloured Peoples, founded in London in 1931 (with Barbour-James as a founder member—he was vice president in 1937), in the agitation over the Italian invasion of Ethiopia and over the Scottsboro Boys, and in the activities of anti-imperialists such as George Padmore and C.L.R. James.

Did the Harlem Renaissance have much impact on that struggle? Many of the Renaissance schemes for Afro-Americans were ended by the economic depression and race segregation. But many of the achievements of Afro-American performers were known to the British black community; and every time Bledsoe or Robeson broadcast, Layton and Johnstone topped the bill, Una Mae Carlisle appeared on the television, or musicians played the local theater, British blacks, still such a numerically inferior group, took pride (Johnson 1986). Pride in the achievements of black folk, the spirit behind the Harlem Renaissance, encouraged all but the most fatalistic of blacks in Britain. By the 1960s much of Britain's tropical empire was politically independent, the struggle having been led and influenced by those who had been touched by the spirit of the Renaissance. It is unlikely that British blacks would have been so forward if there had been no inspiration from their American brothers and sisters and from Garvey's New York activities. The fact that the success in music was so apparent and that such achievers obtained plaudits against extreme odds backed the belief that black people could be masters of their destiny, not supplicants to whites. In that way the Harlem Renaissance was international, belonging to Lenox Avenue, London, Accra, Cardiff, Port of Spain, Howard University, Paris, Freetown, and Kingston: wherever African peoples worked and lived.

NOTES

1. The quatro is a ukelele-like four-stringed instrument tuned as the top four strings of a guitar.

2. Investigating Edmund Jenkins's 1916 sojourn in north Wales in 1980, I was taken to the Grand Theater in Llandudno by an old-timer. A poster from the 1960s came to hand, and I expressed amazement to see the Versatile Three on it. The veteran, who had started his stage career in the 1910s, had recalled the sheer professionalism of Anthony Tuck and his colleagues and, half a century later, gave their name to a poor trio of aspiring white entertainers. A lifetime of stage appearances had not dulled his recollection of the Afro-American trio: some act, surely!

REFERENCES

A.A.C. 1924. A new West African composer. *West Africa* September 13:965–69.
A.P.U. reception and dance. 1924. *West Africa* July 12:704.
African Progress Union reception. 1924. *West Africa* July 5:674.
An African wedding. 1920. *Acton Gazette and Express* October 22:3.
Alcindor, John. 1922. Black troops and white women: Reply to the Countess of Warwick. *Sunday Illustrated* July 2:19.
An "all black" concert. 1929. *Acton Gazette and Express* January 4.
Blackbirds. 1928. *Acton Gazette and Express* September 28:9.
Boisragon, Alan. 1897. *The Benin massacre*. London: Methuen.
Broadcasting in Yoruba. 1924. *West Africa* July 5:674.
Champly, Henry. 1936. *White women, coloured men*. London: John Long.

Chilton, John. 1980. *A jazz nursery: The story of the Jenkins' orphanage bands*. London: Bloomsbury Bookshop.

A coaster's London log. 1924. *West Africa* July 5:673.

Cochran, Charles. 1932. *I had almost forgotten*. London: Hutchinson.

Collier, James. 1984. *Louis Armstrong: A biography*. London: Michael Joseph.

Crescendo. 1919. A jazz band: Banjo effect in Mr. Brahms' Hungarian Dances. *The Star* July 5:10.

Cunard, Nancy, comp. 1934. *Negro: Anthology*. London: Wishart.

The death of Mrs. Simango. 1924. *West Africa* August 2:775.

Deniz, Joe. 1985. Conversations with the author, May 31 and June 15.

E. C. 1924. Gramophone notes. *West Africa* July 12:696.

Ferguson, Blanche. 1966. *Countee Cullen and the Negro Renaissance*. New York: Dodd, Mead.

Fryer, Peter. 1984. *Staying power: The history of black people in Britain*. London: Pluto Press.

Funk, Ray. 1986. Three Afro-American singing groups. In *Under the imperial carpet*, edited by Rainer Lotz and Ian Pegg, 145–63. Crawley, Sussex, England: Rabbit Press.

Geiss, Imanuel. 1974. *The Pan-African movement*. London: Methuen.

Goddard, Chris. 1979. *Jazz away from home*. London: Paddington Press.

Green, Jeffrey. 1982a. *Edmund Thornton Jenkins: The life and times of an American black composer, 1894–1926*. Westport, Conn.: Greenwood Press.

———. 1982b. Roland Hayes in London, 1921. *The Black Perspective in Music* 10, no. 1:29–41.

———. 1984. Conversation with Leslie Thompson. *The Black Perspective in Music* 12, no. 1:98–127.

———. 1986. Dr. J. J. Brown of Hackney (1882–1953). In *Under the imperial carpet*, edited by Rainer Lotz and Ian Pegg, 259–77. Crawley, Sussex, England: Rabbit Press.

Helm, McKinley. 1942. *Angel Mo' and her son, Roland Hayes*. Boston: Little, Brown.

Hough, Richard. [1983] 1985. *Edwina, Countess Mountbatten of Burma*. London: Sphere Books.

Hughes, Langston. 1940. *The big sea*. New York: Alfred A. Knopf.

Hughes, Spike. 1946. *Opening bars: Beginning an autobiography*. London: Pilot Press.

———. 1951. *Second movement: Continuing the autobiography*. London: Museum Press.

Jenkins, Ray. 1986. In pursuit of the African past: John Mensah Sarbah, historian of Ghana. In *Under the imperial carpet*, edited by Rainer Lotz and Ian Pegg, 109–29. Crawley, Sussex, England: Rabbit Press.

Jenkinson, Jacqueline. 1986. The 1919 race riots in Britain: A survey. In *Under the imperial carpet*, edited by Rainer Lotz and Ian Pegg, 182–207. Crawley, Sussex, England: Rabbit Press.

Johnson, Don. 1986. Conversations with the author, March 31 and April 17.

Johnson, James Weldon. 1930. *Black Manhattan*. New York: Alfred A. Knopf.

Kennedy, Carol. 1986. *Mayfair: A social history*. London: Hutchinson.

Lotz, Rainer. 1986. Will Garland's Negro Operetta Company. In *Under the imperial carpet*, edited by Rainer Lotz and Ian Pegg, 130–44. Crawley, Sussex, England: Rabbit Press.

M. B. 1919. Famous orchestra hopes to visit West Africa. *West Africa* August 30:739.

A "Many-millioned cry for justice": London protest against race prejudice and race discrimination. 1919. *African World* August 23. (Courtesy Brian Willan.)

Martin, Tony. 1976. *Race first: The ideological and organizational struggles of Marcus Garvey and the Universal Negro Improvement Association*. Westport, Conn.: Greenwood Press.

———. 1983. *Literary Garveyism: Garvey, black arts, and the Harlem Renaissance*. Dover, Mass.: Majority Press.

McGilchrist, Paul, and Jeffrey Green. 1985. Some recent findings on Samuel Coleridge—Taylor. *The Black Perspective in Music* 13, no. 2:151–78.

Mrs. Maria J. Douglas. 1924. *West Africa* August 30:899.

No racial barrier. 1929. *Acton Gazette and Express* January 18:6.

Plaatje, Sol. 1927. The late Florence Mills. [Kimberley] *Diamond Fields Advertiser* November 14.

The Roland Hayes recital. 1920. *West Africa* November 6:1426.

Rose, Al. 1979. *Eubie Blake*. New York: Schirmer Books.

Rye, Howard. 1983. Eubie Blake and Noble Sissle. *Storyville* 105:88–95.

———. 1984. The *Blackbirds* and their orchestras. *Storyville* 112:133–47.

———. 1986. The Southern Syncopated Orchestra. In *Under the imperial carpet*, edited by Rainer Lotz and Ian Pegg, 217–32. Crawley, Sussex, England: Rabbit Press.

Sampson, Magnus. [1937] 1969. *Gold Coast men of affairs (past and present)*. London: Dawsons of Pall Mall.

Scholes, Theophilus. 1905. *Glimpses of the ages*. Vol. 1. London: John Long.

———. 1908. *Glimpses of the ages*. Vol. 2. London: John Long.

Seroff, Doug. 1986. The Fisk Jubilee Singers. In *Under the imperial carpet*, edited by Rainer Lotz and Ian Pegg, 42–54. Crawley, Sussex, England: Rabbit Press.

A Sierra Leone composer's mission. 1924. *West Africa* August 30:909.

Smith, Ada, with James Haskins. 1983. *Bricktop*. New York: Atheneum.

Southern, Eileen. 1982. *Biographical dictionary of Afro-American and African musicians*. Westport, Conn.: Greenwood Press.

Southern Syncopated Orchestra. 1919. *The Era* July 9:10.

Thompson, Leslie. 1985. *Leslie Thompson: An autobiography as told to Jeffrey P. Green*. Crawley, Sussex, England: Rabbit Press.

Untitled article. 1922. *West India Committee Circular* June 8:258.

Untitled article. 1937. *Outlook* September:165.

Waters, Ethel. 1951. *His eye is on the sparrow*. London: W. H. Allen.

Wilcox, Bert. 1980. Hutch. *Memory Lane* 12, no. 46:11.

Willan, Brian. 1984. *Sol Plaatje, South African nationalist, 1876–1932*. London: Heinemann; Berkeley: University of California Press.

Epilogue

The Harlem Renaissance (which might be more accurately termed "Negro Renaissance") had its beginnings, even before the turn of the century, in towns and cities all across the United States. The attitudes that gave birth to the movement had their genesis in (1) the nationalistic tendencies of the time, (2) the movement of black Americans from slavery to freedom and from rural to city living, (3) Afro-Americans' renewed pride in their African heritage, and (4) the influences of the period "bounded by the close of the Civil War and the economic debacle of the 1930s," the period that Mark Twain called "The Gilded Age" (Gunstream 1986, 5).

While Harlem, New York, is celebrated as the birthplace and focal point of the Renaissance, many scholars have pointed out that the movement was in fact a part of a larger, more geographically widespread and generalized event. The evidence of the activities of William Dawson at Tuskegee Institute, Florence Price in Chicago, Robert Nathaniel Dett at Hampton Institute, *Le Tumulte Noir* in France, and other activities and events across the nation and the world all suggest that such was, in fact, the case. Among the musicians active in the United States during the period were: Camille Nickerson ("The Louisiana Lady") in New Orleans, Walter Dyett in Chicago, Florence Price in Chicago, Carl Diton in Philadelphia, Kemper Harreld in Atlanta, Florence Cole Talbert in Italy and Texas, Helen Hegan in Chicago and New York, Clarence Cameron White in Boston and Hampton, Virginia, Robert Nathaniel Dett in Hampton, Lucie B. Campbell in Memphis, Tennessee, and Edward Boatner in Boston and Chicago. Abroad, Josephine Baker appeared in starring roles in *Revue Nègre*, the *Folies Bergère*, and in Offenbach's *La Creole* (Baker and Bouillon 1977) and also established her own nightclub, *Chez Josephine* (Haney 1981). Roland Hayes toured the concert stages of England, Germany, Spain, France, Italy, Austria,

Czechoslovakia, Russia, and other European countries (Helm 1943); Paul Robeson lived in England, during 1927–1939, where he "discovered" African culture and came to believe strongly in the "oneness of humankind" (Robeson 1958, 49); Amanda Aldridge (a.k.a. Montague Ring) was composing in London; and Bricktop headlined at the Grand Duc and her own "Bricktop's" in Paris, entertaining a select and artistically inclined clientele (Bricktop 1983).

Additionally, the relationships between the writers, visual artists, and musicians of the Renaissance movement, as suggested in the essays by Long and Gordon, indicate the possibility of significant artistic, social, and cultural interaction among the arts and the cultural leaders of the movement. Writers such as Langston Hughes, W.E.B. Du Bois, James Weldon Johnson, Walter White, Zora Neal Hurston, and, of course, Alain Locke, and visual artists such as Archibald Motley, Palmer Hayden, Richmond Barthé, Aaron Douglas, May Jackson, Malvin Johnson, William Johnson, Lois Jones, Augusta Savage, Laura Waring, and Hale Woodruff, all comment on the culture of period; some of them commented importantly upon and were significantly influenced by the music and the musicians of the period; many of them spent time abroad.

The activities and conditions cited above, and others they imply and to which they relate, suggest that further elucidation of the Negro Renaissance as a worldwide movement with signficant relationships among the various art forms would contribute much to our knowledge of Afro-American cultural history and its contributions to world culture. The implications for further study are significant and compelling.

REFERENCES

Baker, Josephine, and Jo Bouillon. 1977. *Josephine*. Translated by Mariana Fitzpatrick. New York: Harper & Row.

Bricktop, with James Haskins. 1983. *Bricktop*. New York: Atheneum.

Gunstream, Robby D. 1986. Yesterday's wind, today's whirlwind. *Design for Arts Education* (May/June):5–15.

Haney, Lynn. 1981. *Naked at the feast: A biography of Josephine Baker*. New York: Dodd, Mead & Company.

Helm, McKinley. 1943. *Angel Mo' and her son, Roland Hayes*. Boston: Little, Brown and Company.

Robeson, Paul. 1958. *Here I stand*. New York: Othello Associates.

Bibliography of the Music:
The Concert Music of the Harlem
Renaissance Composers, 1919–1935

Dominique-René de Lerma

In the period known as the Negro Renaissance, numerous works of music were created by black musicians and composers. The major works of significance in the field of jazz are well known, but most of the concert music remains unknown since little of it, except for arrangements of spirituals, was recorded or widely distributed.

The term "concert music" is intended to represent works designed for concert or recital performance in which improvisation is normally not to be expected. Following that restriction in the case of James P. Johnson, however, was not a comfortable task.

The list contains 725 works by fourteen black composers; those included are Alton Augustus Adams, J. Harold Brown, Harry T. Burleigh, William Levi Dawson, R. Nathaniel Dett, Harry Lawrence Freeman, Edmund Thornton Jenkins, Hall Johnson, James P. Johnson, Florence Price, William Grant Still, Clarence Cameron White, Frederick Jerome Work, and John Wesley Work. The works included are restricted to those written or published by the figures specified between 1919 and 1935 and are representative of art and popular songs, symphonic works, band scores, operas, oratorios, cantatas, choral works and arrangements, instrumental and vocal chamber ensembles, and piano and organ compositions.

Of the composers represented here, Harry T. Burleigh, R. Nathaniel Dett, James P. Johnson, Clarence Cameron White, William Dawson, and Florence Price were the most prolific, with Price producing the most works for instrumental ensemble, large and small, and Dett being the most productive of the composers of choral and art-song literature.

Where appropriate, the elements in these citations are as follows:

1. Composer.
2. Title. When distinctive, the title is transcribed from the publication or secondary source. Uniform titles are offered when the title is not distinctive, as in the case of a sonata or symphony, although modified to satisfy the editorial policies of the Center for Black Music Research.
3. Date of composition.

4. Medium note. If the work is for an instrumental ensemble, the specific performance forces are subsequently provided.

5. Publication data. The city, publisher, and year of publication are stated. The publication date has not been identified in all instances. In these cases, "n.d. [?]" indicates that the research has not determined the date. If there are two or more dates in descending order, the first date is that of the most recent printing.

6. Collation. The last numbered page is identified, plus plate numbers and series note. Multiple volumes are so noted.

7. Series title and number.

8. Text source.

9. Contents.

10. Duration.

11. Instrumentation.

12. Dedication.

13. Awards won, with names and dates.

14. Data on premiere.

15. Holding library. Special notes may be included. Those whose collections have been examined include the following:

Columbia—Center for Black Music Research, Columbia College, Chicago (vertical file photocopies, unless noted);

Fisk—Special Collections, Fisk University, Nashville;

Fleisher—Edwin A. Fleisher Music Collection, Free Library of Philadelphia;

de Lerma—Personal library of the author;

Library of Congress—Music Division, Library of Congress, Washington, D.C.;

Peabody—Library of the Peabody Conservatory, Johns Hopkins University, Baltimore;

Schomburg—Schomburg Collection, New York Public Library;

Spingarn—Spingarn Collection, Howard University, Washington, D.C.;

Yale—James Weldon Johnson Memorial Collection, Yale University, New Haven.

16. Recordings. Label name and number, performers, and date of release are given as appropriate and available. If the label is missing, the recording was not commercially issued.

17. Holding library of recordings. Designations are the same as in item 15 above.

When any of this information is not cited, it is because it has not yet been uncovered. For example, J. Harold Brown's *Allegro* has been included even though the performance medium has not been identified.

ADAMS, ALTON AUGUSTUS, 1889–1987

The governor's own (band). New York: Carl Fischer, 1921. Piano-conductor score and parts: D♭ piccolo, flute, oboe, 4 clarinets, E♭ clarinet, bassoon, 4 cornets, 4 E♭ horns, 3 trombones, 3 saxophones (soprano, alto, tenor), drums, basses. S2350. Plate no. 2253. Dedication: Gov. J. W. Oman. Library: Columbia. Recorded: New World NW-266 (The Goldman Band, Richard Franco Goldman, conductor), 1976. Library: de Lerma.

The spirit of the U.S.N. (band). Boston: Cundy-Bettoney, 1925. 3 p. Piano-conductor score and parts: piccolo, oboe, 3 clarinets, E♭ clarinet, bassoon, 4 cornets, 4 E♭ altos, baritone, 3 saxophones (soprano, alto, tenor), drums, basses. Plate no. C.B.Co. 5183. Dedication: President Coolidge. Library: Columbia.

The Virgin Islands march (band). Boston: Walter Jacobs, 1919. Piano-conductor score and parts: piccolo, oboe, 4 clarinets, Eb clarinet, bassoon, 4 cornets, 4 E♭ altos, 3 trombones, baritone, tuba, 3 saxophones (alto, C melody, tenor, baritone), small drum, bass drum, basses. Also appeared in: *Jacob's orchestra monthly* 10, no. 10 (October 1919). Library: Columbia.

——— (band). Appeared in: *Melody, a monthly magazine for lovers of popular music* 4, no. 3 (March 1920). Library: Columbia.

——— (SATB). New York: Beekman, 1965. 3 p. Library: Columbia.

BROWN, J. HAROLD, 1902–

The African chief (cantata for women's chorus and band). Won: Rodman Wanamaker award, 1930.

Allegro. Won: Rodman Wanamaker award, 1931.

Autumn moods. Won: Rodman Wanamaker honorable mention, 1932.

Fantaisie (piano). 1930.

Invention and chorale (orchestra). 1930.

Job: Oratorio.

Jubilee characteristique: Wade in the water (orchestra). 1928. Won: Rodman Wanamaker first prize, orchestral competition; Harmon contest, first prize.

King Solomon (opera in one act). Premiere: 1951; Karamu House, Cleveland.

Kyrie eleison (SATB, organ, and strings).

Prestidigitation. Won: Rodman Wanamaker award, 1927.

Quartet, strings, A minor. Won: Rodman Wanamaker award, 1931.

Rhapsody. Won: Rodman Wanamaker award, 1928.

The saga of Rip van Winkle (SATB).

BURLEIGH, HARRY T., 1866–1949

Collections

Album of Negro spirituals (high voice and piano). Melville, N.Y.: Belwin Mills, 1969, 1917. 48 p. Plate no. 1432. Contents: (1) By an' by; (2) Couldn't hear nobody pray; (3) De blin' man; (4) Gospel train; (5) Deep river; (6) Ev'ry time I feel de spirit; (7) Nobody knows de trouble; (8) Sometimes I feel like a motherless child; (9) Stan' still Jordan; (10) Wade in de water; (11) Weepin' Mary; (12) Were you there.

———— (for low voice and piano). Melville, N.Y.: Belwin Mills, 1969, 1917. 48 p. Plate no. 1433.

Negro folk songs. New York: G. Ricordi, 1921–1924. 4 vols. Contents: 43 songs.

Old songs hymnal: Words and melodies from the state of Georgia, collected by Dorothy G. Bolton, arranged by Harry T. Burleigh (SATB). New York: Century Co., 1929. x, 208 p. Library: Fisk, Schomburg.

Single Works

Adoration (medium voice and piano). New York: G. Ricordi, 1921. 5 p. Plate no. NY 115. Text: Dora Lawrence Houston. Library: Spingarn.

———— (low voice and piano). New York: G. Ricordi, 1921. 5 p. Plate no. NY 116.

Ain't goin' to study war no mo' (high voice and piano). New York: G. Ricordi, 1922. 6 p. Plate no. NY 268. Library: Spingarn, Yale (manuscript, 3 p.).

———— (TTBB and piano), arranged by Ruggero Vené. New York: Franco Colombo, n.d. [?]. FCC 1737.

Are you smiling? (medium voice and piano). New York: G. Ricordi, 1929. Text: Hector McCarthy.

Balm in Gilead (high voice and piano). New York: Franco Colombo, 1919. 5 p. Plate no. 116578. Text: Jeremiah 8:22. Duration: 2:11. Library: Spingarn. Recorded: (1) Odyssey 23-16-0268 (Paul Robeson, bass, Lawrence Brown, piano) 1968, 1945; (2) Vanguard 2035 (Paul Robeson, bass, Alan Booth, piano) 1965, 1958.

———— (low voice and piano). New York: Franco Colombo, 1919. 5 p. Plate no. 116579. Library: Spingarn. Recorded: (1) Columbia ML-54106 and MM-610 and Odyssey 32-16-02688 (Paul Robeson, bass, Lawrence Brown, piano) 1968, 1945; (2) Vanguard VSD-2035 (Paul Robeson, bass, Alan Booth, piano) 196?, 1958. Library: de Lerma (1–2).

Before meeting (high voice and piano). New York: G. Ricordi, ca. 1921. 7 p. Plate no. NY 64. Text: Arthur Symons. Library: Spingarn.

———— (medium voice and piano). New York: G. Ricordi, ca. 1921. Plate no. NY 63.

Behold that star (medium voice and piano). New York: G. Ricordi, 1944. 7 p. Words and melody from the collection of Thomas W. Talley, Nashville, Tenn. Recorded: RCA LM/LSC-2592 (Marian Anderson, contralto, Franz Rupp, piano) 1962. Library: de Lerma.

———— (SATB and piano or organ). New York: G. Ricordi, 1928. 11 p. G. Ricordi & Co.'s collection of part-songs and choruses for male, female and mixed voices, NY 785; Franco Colombo, Inc., collection of part-songs and choruses.

———— (SAB and piano or organ). New York: Franco Colombo, n.d. [?]. Plate no. 2167.

———— (SSA and piano or organ). New York: Franco Colombo, n.d. [?]. Plate no. 1298.

Bethlehem (medium voice and piano). New York: G. Ricordi, 1929. Text: E. Proctor Clarke.

———— (SATB). New York: G. Ricordi, n.d. [?].

De blin' man stood on de road an' cried (high voice and piano). New York: G. Ricordi, 1928. 6 p. Plate no. NY 743; FC 1433. Text: St. Mark 10:46–52. Library: Spingarn.

——— (low voice and piano). New York: G. Ricordi, 1928. Recorded: (Blanche Foreman, mezzo-soprano, Charles Lloyd, piano) 1982. Library: de Lerma.

Bring her again, O western wind (medium voice and piano). New York: Galaxy Music, 1932. Text: H. E. Henley.

——— (TTBB). New York: Galaxy Music, 1930.

By an' by (high voice and piano). New York: G. Ricordi, 1917. 5 p. Plate no. 116408. Library: Spingarn, Yale. Recorded: (1) (G. Carlton Hines, tenor, André Thomas, piano) 1981; (2) RCA LM-3292 (Paul Robeson, bass, Lawrence Brown, piano) 1972, 1925; (3) Classics Record Library 30-5647 (Paul Robeson, bass, Lawrence Brown, piano) 1976; (4) Odyssey 32-16-0168 (Paul Robeson, bass, Lawrence Brown, piano) 1968, 1945. Library: de Lerma (1).

——— (low voice and piano). New York: G. Ricordi, 1927. 5 p. Duration: 2:16. Recorded: (1) Columbia ML-54106 and MM-610, Odyssey 32-160268, RCA LM-3292, and Classics Record Library 30-5647 (Paul Robeson, bass, Lawrence Brown, piano) 1976, 1968, 1945, 1925; (2) (Blanche Foreman, mezzo-soprano, Charles Lloyd, piano) 1982. Library: de Lerma (1–2).

Christ be with me (medium voice and piano). New York: G. Ricordi, 1929. Text: from St. Patrick's breastplate.

——— (SATB). New York: G. Ricordi, 1906.

Come with me (high voice and piano). New York: G. Ricordi, 1921. 7 p. Plate no. NY 62. Text: L. Kelsey ClenDening. Library: Spingarn.

A corn song (high voice and piano). New York: G. Ricordi, 1920. 11 p. Plate no. 19. Text: Paul Laurence Dunbar. Library: Schomburg, Spingarn.

——— (medium voice and piano). New York: G. Ricordi, 1920. 11 p. Plate no. 20. Library: Schomburg.

Couldn't hear nobody pray (low voice and piano). New York: G. Ricordi, 1922. 6 p. Plate no. NY 240. Library: Yale.

——— (solo high voice and SATB). New York: Franco Colombo, 1922. 7 p. Franco Colombo series, FC 278.

De creation (TTBB). New York: G. Ricordi, 1922.

Dar's a meetin' here tonight (high voice and piano). Boston: Oliver Ditson, 1926. 5 p. Plate no. M-L-3329.

Don't be weary traveler (high voice and piano). New York: G. Ricordi, 1928.

——— (low voice and piano). New York: G. Ricordi, 1928. 5 p. Plate no. NY 744. Library: Spingarn.

Don't you dream of turning back: Folk song (low voice and piano). New York: G. Ricordi, 1921. 5 p. Plate no. 156. Library: Spingarn.

Don't you weep when I'm gone (medium voice and piano). New York: G. Ricordi, 1919. 6 p. Plate no. 116600. Text: Jeremiah 22:10. Library: Spingarn.

Down by the sea (medium voice and piano). New York: G. Ricordi, 1919. 6 p. Plate no. 116540. Text: George F. O'Connell. Library: Schomburg.

——— (low voice and piano). New York: G. Ricordi, 1919. 6 p. Plate no. 116539. Library: Schomburg, Spingarn.

The dream love (high voice and piano). New York: G. Ricordi, 1923. 5 p. Plate no. 363. Text: Alexander Groves. Library: Spingarn.

Dry bones (high voice and piano). New York: Galaxy Music, n.d. [?].

——— (medium voice and piano). New York: G. Ricordi, 1930. 8 p. Text: Ezekiel 37. Dedication: Paul Robeson. Library: Spingarn.

Ethiopia's paean of exaltation (medium voice and piano). New York: G. Ricordi, 1921. Text: Anna J. Cooper.

——— (SATB). New York: G. Ricordi, 1921. Plate no. NY 107.

Ev'ry time I feel the spirit (high voice and piano). New York: G. Ricordi, 1925. 7 p. Plate no. 462. Library: Schomburg, Spingarn, Yale. Recorded: (1) RCA LSC-2600 (Leontyne Price, soprano, orchestra, chorus, Leonard De Paur, conductor, arranged) 1962; (2) (Bruce A. Hubbard, baritone, Stephen Sulich, piano); (3) Victor 2032 (Marian Anderson, contralto, Franz Rupp [?], piano). Library: de Lerma (1–2).

——— (SATB and piano). New York: G. Ricordi, 1925. Plate no. NY 488, FCC 488. Library: Schomburg.

Exile (low voice and piano). New York: G. Ricordi, 1922. 5 p. Plate no. 320. Text: Inez Marie Richardson. Library: Spingarn.

Ezekiel saw de wheel (SATB and piano). New York: G. Ricordi, 1928. Plate no. FCC 768.

——— (SSA and piano). New York: G. Ricordi, 1928. Plate no. FCC 699.

——— (TTBB and piano). New York: G. Ricordi, 1928. Plate no. FCC 700. (Reprinted by Belwin Mills.)

A fatuous tragedy (TTBB). New York: G. Ricordi, 1928. Plate no. 714. Text: Homer Brewer. (May also exist for medium voice and piano.)

Fragments (high voice and piano). New York: G. Ricordi, 1919. Plate no. 116596. Text: Jessie Fauset. Library: Columbia, Spingarn.

——— (low voice and piano). New York: G. Ricordi, 1919. 3 p. Plate no. 116597. Library: Schomburg, Spingarn.

Il giovane guerriero, *See* The young warrior.

Give me Jesus (high voice and piano). New York: G. Ricordi, n.d. [?].

——— (low voice and piano). New York: G. Ricordi, 1926. 5 p. Plate no. NY 594. Library: Spingarn.

Go down, Moses (high voice and piano). New York: G. Ricordi, 1917, 1920. 6 p. Plate no. 116427. Text: Exodus 8. Library: Spingarn. Recorded: Victor 21002 and New World Records NW-247 (Roland Hayes, tenor, Lawrence Brown, piano) 1976, 1922. Library: de Lerma.

——— (low voice and piano). New York: G. Ricordi, 1920. Duration: 2:42. Recorded: (1) Victor 1799 and HMV DA-1560 (Marian Anderson, contralto, Kosti Vehanen, piano) 1937; (2) RCA AVM 1-1735 (Marian Anderson, contralto, Franz Rupp, piano) 1976, 1952; (3) Columbia M 610/17467D and MM-610, Columbia ML-54106, and Odyssey 32-16-0268 (Paul Robeson, bass, Lawrence Brown, piano) 1968, 1945; (4) Colosseum 1008 (Randolph Symonette, baritone, Leslie Harnley, piano). Library: Morgan (2–3).

Go, tell it on the mountain (medium voice and piano). New York: G. Ricordi, 1927. 7 p. Plate no. NY 969. Library: Spingarn.

——— (SATB). New York: G. Ricordi, 1927. Plate no. FCC 817.

De gospel train: Git on bo'd (high voice and piano). New York: G. Ricordi, 1921. 6 p. Plate no. NY 81. Library: Spingarn.

———— (low voice and piano). New York: G. Ricordi. Plate no. NY 80. Recorded: (1) Period SLP-580 (Inez Matthews, mezzo-soprano, Jonathan Brice, piano) 195?; (2) RCA AVM 1-1735 (Marian Anderson, contralto, Franz Rupp, piano) 1976, 1947. Library: de Lerma (1–2).

———— (SATB and piano). New York: G. Ricordi, 1921. Plate no. NY 659; FCC 659.

———— (TTBB and piano). New York: G. Ricordi, n.d. [?]. Title no. FCC 210.

Hard trials (medium voice and piano). New York: G. Ricordi, 1919. 7 p. Plate no. 116582. Text: St. Matthew 8:20, 14:21. Library: Spingarn. Duration: 1:52. Recorded: (1) (Louise Parker, contralto, with piano); (2) KM 1702 (Leroy O. Dorsey, bass, Clyde Parker, piano) 1977; (3) RCA LM/LSC-2592 and Victor M-986 (Marian Anderson, contralto, Franz Rupp, piano) 1962. Library: de Lerma (1–3).

———— (TTBB). New York: G. Ricordi, 1919.

Have you been to Lons? (high voice and piano). New York: G. Ricordi, 1920. 7 p. Plate no. 116490. Text: Gordon Longstone. Library: Schomburg, Spingarn.

———— (medium voice and piano). New York: G. Ricordi, 1920. Plate no. 116265.

He met her in the meadow (high voice and piano). New York: G. Ricordi, 1921. 5 p. Plate no. 220. Library: Spingarn.

———— (SATB). New York: G. Ricordi, 1921. Plate no. NY 234.

———— (SSA). New York: G. Ricordi, n.d. [?].

———— (TTBB). New York: G. Ricordi, n.d. [?]. Plate no. NY 223.

Hear de lambs a crying (medium voice and piano). New York: G. Ricordi, n.d. [?].

———— (solo medium voice and SATB with piano reduction). New York: G. Ricordi, 1927. 13 p. Plate no. NY 652. Text: St. John 21:15–17. Library: Spingarn.

Heav'n, heav'n (medium voice and piano). New York: G. Ricordi, 1921. Plate no. NY 79. Library: Schomburg.

———— (low voice and piano). New York: G. Ricordi, 1921. 6 p. Plate no. NY 78. Library: Schomburg, Spingarn. Duration: 2:37. Recorded: (1) HMV DB-2837, Victor 8958B, Royale 1765, and New World NW-247 (Marian Anderson, contralto, Kosti Vehanen, piano) 1976, 1936; (2) RCA LM/LSC-2592 (Marian Anderson, contralto, Franz Rupp, piano) 1962; (3) Musical Heritage Society MHS-1515 (Inia te Wiata, bass, Maurice Till, piano) 1972. Library: de Lerma (1–3).

———— (SATB). New York: G. Ricordi, n.d. [?]. Plate no. NY 122. Library: Schomburg.

———— (TTBB and piano). New York: G. Ricordi, n.d. [?]. Plate no. FCC 224. Library: Schomburg.

He's jus' de same today (high voice and piano). New York: G. Ricordi, 1919. 7 p. Plate no. 116581. Text: Exodus 14:22; I Samuel 17:49. Library: Spingarn.

———— (medium voice and piano). New York: G. Ricordi, 1914. Plate no. 116580.

Ho, ro, my nut brown maiden (TTB). New York: G. Ricordi, 1930.

I got a home in-a dat rock (low voice and piano). New York: G. Ricordi, 1926. 7 p. Plate no. NY 543. Library: Spingarn.

I hope my mother will be there (SATB). New York: G. Ricordi, 1924.

I know de Lord's laid his hands on me (high voice and piano). New York: G. Ricordi, 1924. 7 p. Plate no. NY 495. Library: Spingarn.

———— (low voice and piano). New York: G. Ricordi, n.d. [?].

———— (SATB). New York: Franco Colombo, n.d. [?]. Plate no. 1801.

I remember all (medium voice and piano). New York: G. Ricordi, 1919. 6 p. Plate no. 116601. Text: Arthur Symons.

———— (low voice and piano). New York: G. Ricordi, 1919. 6 p. Library: Spingarn.

I want to die while you love me (high voice and piano). New York: G. Ricordi, 1919. Plate no. 116598. Text: Georgia Douglas Johnson.

———— (low voice and piano). New York: G. Ricordi, 1919. 6 p. Plate no. 116599. Library: Schomburg.

In the great somewhere (high voice and piano). New York: G. Ricordi, 1919. 7 p. Plate no. 116557. Text: Harold Robè. "Sung by John McCormack at all his engagements." Library: Spingarn.

———— (medium voice and piano). New York: G. Ricordi, 1919. Plate no. 116558.

———— (low voice and piano). New York: G. Ricordi, 1919. Plate no. 116559.

I've been in the storm so long (medium voice and piano). New York: G. Ricordi, 1927. 7 p. Plate no. NY 695. Library: Spingarn.

———— (contralto, SATB, and piano). New York: G. Ricordi, 1927. Plate no. FCC 1310.

Jean (low voice and piano). New York: William Maxwell Music Co., 1903. 6 p. Plate no. 543-4. Text: Frank L. Stanton. Library: Columbia.

Joshua fit de battle of Jericho (medium voice and piano). New York: G. Ricordi, 1935.

———— (SATB). New York: Franco Colombo, n.d. [?]. Plate no. 1630.

Let us cheer the weary traveler (high voice and piano). New York: G. Ricordi, 1919. 6 p. Plate no. 116577. Library: Spingarn.

———— (low voice and piano). New York: G. Ricordi, 1919. 6 p. Plate no. 116576.

Listen to yo' gyardian angel (medium voice and piano). New York: G. Ricordi, 1920. 6 p. Plate no. NY 14. Text: Robert Underwood Johnson. Library: Spingarn.

Little child of Mary: De new-born baby (high voice and piano). New York: G. Ricordi, 1932. 5 p. Plate no. NY 889. Library: Spingarn. Recorded: HMV DA-1427 (John McCormack, tenor, with piano) 1935.

———— (soprano and SATB). New York: Franco Colombo, n.d. [?]. Plate no. 1141.

Little David, play on your harp (high voice and piano). New York: G. Ricordi, 1921. 6 p. Plate no. NY 145. Library: Yale.

———— (low voice and piano). New York: G. Ricordi, n.d. [?]. Plate no. NY 146. Library: Spingarn. Recorded: Avant Garde AV-115 (Eugene Holmes, baritone, Joseph Rezits, piano). Library: de Lerma.

———— (low voice and piano). New York: Belwin-Mills, n.d. [?].

The little house of dreams (high voice and piano). New York: G. Ricordi, 1922. 5 p. Plate no. 340. Text: Arthur Wallace Peach. Library: Spingarn.

Lonesome valley: Go down in the lonesome valley (medium voice and piano). New York: G. Ricordi, 1926. 5 p. Plate no. NY 596. Library: Spingarn.

The Lord's prayer (SATB with piano reduction). New York: G. Ricordi, 1921. Plate no. NY 65.

Love found the way (high voice and piano). New York: G. Ricordi, 1922. 7 p. Plate no. NY 309. Text: Jesse Winne. Library: Spingarn.

—————— (low voice and piano). New York: G. Ricordi, 1922. 7 p. Plate no. NY 310. Library: Spingarn.

A love song (medium voice and piano). Text: John E. Bruce. Library: Schomburg (manuscript).

Love watches: An Irish fragment (high voice and piano). New York: G. Ricordi, 1920. 6 p. Plate no. NY 15. Text: George F. O'Connell. Library: Spingarn.

Lovely dark and lonely one (medium voice and piano). New York: G. Ricordi, 1935. 3 p. Plate no. 1014. Text: "The dream keeper," by Langston Hughes. Library: Spingarn (presentation copy to H. P. Spingarn), Yale. Recorded: (John Patton, tenor, Susan Peters, piano) 1972. Library: de Lerma.

Love's likeness (medium voice and piano). New York: G. Ricordi, 1927. 5 p. Plate no. 694. Text: Madge Marie Miller. Library: Spingarn.

Mister Banjo (SATB). New York: G. Ricordi, 1934. Plate no. 952.

My Lord, what a mornin' (high voice and piano). New York: G. Ricordi, 1918. 6 p. Plate no. 116493. Text: Revelations 8:10. Duration: 3:15. Library: Spingarn. Recorded: (1) (Devonna Barnes Rowe, soprano, McCoy Ransom, piano) 1982; (2) Public 1-29591 (Knoxville College Concert Choir, Nathan Carter, conductor). Library: de Lerma (1).

—————— (low voice and piano). Recorded: (1) Victor B2897 (Paul Robeson, bass, Lawrence Brown, piano); (2) HMV DAe-796 (Marguerite d'Alvarez, contralto, with piano).

—————— (SATTBB and piano). New York: G. Ricordi, 1924. 7 p. Plate no. NY 412; 1713.

—————— (SATTBB and piano). Melville, N.Y.: Belwin-Mills, 1969, 1924. 7 p. Plate no. FCC 412.

My Merlindy Brown (medium voice and piano). New York: G. Schirmer, 1922. *Folk songs of many people,* ed. by Florence Hudson Botsford. Text: James Edwin Campbell.

Nobody knows the trouble I've seen (high voice and piano). New York: G. Ricordi, 1917. 6 p. Plate no. 116436. Library: Spingarn. Recorded: London LPS-182 and Decca LM-4504 (Ellabelle Davis, soprano, Rupert Greenslade, piano) 1950. Library: de Lerma.

—————— (medium voice and piano). New York: G. Schirmer, 1930, 1929, 1922. *Songs of the Americas,* ed. by Florence Hudson Botsford. Recorded: (1) Avant Garde AV-115 (Eugene Holmes, baritone, Joseph Rezits, piano); (2) HMV DAe-796 (Marguerite d'Alvarez, contralto, with piano). Library: de Lerma (1).

—————— (low voice and piano). New York: G. Ricordi, 1917. 6 p.

—————— (SATB and piano). New York: G. Ricordi, 1924. 7 p. G. Ricordi & Co.'s collection of part-songs and choruses for male, female, and mixed voices. Plate NY 406, no. FCC 406.

—————— (TTBB). New York: G. Ricordi, n.d. [?]. Plate no. 845.

—————— (TTBB). New York: Franco Colombo, n.d. [?]. Plate no. FCC 6513.

———— (SSAATTBB), arranged by Fela Sowande. New York: Franco Colombo, n.d. [?]. Plate no. 1896.

O brothers, lift your voices (SATB). New York: G. Ricordi, 1924. Plate no. NY 413. Text: Edward H. Bickersteth.

O Lord, have mercy on me (SATB with piano reduction). New York: G. Ricordi, 1935. 5 p. Plate no. NY 987. Library: Spingarn.

O rocks, don't fall on me (high voice and piano). New York: G. Ricordi, 1922. 7 p. Plate no. NY 270. Library: Spingarn.

———— (low voice and piano). New York: G. Ricordi, 1922.

O Southland (SATB). New York: G. Ricordi, 1919. G. Ricordi & Co.'s collection of part-songs and choruses for mixed voices. Plate 116468; no. 1768. Text: James Weldon Johnson. Library: Schomburg, Yale.

———— (TTBB and piano). New York: G. Ricordi, 1904. 7 p. G. Ricordi & Co.'s collection of part-songs and choruses for male voices. Plate no. 116034. Library: Schomburg.

O wasn't dat a wide ribber? (medium voice and piano). New York: G. Ricordi, 1924. 7 p. Plate no. NY 434. Library: Spingarn. Recorded: (1) RCA LM/LSC-2592 (Marian Anderson, contralto, Franz Rupp, piano) 1962; (2) (Bruce Hubbard, baritone, Stephen Sulich, piano). Library: de Lerma (1–2).

Oh, didn't it rain? (high voice and piano). New York: G. Ricordi, 1919. 6 p. Plate no. 116528. Text: Genesis 7:4. Library: Fisk, Spingarn, Yale.

———— (high voice and piano). In *This is music for today*, vol. 5, ed. by Sur, Tolbert, and Fisher, "offered with accompaniment by Lionel Clexx." Boston: Allyn & Bacon, 1971.

———— (low voice and piano). New York: G. Ricordi, 1919. Plate no. 116527. Duration: 1:28. Library: Fisk. Recorded: (1) Avant Garde AV-115 (Eugene Holmes, baritone, Joseph Rezits, piano); (2) (Bruce Hubbard, baritone, Stephen Sulich, piano); (3) RCA LM/LSC-2592 (Marian Anderson, contralto, Franz Rupp, piano) 1962; (4) (Louise Parker, contralto, Susan Peters, piano) 1972; (5) (Edward Pierson, baritone, Donald Walker, piano); (6) Musical Heritage Society MHS-1515 (Inia te Wiata, bass, Maurice Till, piano) 1972. Library: de Lerma (1–6).

———— (SSA and piano). New York: G. Ricordi, 1919. Plate no. 116552; FCC 1586.

———— (TTBB). New York: G. Ricordi, 1919.

Oh my love (high voice and piano). New York: G. Ricordi, 1919. Plate no. 116591. Text: Harriet Gaylord. Library: Schomburg, Spingarn.

Oh rock me, Julie (high voice and piano). New York: G. Ricordi, 1921. 3 p. Plate no. 152. "Words and melody received by Mr. Krehbiel from Mr. George W. Cable; the melody is based on the whole tone scale." Library: Spingarn. Recorded: (John Patton, tenor, Susan Peters, piano) 1972. Library: de Lerma.

———— (low voice and piano). New York: G. Ricordi, 1921. 3 p. Plate no. 153.

Passing by (TTBB), composed by Edward Purcell, arranged by Harry T. Burleigh. New York: G. Ricordi, 1928. Plate no. 754. Text: Robert Herrick.

Po' lil Lulu (medium voice and piano). New York: G. Schirmer, 1930, 1929, 1922. *Songs of the Americas*, ed. by Florence Hudson Botsford.

The prayer I make for you (high voice and piano). New York: G. Ricordi, 1921. 7 p. Plate no. 117. Text: Harold Robè.

—— (low voice and piano). New York: G. Ricordi, 1921. 7 p. Plate no. 118.

The promis' land: A hallelujah song (high voice and piano). New York: G. Ricordi, 1917. Plate no. 116344. Text: Mrs. N. J. Corey. Library: Spingarn.

—— (SATB). New York: Franco Colombo, n.d. [?]. Plate no. 831.

—— (TTBB). New York: G. Ricordi, 1929.

Ride on, King Jesus (medium voice and piano). New York: G. Ricordi, n.d. [?]. Recorded: (1) RCA AVM 1-1735 (Marian Anderson, contralto, Franz Rupp, piano) 1976, 1947; (2) KM-1702 (Leroy O. Dorsey, bass, Clyde Parker, piano) 1977. Library: de Lerma (1–2).

—— (SATB), arranged by Edward Boatner. New York: Franco Colombo, n.d. [?]. Plate no. 2225.

Run to Jesus (low voice and piano). Boston: Oliver Ditson, 1926. 3 p. Plate no. ML 3308. "This song given to Jubilee Singers by Hon. Frederick Douglass at Washington, D.C., with the interesting statement that it first suggested the thought of escaping from slavery." Library: Spingarn.

Saviour, happy I would be (SATB). New York: G. Ricordi, 1932.

Scandalize my name (low voice and piano). Recorded: (1) Monitor MPS-580 (Paul Robeson, bass, Alan Booth, piano); (2) RCA LM/LSC-2592 (Marian Anderson, contralto, Franz Rupp, piano) 1962. Library: de Lerma (2).

—— (medium voice and piano). New York: G. Ricordi, 1921. 3 p. Library: Yale.

—— (TTBB). 5 p. New York: G. Ricordi, 1921. Library: Spingarn.

Six responses (SATB). New York: St. George's Church, 1926.

Some rival has stolen my true love away (TTBB). New York: G. Ricordi, 1934.

Sometimes I feel like a motherless child (high voice and piano). New York: G. Ricordi, n.d. [?]. Duration: 2:55. Recorded: BRC Productions (Veronica Tyler, soprano, Charles Lloyd, piano) 1980. Library: de Lerma.

—— (medium voice and piano). New York: G. Ricordi, n.d. [?]. Recorded: (1) (Blanche Foreman, mezzo-soprano, Charles Lloyd, piano) 1982; (2) (Bruce Hubbard, baritone, Stephen Sulich, piano). Library: de Lerma (1–2).

—— (low voice and piano). New York: G. Ricordi, 1918. 6 p. Plate no. 116497.

—— (low voice and piano). New York: Franco Colombo, 1958. Plate no. FC 1433. Library: Fisk, Spingarn.

—— (SSA and piano). New York: G. Ricordi, n.d. [?]. Plate no. 116543.

—— (SSA and piano). New York: Franco Colombo, n.d. [?]. Plate no. FCC 1585.

Southern lullaby (soprano and SATB). New York: G. Ricordi, 1920. 8 p. Plate no. NY 22. Text: George V. Hobart. Library: Spingarn.

Stan' still, Jordan (high voice and piano). New York: G. Ricordi, 1926. 7 p. Plate no. NY 598. Duration: 5:50. Recorded: (1) KM-1702 (Daisy Jackson, soprano, Buckner Gamby, piano) 1977; (2) Praise 658 (Isador Oglesby, tenor, John Miller, piano) 1979. Library: de Lerma (1–2).

—— (SATBB), arranged by Fela Sowande. New York: Franco Colombo, n.d. [?]. Plate no. FCC 1893.

Steal away (medium voice and piano). New York: G. Ricordi, 1921. Plate no. NY 158.

—— (medium voice and piano). New York: Belwin-Mills, n.d. [?].

———— (low voice and piano). New York: G. Ricordi, 1921. 6 p. Plate no. NY 157.

———— (low voice and piano). New York: Belwin-Mills, n.d. [?].

———— (SATB). New York: G. Ricordi, n.d. [?]. Plate no. 422, 120940.

———— (SAB). New York: Franco Colombo, n.d. [?]. Plate no. FCC 1830.

Tell me once more (high voice and piano). New York: G. Ricordi, 1920. 7 p. Plate no. 116619. Text: Fred G. Bowles. Dedication: Nessy Cappelli. Library: Spingarn.

———— (low voice and piano). New York: G. Ricordi, 1920. 7 p. Plate no. 116618.

There is a balm in Gilead. *See* Balm in Gilead.

Till I wake (high voice and piano). New York: G. Ricordi, 1926. 7 p. Plate no. 116283. Text: Laurence Hope. "Sung by John McCormack." Library: Spingarn.

The trees have grown so (high voice and piano). New York: G. Ricordi, 1923. 5 p. Plate no. NY 358. Text: John Hanson. Library: Spingarn.

Under a blazing star (high voice and piano). New York: G. Ricordi, 1918. 6 p. Plate no. 116509. Text: Mildred Seitz.

———— (low voice and piano). New York: G. Ricordi, 1918. 6 p. Plate no. 116508. Library: Spingarn.

The victor (high voice and piano). New York: G. Ricordi, 1919. 7 p. Plate no. 116550. Text: George O'Connell. Library: Spingarn.

———— (medium voice and piano). New York: G. Ricordi, 1919. 7 p. Plate no. 116549.

———— (low voice and piano). New York: G. Ricordi, 1919. 7 p. Plate no. 116548.

Wade in de water (high voice and piano). New York: G. Ricordi, 1925. 7 p. Plate no. NY 447. Library: Spingarn.

———— (low voice and piano). New York: Franco Colombo, 1922. Plate no. FCC 1433. Recorded: (Blanche Foreman, mezzo-soprano, Charles Lloyd, piano) 1982. Library: de Lerma.

———— (SATB and piano). New York: Franco Colombo, n.d. [?]. Plate no. FCC 487.

Walk together children (SATB). New York: G. Ricordi, 1938. Plate no. FCC 2065.

———— (SSA). New York: G. Ricordi, n.d. [?]. 5 p. Plate no. 1118. Library: Spingarn.

Were I a star (high voice and piano). New York: G. Ricordi, 1919. 5 p. Plate no. 116547. Text: A. Musgrove Roberts. Library: Spingarn.

———— (medium voice and piano). New York: G. Ricordi, 1919. Plate no. 116546.

Were you there? (high voice and piano). New York: G. Ricordi, 1924. 5 p. Duration: 3:88. Library: Yale. Recorded: (1) London LPS-182 and Decca LM-4504 (Ellabelle Davis, soprano, orchestra, Victor Olof, conductor) 1950; (2) BRC Productions (Veronica Tyler, soprano, Ernest Ragogini, piano) 1980. Library: de Lerma.

———— (medium voice and piano). New York: G. Ricordi, 1924. 6 p. Plate no. NY 446. Duration: 2:56. Library: Spingarn. Recorded: (1) Avant Garde AV-115 (Eugene Holmes, baritone, Joseph Rezits, piano); (2) RCA ARL 1-1402 (Sherrill Milnes, baritone, Jon Sprong, organ) 1976; (3) (Bruce Hubbard, baritone, Stephen Sulich, piano). Library: de Lerma (1-3).

———— (low voice and piano). New York: G. Ricordi, 1924. Library: Yale. Recorded: (1) Victor 1966 and HMV DA-1670 (Marian Anderson, contralto, Kosti

Vehanan, piano) 1938; (2) RCA AVM 1-1735 (Marian Anderson, contralto, Franz Rupp, piano) 1976, 1947; (3) RCA LM-3292 and GB-4480 (Paul Robeson, bass, Lawrence Brown, piano) 1972, 1925; (4) Starline SRS-5193 (Paul Robeson, bass, Rutland Clapham, piano); (5) Columbia X-340 and Columbia WA-6182 (Dame Clara Butt, contralto, with piano). Library: de Lerma (1–4).

—— (SSAATTBB and piano). New York: G. Ricordi, 1924. 7 p. Plate no. 423. Reproduced in "The inclusion of Negro music as a course of study in the school curriculum," by Kenneth Brown Billups (Thesis, M.M., Northwestern University, 1947). Recorded: (1) (Evelyn White Chorale, Evelyn White, conductor); (2) PRC CC-4 (Illinois Wesleyan Choir, Lewis E. Wikehart, conductor). Library: de Lerma (1–2).

—— (SATB and piano, simplified version). New York: G. Ricordi, 1925. 7 p. Franco Colombo's collection of part-songs and choruses for male, female, and mixed voices. Plate no. 592.

—— (SSA). New York: Franco Colombo, n.d. [?]. Plate no. FCC 693.

—— (TTBB and piano). New York: G. Ricordi, n.d. [?]. Plate no. 454.

Who is dat yondah?: Spiritual from the collection of Eva A. Jessye (medium voice and piano). New York: G. Ricordi, 1930. 6 p. Library: Spingarn.

—— (low voice and piano). New York: Galaxy Music, 1930.

You goin' to reap jus' what you sow (SATB). New York: G. Ricordi, 1938. 9 p. Plate no. 1134. Library: Spingarn.

—— (SSA). New York: G. Ricordi, n.d. [?].

The young warrior (low voice and piano). New York: G. Ricordi, 1915. 7 p. and part. Plate no. 116235-6. Text: James Weldon Johnson. Library: Columbia.

DAWSON, WILLIAM LEVI, 1899–

Forever thine (medium voice and piano). Tuskegee: Music Press, 1920. 5 p. Text: William Levi Dawson. Dedication: To Mother. Library: Columbia, Spingarn.

Go to sleep (low voice and piano). Chicago: H. T. FitzSimons, 1926. Text: Vernon N. Ray. Library: Spingarn, Yale (manuscript, with violin).

—— (SATB and piano). Chicago: H. T. FitzSimons, 1920. 5 p. Aeolian series of choral music. Plate no. 1006. Library: Columbia.

—— (SSA and piano). Chicago: H. T. FitzSimons, 1926. 5 p. Aeolian series of choral music. Plate no. 3010. Library: Columbia, Library of Congress.

—— (TTBB and piano). Chicago: H. T. FitzSimons, 1926. 5 p. Aeolian series of choral music. Plate no. 4010. Library: Columbia.

I couldn't hear nobody pray (soprano and SATB with piano reduction). Chicago: H. T. FitzSimons, 1920. 7 p. Aeolian series of choral music. Library: Spingarn. Recorded: Westminster W-9633 and WGM-8154 (Tuskegee Institute Choir, William L. Dawson, conductor) 1968, 1971. Library: de Lerma.

Jesus walked this lonesome valley (high voice and piano). Chicago: Gamble Hinged Music, 1927. 5 p. Plate no. 818. "From the singing of my cousin, Mrs. Blanche Dawson-Roney, Tuskegee Inst., Alabama." Library: Spingarn.

—— (low voice and piano). Chicago: Gamble Hinged Music, 1927. Library: Library of Congress. Recorded: Phase II 8178-1 (Arthur Warner, baritone, J. Spencer Hammond, piano). Library: de Lerma.

—— (SATB and piano). New York: Warner Brothers, 1927. 6 p. Plate G-821.

———— (SSAA and piano). New York: Remick Music, 1950. Remick sacred choral library, 3-G1839. Library: Library of Congress.

Jump back, honey (orchestra). Chicago: H. T. FitzSimons, n.d. [?]. Won: Rodman Wanamaker prize, 1930.

————. (high voice and piano). Kansas City: Wunderlichs Piano Co., 1923. 6 p. Text: Paul Laurence Dunbar. Dedication: Charles Winter Wood. Library: Columbia, Library of Congress.

King Jesus is a-listening (SATB with piano reduction). Chicago: H. T. Fitz-Simons, 1925. 7 p. Aeolian series of choral music, 2004. Library: Library of Congress, Spingarn. Recorded: Westminster W-9633 (Tuskegee Institute Choir, William L. Dawson, conductor) 1978.

———— (SSA with piano reduction). Chicago: H. T. FitzSimons, 1946. Library: Library of Congress.

Lovers plighted. Won: Rodman Wanamaker award, 1931.

The mongrel Yank: A Yankee is a mixture of many races (TTBB and piano), op. 6. Chicago: Gamble Hinged Music, 1930. 14 p. Gamble's selection of secular part-songs for men's voices, 939. Text: Allen Quade. Library: Columbia, Spingarn. *See also:* The rugged Yank (same music, revised text).

My Lord, what a mourning (low voice and piano). Chicago: H. T. FitzSimons, 1927. 5 p. Text: Matthew 24:29. Dedication: Marian Anderson. Library: Spingarn.

Negro folk symphony (1934; rev. 1952). Delaware Water Gap: Shawnee Music Press, 1965, 1963. 162 p. Contents: (1) The bond of Africa; (2) Hope in the night; (3) O le' me shine. Duration: 35:00. Instrumentation: 2 flutes, piccolo, 2 oboes, English horn, 2 clarinets, E♭ clarinet, bass clarinet, 2 bassoons, contrabasoon, 4 horns, 3 trumpets, 3 trombones, tuba, timpani, percussion, harp, strings. Library: Columbia, de Lerma, Library of Congress (LC 66-34572; also 1963 holograph, 52 p.). Recorded: Decca DL-710077, DL-74-1077, and DL-10077 (American Symphony Orchestra, Leopold Stokowski, conductor). Library: de Lerma.

Oh what a beautiful city (medium voice and piano). Recorded: Praise 658 (Isador Oglesby, tenor, John Miller, piano) 1979. Library: de Lerma.

———— (SATB with piano reduction). Tuskegee: Music Press, 1934. 11 p. Tuskegee Choir series, 100. Library: Spingarn, Yale. Recorded: Black Heritage Series vol. 2 0-645 (Virginia State College Choir, Eugene Thamon Simpson, conductor). Library: de Lerma.

———— (SATB with piano reduction). Park Ridge, Ill.: Neil A. Kjos, n.d. [?]. Tuskegee Choir series, T-110.

Out in the fields with God (medium voice and piano). Chicago: Gamble Hinged Music Co., 1929?. 5 p. Plate no. 874. Text: Louise Imogen Guiney. Library: Library of Congress, Spingarn. Recorded: (George Shirley, tenor, Wayne Sanders, piano) 1976. Library: de Lerma.

———— (medium voice and piano). San Diego: Neil A. Kjos, 1957. Plate TH-130.

———— (medium voice and orchestra). Recorded: Desto DC-7107 (Cynthia Bedford, mezzo-soprano, Oakland Youth Orchestra, Robert Hughes, conductor) 1971. Library: de Lerma.

———— (SATB and piano). Chicago: Gamble Hinged Music Co., 1929. Recorded:

Silver Crest MOR-111977 (Morgan State University Choir, Patricia Springer, piano, Nathan Carter, conductor) 1977. Library: de Lerma.

———— (SATB and piano). New York: Remick Music, 1929. 9 p. Library: Library of Congress.

———— (SATB and piano). Tuskegee: Music Press, 1962, 1929. 10 p. Tuskegee Choir series, T-130.

———— (SATB and orchestra). 13 p. Library: Yale (manuscript).

———— (SSAA). Tuskegee: Music Press, 1962, 1929. 8 p. Tuskegee Choir series, T-131.

The rugged Yank (medium voice and piano). San Diego: Neil A. Kjos, n.d. [?]. Plate TH-132. Text: Allen Quade.

———— (TTBB and piano). Tuskegee: Music Press, 1920, 1970. 15 p. Tuskegee Choir series, T-132. Library: Columbia, Library of Congress (1920 imprint). *See also:* The mongrel Yank (same music, earlier text).

Scherzo (orchestra) 1930. Duration: 15:00. Won: Rodman Wanamaker prize, 1930.

Sonata, A major (violin and piano). 1927.

Soon ah will be done (SATB with piano reduction). Tuskegee: Music Press, 1934. 11 p. Tuskegee Choir series, T-102A. Library: Library of Congress, Spingarn, Yale. Recorded: (1) Capitol P-8432 (Roger Wagner Chorale, Roger Wagner, conductor); (2) Monitor MO-576 (Brank Krsmanovich Chorus of Jugoslavia); (3) (Morris Brown College Chorale, J. Weldon Norris, conductor). Library: de Lerma (3).

———— (TTBB with piano reduction). Tuskegee: Music Press, 1947, 1934. 11 p. Tuskegee Choir series, T-101A. Library: Library of Congress. Recorded: Columbia AL-45 (De Paur Infantry Chorus, Leonard De Paur, conductor).

———— (TTBB with piano reduction). Park Ridge, Ill.: Neil A. Kjos, 1962, 1947, 1934. 11 p.

Symphony, no. 1, E flat major (orchestra). 61 p. Library: Yale (manuscript).

Talk about a child that do love Jesus (high voice and piano). Recorded: Victor 4556 (Charles Holland, tenor, Ralph Linsley, piano).

———— (low voice and piano). Chicago: H. T. FitzSimons, 1927. Library: Library of Congress. Recorded: Period SLP-580 (Inez Matthews, mezzo-soprano, Jonathan Brice, piano). Library: de Lerma.

———— (SATB with piano reduction). Chicago: H. T. FitzSimons, 1927. 5 p. Aeolian series of choral music, 2015. Library: Spingarn.

Trio, A major (piano, violin, violoncello). 1925.

You got to reap just what you sow (low voice and piano). Chicago: Gamble Hinged Music Co., 1928. 5 p. Plate no. 839. Dedication: Paul Robeson. Library: Spingarn.

DETT, R. NATHANIEL, 1882–1943

Collections

The collected piano works of R. Nathaniel Dett, with introductions by Dominique-René de Lerma and Vivian Flagg McBrier. Evanston: Summy-Birchard, 1973. xii, 195 p. Contents: (1) Magnolia; (2) In the bottoms; (3) Enchantment;

(4) Cinnamon grove; (5) Tropic winter; (6) Eight Bible vignettes. Library: de Lerma, Library of Congress (72-12872).

Negro spirituals (voice and piano, and SATB). New York: John Church, 1919. 3 vols. Contents: (1) Follow me; (2) Somebody's knocking at your door; (3) I'm so glad trouble don't last alway; (4) Oh, the land I am bound for; (5) Poor me; (6) Zion hallelujah. Library: Library of Congress (voice and piano).

Religious folk-songs of the Negro as sung at Hampton Institute (SATB). Hampton, Va.: Hampton Institute Press, 1927. xxvii, 236 p. Library: Library of Congress (27-10635). Individual titles that have been recorded are listed below.

———— (SATB). New York: AMS Press, 1972, 1927. xxvii, 236 p. Library: Library of Congress (LC 72-1595).

Single Works

As by the streams of Babylon (soprano and SATB), by Thomas Campion, 1567-1620 (from his *First book of ayres*, 1613). New York: G. Schirmer, 1933. 4 p. G. Schirmer's octavo church music and general anthems, 7713. Plate no. 36047. Library: Library of Congress, Spingarn.

As children, walk ye in God's love (soprano and SATB). New York: G. Schirmer, 1930. Schirmer's octavo choruses, 7398. Plate no. 10609. 9 p. Library: Spingarn.

———— (tenor and TTBB). New York: G. Schirmer, 1930. 9 p. Schirmer's octavo choruses, 34911. Library: Spingarn.

Ave Maria, guide me and lead me (baritone and SATB with piano reduction). New York: G. Schirmer, 1930. 7 p. Schirmer's octavo choruses, 7395. Plate no. 34905. Text: Catholic liturgy and Frederick H. Martens. Library: Spingarn.

———— (baritone and SATB with piano reduction). Chapel Hill, N.C.: Hinshaw Music, 1930. 7 p. Plate no. HMC-333.

The chariot jubilee (tenor, SATB, and organ or piano). New York: John Church, 1919. 31 p. Plate no. 18124. Duration: 15:00. Dedication: Syracuse University Chorus, Howard Lyman, conductor. The composer stated in an interview (July 23, 1943) that this was "the first attempt to develop the spiritual into an oratorio form." Library: Columbia, Library of Congress, Spingarn. Recorded: Audio House AHS-30F75 (Morgan State University Choir, James Nathan Jones, tenor, William Partridge, organ, Nathan Carter, conductor) 1975. Library: de Lerma.

———— (tenor, SATB, and orchestra). Instrumentation: solo tenor, SSAATTBB, 2 flutes, 2 oboes, 2 clarinets, 2 bassoons, 4 horns, 2 trumpets, 3 trombones, tuba, timpani, percussion, organ, strings. Commission: Howard Lyman. Premiere: May 14, 1921, Keith's Theatre, Syracuse; Lambert Murphy, tenor, Syracuse Festival Chorus, Cleveland Symphony Orchestra, Howard Wilder Lyman, conductor.

Cinnamon grove suite (piano). 1927. New York: John Church, 1928. Duration: 12:00. Contents: (1) Moderato molto grazioso, on lines from "The dream," by John Donne; (2) Adagio cantabile, on lines from "Gitanjali," by Rabindranath Tagor; (3) Ritmo moderato e con sentimento; Gavotte, on lines from "Epimetheus," by Henry Wadsworth Longfellow; (4) Allegretto, on lines from

"Religious folk songs of the Negro." Library: Library of Congress. Recorded: 2nd movement only, Victor 17912B in set M-764 (Jeanne Behrend, piano). Library: de Lerma.

Concert waltz and ballade (piano). By 1919.

Deep river (SATB). Minneapolis: Hall & McCreary, 1938.

Done paid my vow to the Lord (contralto or baritone, SSA, and piano). Bryn Mawr, Pa.: Theodore Presser, 1919. 8 p. Plate no. 35007-7; 322-35007. Recorded: Richmond Sound Stages RSSWO-626 (Virginia Union University Choir, Odell Hobbs, conductor). Library: de Lerma.

Don't be weary traveller (SATB). New York: John Church, 1921.

Don't you weep no more Mary (SATB with piano reduction). New York: G. Schirmer, 1930. 8 p. Plate no. 34906. Library: Spingarn.

Drink to me only with thine eyes (SATB with piano reduction). New York: J. Fischer, 1933. 12 p. Fischer edition, choruses in octavo form. Plate no. J.F.&B. 6700-11. Text: Ben Johnson. Library: Library of Congress, Spingarn.

Enchantment (piano). 1922. New York: John Church, 1922. 4 vols. Plates no. 18540, 18541, 18542, 18543. Contents: (1) Incantation; (2) Song of the shrine; (3) Dance of desire; (4) Beyond the dream. Library: Library of Congress. Recorded: (Paul Swieten, piano). Library: de Lerma.

—— (orchestra). New York: John Church; Bryn Mawr, Pa.: Theodore Presser, n.d. [?]. Instrumentation: 3 flutes and piccolo, 2 oboes, 2 clarinets, 2 bassoons, timpani, percussion, harp, piano, strings. Duration: 18:00. Library: Fleisher (3627).

—— (high voice and piano). Recorded: Praise 658 (Isador Oglesby, tenor, John Miller, piano) 1979. Library: de Lerma.

Follow me (low voice and piano). New York: John Church, 1919. 8 p. Plate no. 18209. Arranged from the collection of Mrs. Catherine Fields-Gay. Library: Spingarn. Recorded: Victor 6472 (Reinald Werrenrath, baritone, with orchestra). Library: de Lerma.

Gently Lord, O gently lead us: Melody from Bahama songs and stories, text from a hymn (SATB with piano reduction). Cincinnati: John Church, 1924. 17 p. The John Church Co. anthems for mixed voices, 2743. Plate no. 18766-8. Library: Library of Congress.

Go not far from me, O God (SATB with piano reduction). New York: J. Fischer & Bro., 1933. 11 p. Fischer edition, 6698. Plate no. J.F.&B. 6698-10. Library: Library of Congress.

God understands (medium voice and piano). Cincinnati: The John Church Co., 1926. 5 p. Plate no. 19061-3. Text: Katrina Trask. Library: Library of Congress.

I couldn't hear nobody pray (SATB). In *Religious folk-songs of the Negro as sung at Hampton Institute*, appendix, 202. New York: AMS Press, 1972, 1927. Recorded: Victor M-879 and RCA Camden CAL-344 (Dorothy Maynor, soprano, with male chorus). Library: de Lerma.

I want to be ready (SATB). In *Lift every voice and sing*, ed. by Irene J. Brown, no. 81. New York: Church Hymnal Corporation, 1981.

I'm a-goin' to see my friends ag'in (high voice and piano). New York: John Church, 1924. 5 p. Plate no. 18764. From the singing of Rev. J. Fletcher Bryant. Library: Library of Congress, Spingarn.

—— (SATB). New York: John Church, 1924.

I'm a-trav'ling to the grave (high voice and piano). New York: Mills, 1943. 5 p. Dedication: Dorothy Maynor. Library: Spingarn. Recorded: (1) London LPS-182 (Ellabelle Davis, soprano, Rupert Greenslade, piano); (2) Praise 658 (Isador Oglesby, tenor, John Miller, piano); (3) (Ben Holt, baritone, Cliff Jackson, piano); (4) (John Patton, tenor, C. Edward Thomas, piano). Library: Schomburg (1), de Lerma (1–4).

—— (high voice and piano). In *Spirituals for voice and piano*. New York: Mills Music, 1942.

I'm so glad trouble don't last alway (medium voice and piano). New York: John Church, 1919. 5 p. Plate no. 18150. Library: Spingarn.

—— (SSAA). Bryn Mawr, Pa.: John Church, Theodore Presser, 1919. 4 p. Plate no. 322-35123.

In dat great gittin'-up mornin' (SATB). In *Religious folk-songs of the Negro as sung at Hampton Institute*, 154. New York: AMS Press, 1972, 1927. Recorded: Victor M-879 (Dorothy Maynor, soprano, with male chorus).

In the bottoms (piano). Chicago: Clayton F. Summy, 1913. 26 p. Summy edition, 61. Plate no. 1465. Contents: (1) Prelude; Night; (2) His song; (3) Honey; (4) Barcarolle; (5) Juba. Duration: 15:00. Premiere: 1913, Music Hall, Chicago; Fannie Bloomfield-Zeisler, piano. Library: Library of Congress, Spingarn. Recorded: (1) Philips 9500 096 (Clive Lythgoe, piano); (2) Desto DC-7102/3 (Natalie Hinderas, piano); (3) (Mildred Ellis, piano, contains nos. 2, 3, and 5); (4) Decca 24159 in album A-586 (matrix 73059; Percy Grainger, piano, first movement only) September 5, 1945; (5) Gustafson Piano Library Tape GLP-102 (Percy Grainger, piano). Library: de Lerma (1–3, 5).

Iorana: Tahitian maiden's love song (medium voice and piano). Chicago: Clayton F. Summy, 1935. 7 p. Plate no. 3019. Text: J. Henry Quine. Library: Library of Congress, Spingarn. Recorded: (George Shirley, tenor, Wayne Sanders, piano). Library: de Lerma.

—— (medium voice and piano). In *Negro art songs*, edited by Edgar Rogie Clark. New York: Edward B. Marks Music Corporation, 1946; Ann Arbor: University Microfilms, 1973, 1946.

Juba, from *In the bottoms* (piano). Chicago: Clayton F. Summy. Duration: 4:00. Recorded: (1) unidentified piano roll 6339 (Percy Grainger?, piano) 1920; (2) Decca album A-386 (matrix 73059; Percy Grainger, piano); (3) Gustafson Piano Library Tape GLP-102 (Percy Grainger, piano; contains two performance versions); (4) Columbia 7000M in album A-6145 (Percy Grainger, piano) between 1919 and 1925; (5) University of Washington Press OLY-104 (Victor Steinhart, piano, 1975). Library: de Lerma (1–5).

—— (piano, simplified). Chicago: Summy, 1926. 5 p. Plate no. CFSCo. 2401-4. Library: Library of Congress.

—— (2 pianos). Recorded: (Wilfred Delphin, Edwin Romain, pianos). Library: de Lerma.

—— (SATB and piano). Chicago: Summy, 1934. 17 p. Plate no. CFSCo 2978. Text: R. Nathaniel Dett. Dedication: Inter-Hi Chorus of Rochester, Alfred Spouse, director. Library: Columbia, Library of Congress.

—— (orchestra). Recorded: RCA Victor E-76 (RCA Victor Orchestra, Ardon Cornwell, conductor). Library: de Lerma.

Lead gently, O Lord, and slow (SATB). Cincinnati: John Church, 1924. Library: Spingarn.

Let us cheer the weary traveler (SATB). Bryn Mawr, Pa.: John Church, 1926. 11 p. Plate no. 322-35044.

Listen to the lambs. 1923; revised 1936. Recorded: Columbia ML-6235, MS-6835 (Mormon Tabernacle Choir, Richard P. Condie, conductor) 1965. Library: de Lerma.

Magic moon of molten gold (high voice and piano). New York: John Church, 1919. 17 p. Plate no. 18211. Text: Frederick H. Martens. Library: Columbia, Spingarn.

Magnolia suite (piano). Chicago: Clayton F. Summy, 1912. Contents: (1) Magnolias; (2) The deserted cabin; (3) My lady love; (4) Mammy; (5) The place where the rainbow ends. Recorded: (Hildred Roach, piano; no. 2 only). Library: de Lerma.

A man goin' roun' takin' names (low voice and piano). New York: John Church, 1924. 5 p. Plate no. 18765. "From the singing of Capt. Walter R. Brown of Hampton Inst." Library: Library of Congress, Spingarn.

My day (medium voice and piano). New York: John Church, 1929. 5 p. Plate no. 19311. Text: Daniel S. Twohig. Library: Columbia, Library of Congress, Spingarn.

My way's cloudy (SATB). In *Religious folk-songs of the Negro as sung at Hampton Institute*, 231. New York: AMS Press, 1972, 1927. Recorded: Vonna Records VR-1601 (Morgan State College Choral Union, Orville Mosely, conductor) ca. 1950. Library: de Lerma.

Nepenthe and the muse (piano). New York: John Church, 1922. 6 p. Plate no. 18544. Library: Spingarn.

Nobody knows de trouble I've seen (SATB). In *Religious folk-songs of the Negro as sung at Hampton Institute*, 232. New York: AMS Press, 1972, 1927. Recorded: Victor M-879 (Dorothy Maynor, soprano, with male chorus).

Now rest beneath night's shadows (SSAA). New York: J. Fischer & Bro., 1938. 8 p. Plate no. 7399. Text: Paul Gerhardt (1656).

O hear the lambs a-crying (SATB). New York: John Church, 1927.

O Lord, the hard-won miles (high voice and piano). New York: G. Schirmer, 1934. 5 p. Plate no. 36034. Text: Paul Laurence Dunbar. Library: Spingarn.

—— (low voice and piano). New York: G. Schirmer, 1934. 5 p. Plate no. 36033. Library: Spingarn.

Oh Mary, don't you weep (SATB). Boston: C. C. Birchard, 1919. 4 p. Laurel octavo, 3d series, 134. Library: Library of Congress.

Oh, the land I'm bound for (low voice and piano). New York: John Church, 1923. 5 p. Plate no. 18658. Library: Spingarn.

Ole-time religion (SATB). In *Religious folk-songs of the Negro as sung at Hampton Institute*, 200. New York: AMS Press, 1972, 1927. Recorded: Victor M-879 (Dorothy Maynor, soprano, with male chorus).

Open yo' eyes (high voice and piano). Philadelphia: Theodore Presser, 1923. 7 p.

Plate no. 19031. Text: "The album of a heart," by R. Nathaniel Dett. Library: Columbia, Library of Congress (1924 imprint, Plate no. 19496), Spingarn.

———— (low voice and piano). Philadelphia: Theodore Presser, 1923. 7 p. Plate no. 19496.

The ordering of Moses: Biblical folk scene. 1932. Text: Bible and folklore. Duration: 60:00. Instrumentation: SATB soli, SSAATTBB, 2 flutes and piccolo, 2 oboes, 2 clarinets, 2 bassoons, 4 horns, 3 trumpets, 2 trombones, tuba, timpani, harp, organ, strings. Dedication: George Foster Peabody. Premiere: May 7, 1939, Cincinnati Festival; Eugene Goossens, conductor. Original title, as M.M. thesis, Eastman School of Music, 1932: Sacred cantata for soli, chorus and orchestra. Library: Schomburg. Recorded: (1) U.S. State Department; (2) Silver Crest TAL-42868-S (Jeannette Walters, soprano, Carol Brice, contralto, John Miles, tenor, John Work, IV, baritone, The Talladega College Choir, Mobile Symphony Orchestra, William L. Dawson, conductor); (3) (Elizabeth Hogue, soprano, Shirley Hughes and Dorothy Fleming, mezzo-sopranos, James Bradley and Charles Sullivan, tenors, Garymichael Murphy and Stanley Thurston, baritones, Kevin Short, bass, Morgan State University Choir, Nathan Carter, conductor). Library: de Lerma (2–3).

———— (piano-vocal score). Melville, N.Y.: J. Fischer & Bro., 1965, 1939. 123 p. Fischer ed. 7230. Library: Columbia, de Lerma, Library of Congress (1937 imprint), Schomberg, Spingarn, Yale (1937 imprint).

Poor me (medium voice and piano). New York: John Church, 1923. 5 p. Plate no. 18656. Dedication: Marian Anderson. "Melody taken from Folk songs of the American Negro, by the Work brothers." Library: Spingarn. Recorded: Victor 10-1278 (Marian Anderson, contralto, Franz Rupp, piano). Library: de Lerma.

———— (SATB). New York: John Church, 1919. Library: Spingarn.

Ramah (violin and piano). Boston: Boston Music Co., 1923. 7 p. and parts. Plate no. 6941. Library: Library of Congress.

Ride on, Jesus (high voice and piano). New York: J. Fischer & Bro., 1940. 4 p. Plate no. J.F.&B. 7695. "Setting requested and made especially for Miss Dorothy Maynor." Library: Spingarn.

Ride on, King Jesus (high voice and piano). Recorded: BRC Productions (Veronica Tyler, soprano, Charles Lloyd, piano) 1980. Library: de Lerma.

Rise up shepherd an' foller (solo voice, SATB, and organ). Glen Rock, N.J.: J. Fischer & Bro., 1964, 1936. 7 p. Plate no. 7218. Library: Library of Congress (1936 imprint), Spingarn (1936 imprint).

———— (tenor, TTBB, and piano). Glen Rock, N.J.: J. Fischer & Bro., 1936. 7 p. Plate no. 7219-6. Library: Library of Congress. Recorded: Victor M-879 and RCA Camden CAL-3444 (Dorothy Maynor, soprano, with male chorus). Library: de Lerma.

Sit down servant (medium voice and piano). New York: G. Schirmer, 1932. Plate no. 35805. Library: Library of Congress, Spingarn.

———— (solo voice and SATB). New York: G. Schirmer, 1936. G. Schirmer octavo, 7931. Plate no. 36912. Library: Library of Congress.

Somebody's knocking at your door (medium voice and piano). New York: John Church, 1919. 9 p. Plate no. 18210. Library: Spingarn.

———— (SATB). Cincinnati: John Church, 1919.

—— (SATB). Philadelphia: Theodore Presser, 1932. 15 p. Theodore Presser Co. part-songs for mixed voices, 35197. Plate no. 35197-14. Library: Library of Congress.

—— (SSAA). Cincinnati: John Church, 1919.

Sonata, no. 1, F minor (piano). By 1924.

Sonata, no. 2, E minor (piano). By 1925.

Steal away to Jesus (SATB). In *Religious folk-songs of the Negro as sung at Hampton Institute,* appendix vii, 111. New York: AMS Press, 1972, 1927. Recorded: Victor M-879 and RCA Camden CAL-344 (Dorothy Maynor, soprano, with male chorus). Library: de Lerma.

Symphonic suite, E minor (piano). Duration: 23:00.

Symphony, E minor (orchestra).

There is a balm in Gilead (SATB). In *Lift every voice and sing,* ed. by Irene J. Brown, no. 14. New York: Church Hymnal Corporation, 1981. Recorded: Period SPL-580 (Inez Matthews, mezzo-soprano, Jonathan Brice, piano). Library: de Lerma.

There's a man goin' 'round takin' names (solo voice and SATB). Cincinnati: John Church, 1924.

There's a meeting here tonight (SSA). Cincinnati: John Church, 1921.

A thousand years ago or more (high voice and piano). New York: John Church, 1919. 9 p. Plate no. 18212. Text: Frederick H. Martens. Library: Columbia, Spingarn.

Tropic winter (piano). Contents: (1) The daybreak charioteer; (2) A bayou garden; (3) Pompons and fans; (4) Legend of the atoll; (5) To a closed casement; (6) Noon siesta; (7) Parade of the jasmine banners. Chicago: Clayton F. Summy, 1938. Recorded: (Hildred Roach, piano; contains no. 1 only). Library: de Lerma.

The voice of the sea (low voice and piano). New York: John Church, 1924. 5 p. Plate no. 18819-4. Text: from "The album of a heart," by R. Nathaniel Dett. Dedication: Kathryn Mesile, contralto. Library: Columbia, Library of Congress, Spingarn.

Wasn't that a mighty day? (SATBB). New York: G. Schirmer, 1933. 9 p. G. Schirmer octavo choruses, 7712. Plate no. 36042. Library: Library of Congress, Spingarn.

Were thou the moon (low voice and piano). Cincinnati: John Church, 1924. 5 p. Plate no. 18818. Text: from "Album of a heart," by R. Nathaniel Dett. Library: Library of Congress, Spingarn.

Were you there when they crucified my Lord? (SATB). In *Religious folk-songs of the Negro as sung at Hampton Institute,* appendix vi, 106. New York: AMS Press, 1972, 1927. Recorded: Victor M-879 and RCA Camden CAL-344 (Dorothy Maynor, soprano, with male chorus). Library: de Lerma.

The winding road (low voice and piano). Philadelphia: Theodore Presser, 1923. 7 p. Plate no. 19030. Text: Tertius van Dyke. Library: Columbia, Library of Congress, Spingarn.

Zion, hallelujah (medium voice and piano). New York: John Church, 1923. 5 p. Plate no. 18657. "As sung by Miss Baytop." Library: Spingarn.

FREEMAN, HARRY LAWRENCE, 1869–1954

An American romance: Opera. 1927. Text: Harry Lawrence Freeman.

Down where the Yazoo River flows (voice and piano). 1924. 4 p. Text: Harry Lawrence Freeman. Library: Columbia (photocopy of manuscript).

The flapper: Opera. 1929. Text: Harry Lawrence Freeman.

I'd choose a southern girl (voice and piano). New York: Jerome H. Remick, 1910. 5 p. Text: Chas. A. Isbell. Library: Columbia.

If thou did'st love (high voice and piano). New York: Handy Brothers, 1935. 6 p. Library: Atlanta, Columbia, Spingarn.

Leah Kleschna: Opera. 1931. Text: Harry Lawrence Freeman.

The slave (orchestra). 1925.

The slave ballet from *Salomé: Ballet* (chorus and orchestra). 1923. Text: Harry Lawrence Freeman.

Uzziah: Opera. 1934. Text: Harry Lawrence Freeman.

Vendetta: Opera. 1923. Text: Harry Lawrence Freeman. Library: Columbia (libretto; n.p.: The Negro Grand Opera Company, 1923).

Voodoo: A grand opera in three acts. 1926. Text: Harry Lawrence Freeman. Library: Columbia (libretto; n.p.: The Negro Grand Opera Company, 1926).

————, Act III (soprano, tenor, SATB, and piano). Library: Columbia (photocopy of manuscript).

Whither (high voice and piano). New York: Handy Brothers, 1935. 4 p. Text: Harry Lawrence Freeman. Library: Columbia, Spingarn.

JENKINS, EDMUND THORNTON, 1894–1926

Afram: Opera in 3 acts. 1924. Contents (not assumed to be in order): (1) Beneath the palmettos and pines; (2) Blues des contrebaniers et des policiers; (3) The Carolina strut; (4) Chanson du prince; (5) Chanson nègre: O bye and bye; (6) Dance of the cotton pickers; (7) Danse d'amour; (8) Kentucky Kate; (9) Lamentation; (10) L'il Liza Jane; (11) Nobody knows de trouble I see; (12) Pretty kids; (13) Tableau de la plantation.

African war dance (orchestra). 1925. Won: Casper Holstein award, first prize, 1926.

Amber eyes. 1925.

Baby darling, baby mine (medium voice and piano). 1919. Text: William Archer Plowright. Premiere: August 8, 1919, Albert Rooms, London; Evelyn Dove, soprano.

Charlestonia, op. 12: Rhapsody, no. 1 (orchestra). 1925. Premiere: July 1925, Kursaal, Ostend, Belgium; F. Rasse, conductor.

Folk rhapsody, no. 2: Rapsodie spirituelle (orchestra). 1923. Premiere: November 2, 1919, Wigmore Hall, London; Edmund Jenkins, conductor.

If I were to tell you I love you. 1925.

A prayer (medium voice and piano). 1925. Paris: Anglo-Continental-Américan Music Press, 1925. 8 p. Plate A.C.A. (CL)5. Text: Benjamin G. Brawley. Library: Columbia.

Rêverie phantasie (violin and piano). 1919. Premiere: August 8, 1919, Albert Rooms, London; Angelita Riveira, violin, Edmund Jenkins, piano.

The saxophora strut. 1925.

Slow movement and rondo (woodwind quartet and piano). 1919. Instrumentation: flute, 2 clarinets, horn, and piano. Premiere: March 5, 1919; Mary Underwood, flute?, G. Stutely, clarinet?, Edmund Jenkins, clarinet, Francis Bradley, horn?, Marjorie Herman, piano? Won: Battison Haynes Prize, 1919.

Sonata, A major (violoncello). 1925. Won: Casper Holstein award, 2d prize, 1925.

Spring fancies (piano). 1920. Paris: Anglo-Continental-Américan Music Press, 1925. 7 p. Plate A.C.A.(CL)10. Library: Columbia.

Symphony, op. 14 (orchestra). 1926. 50 p. Duration: 25:00 to 30:00. Possibly left unorchestrated.

That place called Italy. 1925.

JOHNSON, HALL, 1888–1970

Cert'n'y Lord (tenor, bass, and SATB with piano reduction). New York: Carl Fischer, 1952, 1930. 11 p. Plate no. CM 6641. Library: Library of Congress (1952 imprint). Recorded: Black Heritage Recordings 90671 (Rufus Graves, baritone, Reginald Henderson, bass, Virginia State College Choir, Eugene Thamon Simpson, conductor). Library: de Lerma.

City called heaven (medium voice and piano). New York: Robbins, 1930. Duration: 4:31. Library: Spingarn. Recorded: (1) Victor 895B and HMV DB-2837 (Marian Anderson, contralto, Kosti Vehanan, piano); (2) (David Hudson, tenor, Hayward Mickens, piano) 1974. Library: de Lerma (1–2).

———— (SATB). New York: Robbins, 1947, 1930. 7 p. Plate no. R3303. Recorded: (1) Black Heritage Recordings 90671 (Virginia State College Choir, Eugene Thamon Simpson, conductor); (2) (Evelyn White Chorale, Evelyn White, conductor). Library: de Lerma (1–2).

———— (TTBB). New York: Big Three, n.d. [?].

Fi-yer: Opera. 1933.

Go down, Moses, from *The green pastures* (baritone and SATB). New York: Carl Fischer, 1930. 7 p. Plate no. CM 6739. Library: Library of Congress. Recorded: HMV DA-6032 (Hall Johnson Choir).

The green pastures: Musical. 1930. Contents (in show and publication order): (1) Oh rise an' shine; (2) When de saints come marchin' in; (3) Cert'n'y Lord; (4) My God is so high; (5) Hallelujah; (6) In the bright mansions above; (7) Doncher let nobody turn you roun'; (8) Run sinner, run; (9) You better min'; (10) Dere's no hidin' place down here; (11) Some o' these days; (12) I want to be ready; (13) De ol' ark's a-moverin'; (14) Witness; (15) My Lord's a-writin' all de time; (16) Go down, Moses; (17) Oh Mary, doncher weep; (18) Lord, I don't feel noways tired; (19) Joshua fit de battle ob Jericho; (20) I can't stay away; (21) Hail de king of Babylon; (22) Death's g'on ter lay his col' icy hands on me; (23) De blin' man stood on de road an' cried; (24) Hallelujah, King Jesus. Text (of play): Marc Connely, after "Ol' man Adam an' his chillun" by Roark Bradford. Premiere: February 26, 1930, Mansfield Theatre, New York (640 performances); Hall Johnson Choir, Hall Johnson, conductor. Recorded: (1) Victor 4460 (Hall Johnson Choir; Joshua fit de battle of Jericho, only); (2)

(Hall Johnson Choir; Hall Johnson, conductor; excerpts of the play from a radio broadcast) 1940. Library: de Lerma (2).

—————— (medium voice and piano). New York: Carl Fischer, 1930. 40 p. Plate O-480; 02069-8; #25807-38. Library: Library of Congress (36-2627), Schomburg, Spingarn.

—————— (medium voice and piano). New York: Farrar & Rinehart, 1930. vi, 40 p. Library: Library of Congress (36-2630), Schomburg.

His name so sweet (high voice and piano). New York: Carl Fischer, 1934. 7 p. Sheet music edition, V 1222. Plate no. 26646-5. Library: Library of Congress, Spingarn. Recorded: (1) Period SPL-580 (Inez Matthews, mezzo-soprano, Jonathan Brice, piano) 195?; (2) Avant Garde AV-115 (Eugene Holmes, baritone, Joseph Rezits, piano); (3) (Louise Parker, contralto, Susan Peters, piano) 1972. Library: de Lerma (1–3).

—————— (SATB). New York: Carl Fischer, 1935. 2 p. Folklore choral series, 4580. Recorded: (1) Black Heritage Recordings 90671 (Virginia State College Choir, Eugene Thamon Simpson, conductor); (2) RCA LSC-2600 (Leontyne Price, soprano, orchestra and chorus, Leonard De Paur, conductor) 1962. Library: de Lerma (1–2).

—————— (SSA). New York: Carl Fischer, 1935. 3 p. Plate no. CM 5213.

—————— (TTBB). New York: Carl Fischer, 1935. 3 p. Plate no. CM 2183. Recorded: Columbia ML-2119 (De Paur Infantry Chorus, Leonard De Paur, conductor) 1950.

Hold on (medium voice and piano). New York: Robbins, 1930. Recorded: (1) Period SPL-580 (Inez Matthews, mezzo-soprano, Jonathan Brice, piano) 195?; (2) RCA LM/LSC-2592 (Marian Anderson, contralto, Franz Rupp, piano) 1962. Library: de Lerma (1–2).

—————— (low voice and piano). New York: Carl Fischer, 1941. 7 p. Sheet music edition V 1502. Plate no. CC 29105. Library: Columbia.

—————— (tenor and SATB). New York: Robbins, 1958, 1930. 9 p. Plate no. 3299.

Honor, honor (high voice and piano). New York: Carl Fischer, 1930. 7 p. Sheet music edition, V 1220. Plate no. 26644. Duration: 1:40. Library: Library of Congress, Spingarn. Recorded: (1) Tioch Digital TD-1009 (Wilhelmenia Fernandez, soprano, George Darden, piano); (2) (G. Carlton Hines, tenor, André Thomas, piano) 1981; (3) Marble Arch LS-1181 (Paul Spencer Adkins, tenor, with piano) ca. 1981. Library: de Lerma (1–3).

—————— (low voice and piano). New York: Carl Fischer, 1930. Sheet music edition V 1502. Recorded: (1) RCA AVM-1-1735 (Marian Anderson, contralto, Franz Rupp, piano) 1974, 1947; (2) (Marian Anderson, contralto, NBC Symphony Orchestra, Frank Black, conductor) 1944. Library: de Lerma (1–2).

—————— (tenor and SATB). New York: Carl Fischer, 1935. 4 p. Folklore choral series, CM 4579. Recorded: (1) Black Heritage Recordings 90671 (Virginia State College Choir, Eugene Thamon Simpson, conductor); (2) RCA LSC-2600 (Leontyne Price, soprano, orchestra and chorus, Leonard De Paur, conductor) 1962. Library: de Lerma (1–2).

—————— (SSA and piano). New York: Carl Fischer, 1935. 6 p. Plate no. CM 5215.

—————— (TTBB). New York: Carl Fischer, 1935. 6 p. Plate no. CM 21826. Recorded:

Columbia ML-2119 (De Paur Infantry Chorus, Leonard De Paur, conductor) 1950.

Jesus, lay yo' head in de winder (medium voice and piano). New York: Robbins, 1930. 5 p. Plate no. 541. Library: Spingarn.

——— (tenor and SATB). New York: Robbins, 1958, 1930. 8 p. Plate no. R 3301.

Lord, I don't feel no-ways tired (tenor and SATB with piano reduction) from "Green pastures." New York: Carl Fischer, 1950. Folklore series, CM 6502. Recorded: Black Heritage Recordings 90671 (Virginia State College Choir, Eugene Thamon Simpson, conductor). Library: de Lerma.

Steal away (medium voice and piano). New York: Carl Fischer, 1934. 5 p. Sheet music edition, V 1221. Plate no. 26645-4. Library: Library of Congress, Spingarn.

——— (SATB). New York: Carl Fischer, 1935. 2 p. Folklore choral series, 458.

——— (SSA and piano). New York: Carl Fischer, 1935. 3 p. Plate 5214.

——— (TTBB). New York: Carl Fischer, 1935. 2 p. Plate CM 2148.

Tradition (low voice and piano), by Ismay Andrews, arranged for dance interpreted by Emilia Caesar. New York: Handy Brothers, 1935. 7 p. Dedication: Hall Johnson. Library: Spingarn.

Way up in heaven (medium voice and piano). New York: Robbins, 1930. Library: Spingarn.

——— (SATB and piano). New York: Robbins, 1930. 5 p. Plate R 3300.

JOHNSON, JAMES P., 1891–1955

Collections

Dixieland echoes: A collection of five descriptive Negro songs (medium voice and piano), composed and edited by Perry Bradford and James P. Johnson. New York: Perry Bradford, 1928. 24 p. Contents: (1) Echoes of ole Dixie land; (2) Honey; (3) Mississippi River flood; (4) Cotton pickin'; Jubilee song; (5) Liza Jane's weddin'. Library: Library of Congress, Schomburg (inscribed by both composers to Arthur Schomburg), Spingarn.

Piano solos. New York: Clarence Williams, 1945. 28 p. Contents: (1) Snowy mornin' blues; (2) Riffs; (3) Carolina shout; (4) Over the bass; (5) Keep off the grass. Library: Columbia, Library of Congress.

Single Works

After hours: Novelty piano solo. New York: Jack Mills, 1923. 5 p. Library: Columbia.

Ain't cha got music, from *Harlem hotcha* (SSAATTBB and piano), arranged by W. C. Handy. New York: W. C. Handy, 1932. 15 p. Text: Andy Razaf. Library: Spingarn, Yale.

Alabama stomp (medium voice and piano). New York: Robbins-Engel, 1926. 5 p. Plate no. SH 317. Text: Henry Creamer. Used in "Earl Carroll's vanities of 1926." Library: Spingarn.

Blackbirds of 1939: Musical. 1939. Vocal arrangements by James P. Johnson. Premiere: February 11, 1939, Hudson Theater, New York (9 performances).

Charleston, from *Runnin' wild* (medium voice and piano). New York: T. B. Harms, 1923. 5 p. Used in Toller Cranston's "The ice show" (1977). Library: Spingarn, Yale. Recorded: (1) Columbia M-33706 (band, Dick Hyman, conductor) 1975; (2) (The California Ramblers) ca. 1925. Library: de Lerma (1).

———— (medium voice and piano). Berlin: Rondo-Verlag, 1925. 3 p. Plate no. R.-V. 521. Text: Artur Rebner. Issued as "Der original Charleston, der neue Modetanz mit Tanzbeschreibung." Library: Library of Congress.

Charleston dance (medium voice and piano). New York: Jack Mills, 1923. Text: James P. Johnson. Recorded: CM 33706 (Dick Hyman, piano).

Chicago loop: Musical in 2 acts. 1926. New York: Henry Creamer, 1926. Text: Henry Creamer and Ted Wing.

Chicago stomp down (medium voice and piano). New York: Jack Mills, 1927. Text: Henry Creamer.

Clementine (for medium voice and piano), by James P. Johnson and Harry Warren. New York: Shapiro, Bernstein, 1927. Text: Henry Creamer.

Day dreams (medium voice and piano). 1920. New York: Irving Berlin, 1929. Text: Saul Bernie and Stella Unger.

Desperate blues (medium voice and piano), arranged by H. Qualli Clark. 1922. New York: Sphinx Music, 1922. Text: Alex Rogers.

Don't cry, baby (medium voice and piano). New York: Saul Bernie, 1929. 4 p. Text: Saul Bernie and Stella Unger. Library: Spingarn.

Don't need nobody to tell me that I'm in bad (medium voice and piano). New York: Irving Berlin, 1923. Text: Mercedes Gilbert.

Don't never tell nobody what your good man can do (medium voice and piano). 1923. New York: Irving Berlin, 1923. Text: Mercedes Gilbert.

Ebony dream (piano). New York: Perry Bradford, 1928. 6 p. Library: Spingarn.

Eccentricity waltz (piano). About 1917. New York: Clarence Williams, 1926. 4 p. Duration: 3:17. Library: Columbia. Recorded: (1) QRS piano roll 101000 (James P. Johnson, piano); (2) Olympic 7132 (James P. Johnson, piano) 1974, 1921; (3) Columbia M-33706 (Ruby Braff, cornet, Dick Hyman, piano) 1975; (4) Musical Heritage Society MHS-4022 (William Albright, piano) 1979. Library: de Lerma (2–4).

Everybody's doing the Charleston now (medium voice and piano), by James P. Johnson, Cecil Mack, Bud Green, and Elmore White. New York: Irving Berlin, 1925. Original title: Everybody does the Charleston now.

Exhortation theme, from *Yamekraw* (medium voice and piano). New York: Perry Bradford, 1928. Text: Henry Creamer.

The fight, from *Runnin' wild.* Recorded: Okeh 40186 and New World NW-260 (Aubrey Lyles and Flournoy Miller). Library: de Lerma.

Geechie: A dusky romance: Musical in 3 acts. 1926. New York: Henry Creamer, 1926. Text: Henry Creamer.

Ginger Brown, from *Runnin' wild* (medium voice and piano). New York: T. B. Harms, 1923. Recorded: CM 33706 (Dick Hyman, piano).

Give me the sunshine, from *Keep shufflin'* (medium voice and piano). New York: T. B. Harms, 1928. 5 p. Plate no. 8146. Library: Spingarn.

Go Harlem (medium voice and piano). Text: Andy Razaf. Recorded: Time-Life

STL-J18 and Columbia (Jimmy Johnson and His Orchestra) 1981, 1931. Library: de Lerma.

Harlem choc'late babies on parade (piano). 1926. New York: Henry Creamer, 1926. Duration: 2:52. Recorded: Olympic 7132 (James P. Johnson, piano) 1974, 1926. Library: de Lerma.

Harlem hotcha: Musical. 1932. Text: Andy Razaf.

Harlem hotcha, from *Harlem hotcha*. Text: Andy Razaf. Recorded: Time-Life STL-J18 and Disc (The Carnival Three) 1981, 1945. Library: de Lerma.

Harlem symphony (orchestra). 1932. New York: Robbins Music, 1932. Contents: (1) Subway journey; (2) Song of Harlem; (3) Night club; (4) Baptist mission.

Heart-breakin' Joe, from *Runnin' wild* (medium voice and piano). Text: Jo Trent.

Hot diggity dog (medium voice and piano). New York: Jack Mills Music, 1923. Text: Henry Creamer.

Hot Harlem, from *Sugar hill*. Recorded: Time-Life STL-J18 and Asch (James P. Johnson's New York Orchestra) 1981, 1944. Library: de Lerma.

I don't know nobody, from *Runnin' wild*. Library: Library of Congress.

I don't love nobody but you, from *Messin' around* (low voice and piano). New York: Witmark, 1929. 5 p. Plate no. 8683. Text: Perry Bradford. Library: Spingarn.

I need lovin' (medium voice and piano). New York: Jerome H. Remick, 1926. 5 p. Plate no. 274. Library: Spingarn, Yale.

I need you, from *Messin' around* (medium voice and piano). New York: Witmark, 1929. 5 p. Plate no. 8684. Text: Perry Bradford. Library: Spingarn.

I was so weak, love was so strong, from *Harlem hotcha* (medium voice and piano). New York: W. C. Handy, 1932. 5 p. Text: Andy Razaf. Library: Spingarn, Yale.

If I could be with you one hour tonight (medium voice and piano with plectral tablature). New York: Jerome H. Remick, 1926. 5 p. Plate no. 232. Text: Henry Creamer and James P. Johnson. Library: Columbia, Spingarn, Yale. Recorded: (1) QRS piano roll 3818 (James P. Johnson, Fats Waller, piano); (2) Columbia M-33706 (Ruby Braff, cornet, Dick Hyman, piano); (3) Time-Life STL-J18 and Decca (James P. Johnson, piano, Eddie Dougherty, drums) 1981, 1944. Library: de Lerma (2–3).

Ivy, cling to me (medium voice and piano) by James P. Johnson and Isham Jones, arranged by H. Qualli Clark. New York: Irving Berlin, 1922. 5 p. Text: Alex Rogers. Library: Spingarn.

Jasmine concerto: Jazz-o-mine (piano and orchestra). 1935. New York: Mills Music, 1935. Contents: 3 movements.

————, 2nd movement (piano solo). New York: Mills Music, 1949. Library: Library of Congress.

Jingles (piano). 1926. New York: Clarence Williams, 1926. Recorded: (1) Time-Life STL-J18 and Brunswick (James P. Johnson, piano) 1981, 1930; (2) Columbia M-33706 (band, Dick Hyman, conductor). Library: de Lerma (1–2).

Jungle nymphs: A novelette (piano). 1924. New York: Jack Mills, 1924. 6 p. Library: Columbia, Spingarn.

Keep off the grass (piano) 1926. New York: Clarence Williams, 1926. Recorded:

Time-Life STL-J18 and OKeh (James P. Johnson, piano) 1981, 1921. Library: de Lerma.

Keep shufflin': Musical. 1928. Text: Con Conrad and Henry Creamer. Contents, in show order (some tunes by or with Fats Waller or Will Vodery): (1) Teasing mama; (2) Choc'late bar; (3) Labor Day parade; (4) Give me the sunshine; (5) Leg it; (6) Exhortation theme; (7) Sippi; (8) How jazz was born; (9) Keep shufflin'; (10) Everybody's happy in Jimtown; (11) Dusky love; (12) Charlie my back door man; (13) On the levee; (14) Skiddle de scow.

Kitchen opera: Musical.

Lock and key (medium voice and piano). New York: Henry Creamer, 1927. Text: Henry Creamer. Recorded: Time-Life STL-J20 (Bessie Smith, vocal, James P. Johnson, piano) 1982, 1927. Library: de Lerma.

Love bug, from *Runnin' wild* (low voice and piano). New York: T. B. Harms, 1923. 5 p. Plate no. 6873. Recorded: CM 33706 (Dick Hyman, piano).

Manhattan street scene: Ballet.

Meet Miss Jones: Musical. Library: Library of Congress (uncataloged selections).

Messin' around: Musical. 1929. Text: Perry Bradford. Contents (in show order): (1) On to Harlem; (2) Harlem town; (3) Skiddle de scow; (4) Get away from my window; (5) Your love is all I crave; (6) Shout on; (7) I don't love nobody; (8) Roustabouts; (9) Mississippi; (10) Circus days; (11) Sorry; (12) Put your mind right on it; (13) Yamekraw; (14) Messin' around.

Mississippi moon, from *Messin' around* (orchestra).

Mistah Jim (medium voice and piano). New York: Irving Berlin, 1925. Text: Cecil Mack.

Mule walk stomp (piano). Before 1939. Recorded: (1) Time-Life STL-J18 and Blue Note (James P. Johnson, piano) 1981, 1943; (2) Musical Heritage Society MHS-4022 (William Albright, piano) 1979. Library: de Lerma (1–2).

Oh Georgie, look what you've done to me (medium voice and piano). New York: Witmark, 1927. Text: Henry Creamer.

Oh Malinda (medium voice and piano). New York: Bud Allen, 1927. Text: Andy Razaf.

Old-fashioned love, from *Runnin' wild* (medium voice and piano). New York: T. B. Harms, 1923. 5 p. Text: Cecil Mack. Library: Columbia, Spingarn. Duration: 3:04. Recorded: (1) Time-Life STL-J18 and Columbia (Jimmy Johnson and His Orchestra) 1981, 1939; (2) Columbia M-33706 (Dick Hyman, piano); (3) New World Records NW-269 and OKeh 4993 (Clarence Williams' Blue Five) 1977, 1923; (4) Monmouth-Evergreen MES-7080 (Adelaide Hall, vocal). Library: de Lerma (1–3).

Open your heart, from *Runnin' wild* (medium voice and piano), by Springfield and Westlake. New York: T. B. Harms, 1923. 5 p. Plate no. 6866. Library: Spingarn. Recorded: CM 33706 (Dick Hyman, piano).

Overture, from *Runnin' wild.* Recorded: (Newport Jazz Festival band) 1979. Library: de Lerma.

A porter's love song to a chambermaid (medium voice and piano). New York: Joe Davis, 1922. 3 p. Text: Andy Razaf.

———— (medium voice and piano). In *The best of blues in songs and stories*. New York: Charles Hansen, n.d.

Reflections (orchestra). 1935.

———— (piano). New York: Mills Music, 1935. Library: Library of Congress.

Riffs (piano). n.p.: Acme Music, 1930. Recorded: Time-Life STL-J18 and OKeh (James P. Johnson, piano). Library: de Lerma.

Runnin' wild: Musical. 1923. Contents (in show order): (1) Open your heart; (2) Log cabin days; (3) Old-fashioned love; (4) Love bug; (5) Ginger Brown; (6) Charleston; (7) Juba dance; (8) Keep movin'; (9) Sun kist Rose; (10) Show time; (11) Heart Breaking Joe; (12) Banjoland; (13) Pay day on levee; (14) Slow an' easy goin' man; (15) The sheik of Alabam'; (16) A brown-skin vamp. Premiere: October 29, 1923, Colonial Theatre, New York (213 performances). Recorded: (1) Columbia C2S-847 (Eubie Blake, piano [Charleston, Old-fashioned love, and If I could be with you]) 1969; (2) Columbia M-33706 (band, Dick Hyman, conductor [Ginger Brown, Old-fashioned love, Charleston, Love bug, Open your heart]) 1975; (3) Olympic 7132 (James P. Johnson, piano [Charleston, Old-fashioned love, Open your heart, Love bug]) 1974, 1924. Library: de Lerma (1–3).

Scalin' the blues (piano). 1926. New York: Clarence Williams, 1926.

Scoutin around (piano). In *Jazzopation: A study in jazz by the masters, six hot piano solos just off the stove*. New York: Perry Bradford, 1927.

Sefronia's dream: Ballet.

[Selections] Medley, from *Runnin' wild* (piano). Contents: (1) Charleston; (2) Old-fashioned love; (3) Open your heart; (4) Love bug. Recorded: QRS piano roll 10107 (James P. Johnson, piano).

She's the hottest gal in Tennessee (medium voice and piano). New York: Shapiro, Bernstein, 1926. 5 p. Text: Henry Creamer. Used in Paramount film, "The lady fare." Library: Spingarn.

Sippi, from *Keep shufflin'*. 1928. New York: T. B. Harms, 1928. 6 p. Plate no. 8147. Library: Spingarn.

Skiddle de skow, from *Messin' around* and *Runnin' wild* (medium voice and piano). New York: Witmark, 1929. 5 p. Plate no. 8685. Text: Perry Bradford. Library: Spingarn.

Slippery hips (medium voice and piano). New York: Jewell Music, 1930. Text: Andy Razaf.

Snowy morning blues (piano). 1927. New York: Perry Bradford, 1927. Duration: 3:01. Recorded: (1) Folkways FJ-2809 (James P. Johnson, piano) 1960, 1943; (2) Musical Heritage Society MHS-4022 (William Albright, piano) 1979; (3) Time-Life STL-J18 and Columbia (James P. Johnson, piano) 1981, 1927; (4) Columbia M-33706 (Ruby Braff, cornet, Dick Hyman, piano). Library: de Lerma (1–3).

Sorry that I strayed away from you, from *Messin' around* (medium voice and piano). New York: Witmark, 1929. 5 p. Plate no. 8686. Text: Perry Bradford. Library: Spingarn.

The Spanish in my eyes (high voice and piano), by James P. Johnson and Enrico Madriguera. New York: Haviland, 1934. 5 p. Library: Spingarn.

Stop that dog, from *Harlem hotcha* (medium voice and piano). New York: W. C. Handy, 1932. 5 p. Text: Andy Razaf. Library: Spingarn, Yale.

Sugar hill: Musical. 1931. Text: Flournoy Miller and Jo Trent. Contents (listed in alphabetical order): (1) Apple jack; (2) Far away love; (3) Fate misunderstood me; (4) Hot Harlem; (5) I don't want any labor in my job; (6) Keep 'em guessin'; (7) My sweet hunk o' trash; (8) Peace, sister, peace; (9) Shivaree; (10) Smilin' through my tears; (11) Stay out of the kitchen; (12) Sugar hill; (13) Yes, I love you honey; (14) You can't lose a broken heart. Library: Library of Congress (uncataloged selections).

Sunny side (medium voice and piano). 1929. New York: Saul Bernie, 1929. Text: Saul Bernie and Stella Unger.

Sweet mistreater (medium voice and piano). New York: Henry Creamer, 1927. Text: Henry Creamer.

Symphonic Harlem (orchestra).

Symphony in brown (orchestra).

There goes my headache, from *Harlem hotcha* (medium voice and piano). New York: W. C. Handy, 1932. 5 p. Text: Andy Razaf. Library: Spingarn, Yale.

Toddlin' home (piano). In *Jazzopation: A study in jazz by the masters, six hot piano solos just off the stove.* New York: Perry Bradford, 1927.

Ukulele blues (medium voice and piano), arranged by H. Qualli Clark. 1922. New York: Sphinx Music, 1922. Text: Merton H. Bories.

Weepin' blues (piano), arranged by Phil Worde. 1923. New York: Perry Bradford, 1923.

When I can't be with you (medium voice and piano). New York: Southern, 1931. 5 p. Text: Andy Razaf.

Why did Minnie ha ha? (medium voice and piano). New York: Shapiro, Bernstein, 1926. Text: Henry Creamer.

Worried and lonesome blues (piano), arranged by Phil Worde. 1923. New York: Perry Bradford, 1923.

Yamekraw: Negro rhapsody (piano). New York: Perry Bradford, 1927. 26 p. Library: Columbia, Spingarn (both copies inscribed "Presented to Arthur B. Spingarn, great friend of the Negro race, with the best wishes of the composer, James P. Johnson, Jan. 30 1936"), Yale. Originally for orchestra. Recorded: Folkways FJ-2842 (James P. Johnson, piano).

———— (small orchestra). Instrumentation: 2 cornets, trombone, 2 alto saxophones, 1 tenor saxophone, banjo, piano, drums, violin, double bass/tuba, piano-conductor.

———— (theater orchestra). Instrumentation same as above, plus flute, clarinet, violin 2, viola, and violoncello.

———— (full orchestra). Instrumentation same as above, plus oboe, bassoon, clarinet 2, horns.

———— (orchestra), arranged by William Grant Still. 1928. New York: Alfred, 1928. 19 p. (piano-conductor) and 19 parts. Library: Columbia, Library of Congress.

Yes, I love you honey, from *Sugar hill* (medium voice and piano). New York: T. B. Harms, 1931. 5 p. Plate no. 8772. Text: Jo Trent. Library: Spingarn.

You can't do what my last man did (medium voice and piano). 1923. New York: James P. Johnson, 1923. Text: A. Moore. Composer may have been J. C. Johnson. Recorded: Murray Hill 927942 and Victor 19123 (James P. Johnson, piano), n.d., 1923. Library: de Lerma.

You don't understand (medium voice and piano). 1929. New York: Clarence Williams, 1929. Text: Clarence Williams and Spencer Williams. Recorded: Time-Life STL-J20 (Bessie Smith, vocal, James P. Johnson, piano) 1982, 1929. Library: de Lerma.

You for me, me for you, from now on (medium voice and piano). 1925. New York: Clarence Williams, 1925, 1926. Text: Cecil Mack. Library: Spingarn.

You just can't have no one man by yourself (medium voice and piano). 1923. New York: Clarence Williams, 1923. Text: Mercedes Gilbert.

You said you wouldn't but you done it (medium voice and piano). 1923. New York: Jack Mills, 1923. Text: Henry Creamer.

Your love is all that I crave, from *Messin' around* (medium voice and piano). New York: Witmark, 1929. 5 p. Plate no. 8757. Text: Perry Bradford and M. Dubin. Also used in Warner Brothers film "Show of shows." Library: Spingarn.

Yours, all yours, from *Harlem hotcha* (medium voice and piano). New York: W. C. Handy, 1932. 5 p. Text: Andy Razaf. Library: Spingarn, Yale.

You've got to be modernistic (piano). New York: Clarence Williams, 1930. Duration: 3:03. Recorded: (1) Time-Life STL-J18, Decca DXSF-7140, and Brunswick (James P. Johnson, piano) 1982, 1930; (2) Columbia M-33706 (band, Dick Hyman, conductor); (3) Musical Heritage Society MHS-4022 (William Albright, piano) 1979. Library: de Lerma (1–3).

You've got what I've been looking for (medium voice and piano), arranged by H. Qualli Clark. 1922. New York: Sphinx Music, 1922. Text: Merton H. Bories.

You've lost your loving baby now (medium voice and piano). New York: Witmark, 1927. Text: Henry Creamer.

PRICE, FLORENCE, 1888–1953

Adoration (organ). Dayton: Lorenz Music, n.d. [?].

American folksongs in counterpoint (string quartet). Also known as Negro folksongs in counterpoint.

At the cotton gin: A southern sketch (piano). New York: G. Schirmer, 1927. 5 p. Plate no. 33200c. Library: Columbia, Spingarn.

The butterfly (piano). New York: Carl Fischer, 1936. 5 p. Sheet music edition, P2100. Plate no. 27643. Library: Spingarn.

Chicago suite (orchestra).

Concert overture based on "Sinner please don't let this harvest pass" (orchestra).

Concert overture on Negro spirituals, no. 1 (orchestra). Duration: 10:00. Instrumentation: 3 flutes, piccolo, 2 oboes, 2 clarinets, 2 bassoons, 3 horns, 2 trumpets, 2 trombones, tuba, timpani, 4–5 percussion, strings.

Concert overture on Negro spirituals, no. 2 (orchestra). Duration: 12:00. Instrumentation: 3 flutes and piccolo, 2 oboes and English horn, 2 clarinets and bass clarinet, 2 bassoons, 4 horns, 3 trumpets, 3 trombones, tuba, timpani, percussion, harp, strings.

Concerto, piano, F minor (1932). Contents: one movement. Duration: 12:00. Instrumentation: flute, oboe, 2 clarinets, bassoon, 2 horns, 2 trumpets, 2 trombones, timpani, 2 percussion, strings. Premiere: 1932; Florence Price, piano, Chicago Symphony Orchestra, Frederick Stock, conductor.

Concerto, violin, D major. Duration: 16:00. Instrumentation: 2 flutes, 2 oboes, 2 clarinets, 2 bassoons, 2 trumpets, timpani, strings.

Cotton dance (piano). Won: Rodman Wanamaker honorable mention, 1931.

Dreamin' town (medium voice and piano). 1934. 4 p. Text: Paul Laurence Dunbar. Duration: 2:00. Library: University of Arkansas (facsimile of holograph).

The envious wren (medium voice and piano). 6 p. Text: Alice Carey and Phoebe Carey. Library: University of Arkansas (facsimile of holograph).

Ethiopia's shadow in America (orchestra). Won: Rodman Wanamaker honorable mention, 1932.

Evening (organ).

Fantasy, no. 1 (piano).

Fantasy, no. 2 (piano).

Fantasy, no. 3 (piano).

Fantasy, no. 4 (piano). Won: Rodman Wanamaker honorable mention, 1932.

Fantasy in purple (medium voice and piano). 3 p. Text: Langston Hughes. Duration: 2:00. Library: University of Arkansas (facsimile of holograph).

Five easy pieces for grade 2 (piano). Chicago: McKinley Music, 1928. Plate no. 2241/2242/2243/2244/2245. Contents: (1) Anticipation: A study in phrasing; (2) Doll waltz: Vals de la muneca: A study in rests; (3) The engine: La maquine de vapor: A study in staccato and short phrases; (4) The waltzing fairy: El duende valsante: A study in legato, staccato, and phrasing; (5) The waterfall: La cascada: A study in arpeggio forms. Library: Spingarn.

Forever (medium voice and piano). 3 p. Text: Paul Laurence Dunbar. Duration: 2:00. Library: University of Arkansas (facsimile of holograph).

The gnat and the bee (piano). New York: Carl Fischer, 1936. 5 p. Sheet music edition, P2098. Plate no. 27642. Library: Spingarn.

Hourglass: Sandman (organ).

Impromptu (organ).

In quiet mood (organ). New York: Galaxy Music, 1951. 5 p. Plate no. G.M. 1822-4. Duration: 3:00. Library: Library of Congress.

In the land of cotton (piano).

Mellow twilight: El crepúscolo suave (piano). Chicago: McKinley, 1929. 5 p. Plate no. 2303-3. Library: Columbia, Spingarn.

Mississippi River (orchestra). Duration: 10:00. Instrumentation: 3 flutes and piccolo, 2 oboes and English horn, 2 clarinets and bass clarinet, 2 bassoons and contrabassoon, 4 horns, 3 trumpets, 3 trombones, tuba, timpani, percussion, harp, strings.

Moonbridge (high voice and piano). Chicago: Gamble Hinged Music, 1930. 6 p. Plate no. 937. Text: Mary Rolofson Gamble. Duration: 2:00. Library: Columbia, Spingarn.

———— (SSA and piano). New York: Remick Music, 1930. 7 p. Plate no. G-1847-6.

The new moon (SSAA and piano 4 hands). Chicago: Gamble Hinged Music, 1930. 12 p. Plate no. 964-11. Duration: 3:00. Text: anonymous. Dedication: Estella C. Bonds. Library: Columbia.

The oak (orchestra). Duration: 7:00. Instrumentation: 3 flutes and piccolo, English horn, 2 clarinets and bass clarinet, 2 bassoons, 4 horns, 3 trumpets, 3 trombones, tuba, timpani, percussion, harp, strings.

Offertory (organ).

Overture, no. 1 (orchestra).

Overture, no. 2 (orchestra).

Passacaglia and fugue (organ).

Quartet (strings).

Quintet (piano and strings).

Retrospection: An elf on a moonbeam (organ).

Rhapsody (piano and orchestra).

The rose (piano). New York: Carl Fischer, 1936. 5 p. Sheet music edition, P2091. Plate no. 27638. Library: Spingarn.

A sachem's pipe (piano). New York: Carl Fischer, 1935. 5 p. Sheet music edition, P2060. Plate no. 27275. Library: Spingarn.

Sandman, See Hourglass.

Seagulls (SSAA, flute, violin, viola, violoncello, and piano). Won: Lake Vie Musical Society contest.

Sonata (organ).

Sonata, E minor (piano). Contents: (1) Allegro con furia; (2) Adagietto; (3) Allegro deciso. Won: Rodman Wanamaker prize, 1932.

Song of the oak (orchestra). Duration: 12:00. Instrumentation: 3 flutes and piccolo, 2 oboes and English horn, 2 clarinets and bass clarinet, 2 bassoons and contrabassoon, 4 horns, 3 trumpets, 4 trombones, tuba, timpani, 5–6 percussion, harp, organ (ad lib.), strings.

Suite (organ).

Symphonic tone poem (orchestra).

Symphony, no. 1, E minor (orchestra). 1932. Duration: 20:00. Instrumentation: 2 flutes, 2 oboes, 2 clarinets, 2 bassoons, 4 horns, 2 trumpets, 3 trombones, tuba, timpani, 3 percussion, strings. Won: Rodman Wanamaker prize, 1932.

Symphony, no. 2, G minor (orchestra). Duration: 25:00. Instrumentation: 3 flutes and piccolo, 2 oboes and English horn, 2 clarinets and bass clarinet, 2 bassoons and contrabassoon, 3 horns, 2 trumpets, 4 trombones, timpani, 3 percussion, harp, strings.

Symphony, no. 3, C minor (orchestra). 110 p. Duration: 22:00. Instrumentation: 3 flutes and piccolo, 2 oboes and English horn, 2 clarinets and bass clarinet, 2 bassoons, 4 horns, 3 trumpets, 3 trombones, tuba, timpani, percussion, harp, strings. Library: Yale (manuscript).

Symphony, [no. 4?], D minor (orchestra). Duration: 20:00. Instrumentation: 3 flutes and piccolo, 2 oboes and English horn, 2 clarinets and bass clarinet, 2 bassoons, 4 horns, 3 trumpets, 3 trombones, tuba, timpani, 3–5 percussion, harp, strings.

Tecumseh (piano). New York: Carl Fischer, 1935. 5 p. Sheet music edition, P2062. Plate no. 27277. Library: Spingarn.

Three little Negro dances (piano). Bryn Mawr, Pa.: Theodore Presser, 1933. Plate no. 26030/26031/26032. Contents: (1) Hoe cake; (2) Rabbit foot; (3) Ticklin' toes. Library: Spingarn.

———— (band, reduced score), arranged by Eric W. G. Leidzén. New York: Theodore Presser, 1939. 8 p. Plate no. 26788-94. Recorded: Vonna Records VR-1610 (Morgan State College Concert Band, R. Hayes Strider, conductor) ca. 1950. Library: de Lerma.

Tropical moon (piano).

The winds and the sea (SATB and orchestra).

The zephyr: El cefiro, Mexican folk song (piano). Chicago: Gamble Hinged Music, 1928. 5 p. Plate no. 2279. "A study in phrasing and pedaling." Library: Spingarn.

STILL, WILLIAM GRANT, 1895–1978[1]

Africa: Suite (orchestra). 1930. Manuscript (copyright, 1934, held by Robbins Music Corporation). Contents: (1) Land of peace; (2) Land of romance; (3) Land of superstition. Instrumentation: 3 flutes and piccolo, 2 oboes and English horn, 3 clarinets and bass clarinet, 3 bassoons, 4 horns, 3 trumpets, 3 trombones, tuba, timpani, 3 percussion, celeste, harp, piano, strings. Duration: 23:00–30:00. Premiere: 1930; Little Symphony, Georges Barrère, conductor. Withdrawn. Library: Columbia (9 p. lead sheet), Library of Congress (74-226251; holograph, 101 p., gift of I. Schwerke, March 1966; 3 p. penciled note on stationery having monogram "RL" mentioning the composer's invention of fingernail pizzicato, use of tom-toms and of Harmon and fibre mutes for trumpets and trombones; also manuscript of 9 p. dated 1934 and lead sheet of 5 p. dated 1937).

———— (orchestra). 1931 reorchestration. Premiere: Rochester, American Composers Concert, Eastman School of Music.

Afro-American symphony, *See* Symphony no. 1.

Animato: Humor, from *Afro-American symphony* (reduced orchestra, piano score). New York: J. Fischer, 1937. 7 p. Plate no. J.F.&B. 0366. Library: Spingarn. Recorded: (1) Victor 1059B (Eastman-Rochester Symphony Orchestra, Howard Hanson, conductor) 1941; (2) Columbia 11992B (All-American Youth Orchestra, Leopold Stokowski, conductor); (3) (NBC Symphony Orchestra, Max Reiter, conductor). Library: de Lerma (3).

Black bottom (chamber orchestra). 1922. Manuscript (copyright, 1937, held by Robbins Music Corporation). Duration: 10:00. Withdrawn. Library: Columbia (1 p. lead sheet).

The black man dances: Suite (orchestra). Manuscript. Contents: 3 movements. Duration: 10:00. Withdrawn.

Blue steel: Opera in 3 acts. 1935. Manuscript. Text: Bruce Forsythe, based on a story by Carlton Moss. Duration: 120:00. Withdrawn following performance of excerpts. Library: Library of Congress (piano-vocal score, 59 p.).

The breath of a rose (medium voice and piano). New York: G. Schirmer, 1928. 5 p. Plate no. 33804. Text: Langston Hughes. Library: Columbia, Library of Congress, Schomburg, Spingarn. Recorded: (Helene Oatts, soprano, Robert L. Morris, piano) 1969. Library: de Lerma.

———— (medium voice and piano). In *A new anthology of American song.* New York: G. Schirmer, 1942. Plate no. 39640.

Brown baby (medium voice and piano), by Willie M. Grant [pseud.]. New York:

Edward B. Marks, 1923. 5 p. Plate no. 9111. Text: Paul Henry [pseud.]. Library: Spingarn.

Darker America (orchestra). 1924. Boston: C. C. Birchard, for the Eastman School of Music, 1928. 4, 47 p. Duration: 11:58. Instrumentation: 2 flutes and piccolo, oboe, English horn, 2 clarinets, 2 bassoons, horn, trumpet, trombone, percussion, piano, strings. Premiere: November 28, 1926, Aeolian Hall, New York, International Composers Guild Concert; Eugene Goossens, conductor. Library: Columbia, Library of Congress. Recorded: Turnabout TVS-34546 (Music for Westchester Symphony Orchestra, Siegfried Landau, conductor) 1974. Library: de Lerma.

A deserted plantation (chamber orchestra). 1933. New York: Robbins, 1934. 4 p. Contents: (1) Spiritual: I want Jesus to walk with me; (2) Young Missy; (3) Dance. Duration: 15:00. Premiere: December 15, 1933, Metropolitan Opera House; Paul Whiteman, conductor. Library: Library of Congress.

———— (piano). New York: Robbins Music, 1936. Library: Spingarn.

Dismal swamp (orchestra). ca. 1936. San Francisco: The New Music Society of California, 1937. 32 p. New music orchestra series, no. 2, January 1937. Instrumentation: 3 flutes, 2 oboes and English horn, 3 clarinets and bass clarinet, 2 bassoons and contrabassoon, 4 horns, 4 trumpets, 3 trombones, tuba, timpani, vibraphone, piano, strings. Duration: 15:00. Premiere: October 30, 1936, Rochester, New York; Howard Hanson, conductor. After the poem by Verna Arvey. Library: Library of Congress (A45-1269).

Ebon chronicle (orchestra). 1936. Manuscript. Duration: 9:00. Premiere: November 3, 1936, Fort Worth Symphony Orchestra; Paul Whiteman, conductor. Library: Library of Congress (lead sheet), Fleisher (2767).

Entrance of les porteuses, from *La guiablesse.* Recorded: Glendale GL-8011 (San Francisco Symphony Orchestra, William Grant Still, conductor) 1984, 1940. Library: de Lerma.

From the black belt (orchestra; piano score). 1925. New York: Carl Fischer, 1946. 15 p. Contents: (1) Li'l scamp; (2) Honeysuckle; (3) Dance; (4) Mah bones is creakin'; (5) Blues; (6) Brown girl; (7) Clap yo' han's. Duration: 11:14. Instrumentation: 2 flutes, 2 oboes, 2 clarinets, 2 bassoons, 4 horns, 3 trumpets, 2 trombones, tuba, timpani, percussion, harp, strings. Premiere: March 20, 1927, Henry Miller Theatre, New York; Little Symphony, George Barrère, conducting. Recorded: Turnabout TVS-34546 (Music for Westchester Symphony Orchestra, Siegfried Landau, conductor), 1974. Library: de Lerma.

From the heart of a believer (orchestra). 1927. Manuscript. Duration: 10:00. Withdrawn.

From the journal of a wanderer (orchestra). 1925. Manuscript. Contents: (1) Phantom trail; (2) Magic bells; (3) Valley of echoes; (4) Mystic moon; (5) Devil's hollow. Duration: 20:00. Premiere: 1926, North Shore Festival, Chicago; Chicago Symphony Orchestra, Frederick Stock, conductor. Withdrawn. Library: Fleisher (2830).

From the land of dreams (SSA and chamber orchestra). 1924. Manuscript. Duration: 8:00. Premiere: February 8, 1925; International Composers Guild, Vladimir Shavitz, conductor.

La guiablesse: Ballet. 1927. New York: Carl Fischer, n.d. [?]. Scenario: Ruth Page, after Lafcadio Hearn. Duration: 30:00. Library: Fisk (holograph).

——— (piano). 1941. 38 p. Library: Library of Congress.

Gwinter sing all along de way, from *Twelve Negro spirituals* (SATB). New York: Handy Brothers, n.d. [?].

Kaintuck' (piano and orchestra). 1935. Mission Viejo, Calif.: WGS Music. 30 p. Duration: 14:00. Instrumentation: 3 flutes and piccolo, 2 oboes, 3 clarinets, 2 bassoons, 4 horns, 3 trumpets, 3 trombones, tuba, timpani, percussion, strings. Commission: League of Composers. Dedication: To my wife, Verna Arvey. Library: Columbia (lead sheet, 1937), de Lerma, Library of Congress (lead sheet, 1937), Yale (manuscript).

——— (2 pianos). 1935. Premiere: October 28, 1935, Los Angeles Pro Musica. Recorded: Orion ORS-82442 (Richard Fields, Gary Steigerwalt, pianos) 1982. Library: de Lerma.

Keep me from sinkin' down, from *Twelve Negro spirituals* (SATB). New York: Handy Brothers, n.d. [?].

Lawd, ah wants to be a Christian, from *Twelve Negro spirituals* (medium voice and piano). Recorded: Narthex (John Patton, tenor, C. Edward Thomas, piano). Library: de Lerma.

——— (SATB). New York: Handy Brothers, n.d. [?].

Levee land (soprano and orchestra). 1925. Text: William Grant Still. Contents: 4 songs. Duration: 10:00. Instrumentation: 2 flutes, 2 oboes, tenor banjo, piano, percussion, 2 violins. Premiere: January 24, 1926, Aeolian Hall, New York, International Composers Guild Concert; Florence Mills, soprano, orchestra, Eugene Goossens, conductor. For work bearing same title, *See* The American scene, suite II.

Log cabin ballads (orchestra). 1927. Manuscript. Contents: (1) Long to'ds night; (2) Beneaf de willer; (3) Miss Malindy. Duration: 10:00. Premiere: March 15, 1928, Booth Theatre, New York; Little Symphony, Georges Barrère, conductor.

Memphis man (medium voice and piano), by Willy Grant [pseud.]. New York: Edward B. Marks, 1923. 5 p. Plate no. 8193. Text: Paul Henry [pseud.]. Library: Spingarn.

Moderato assai: Longing, from *Afro-American symphony* (band), arranged by Melvin Miles. Thesis (M.A., music education), Morgan State University, 1978 ("A transcription for concert band of the first movement from William Grant Still's Afro-American Symphony"). Library: de Lerma.

Sahjdi (dancers, baritone, SATB, and orchestra). 1931. New York: Carl Fischer, n.d. [?]. Scenario: Richard Bruce Nugent and Alain Locke. Duration: 45:00. Instrumentation: 2 flutes and piccolo, 2 oboes and English horn, 2 clarinets, E♭ clarinet, bass clarinet, 2 bassoons, 4 horns, 2 trumpets, 2 trombones, tuba, timpani, 3 percussion, strings. Dedication: Howard Hanson. Premiere: May 22, 1931, Rochester; Thelma Biracree, solo dancer, Howard Hanson, conductor. Library: Columbia (incomplete lead sheet, 2 p.), Library of Congress (LC 65-80155/M), Yale (manuscript). Recorded: (1) Mercury MG-50257 and SR-90257 (Eastman School of Music Chorus, Eastman-Rochester Symphony Orchestra, Howard Hanson, conductor) 1960; (2) Columbia M-3343 (Morgan State University Choir, London Symphony Orchestra, Paul Freeman, conductor) 1975 (reissued by the College Music Society in 1978 in album P9 19414); (3) (Morgan State University Choir, Baltimore Symphony Orchestra, Paul Freeman, conductor) 1973; (4) (Indianapolis Symphony Orchestra, Kenneth Billups Chorus, Everett Lee, conductor) 1976; (5) Audio House AHS-30F75 (Morgan State University Choir, Annette Houston, piano, George Gray, percussion, Nathan Carter, conductor) 1975; (6) (Morgan State University Choir, Nathan Carter, conductor, contains excerpts) 1976. Library: de Lerma (1–6).

———— (typescript scenario). Library: Columbia.

———— (piano-vocal score). New York: Carl Fischer, 1941. 63 p. Library: Library of Congress.

———— (piano-vocal score). New York: Carl Fischer, 1961, 1941. 47 p. American composers edition. Library: Columbia (incomplete), Library of Congress (65-80155/M; also reproduction of holograph).

Suite, from *La guiablesse.* 27 p. Contents: (1) First dance of the children; (2) Dance of Yzore and Adou; (3) Entrance of les porteuses. Instrumentation: 3 flutes and piccolo, 2 oboes and English horn, 2 clarinets and bass clarinet, 2 bassoons, 4 horns, 3 trumpets, 3 trombones, tuba, timpani, percussion, harp, strings. Premiere: May 5, 1933, Third Annual Festival of American Music, Rochester, New York; Thelma Biracree, dancer, Howard Hanson, conductor. Library: de Lerma (includes note from the composer to Paul Freeman).

Suite, from *Sahjdi.* Duration: 20:30.

[Symphony, no. 1] Afro-American symphony (orchestra). 1930. New York: J. Fischer & Bro., 1935. 88 p. Contents: (1) Moderato assai; Longing [7:15]; (2) Adagio; Sorrow [5:14]; (3) Animato; Humor [4:00]; (4) Lento con resoluzione; Aspiration [7:15]. Duration: 23:45. Instrumentation: 3 flutes and piccolo, 2 oboes and English horn, 2 clarinets and bass clarinet, 2 bassoons, 4 horns, 3 trumpets, 3 trombones, tuba, 3 percussion, celeste, harp, tenor banjo, strings. Dedication: Irving Schwerke. Premiere: October 29, 1931, Eastman School of Music, Rochester, New York, American Composers Concert; Rochester Philharmonic, Howard Hanson, conductor. Library: de Lerma (violin 1 and cello parts, with rubber stamp "revised"), Library of Congress (holograph, 101 p. 74-226255). Recorded: (1) New Records NRLP-105 (Vienna State Opera Orchestra, Karl Krueger, conductor); (2) Society for the Preservation of the American Musical Heritage MIA-118 (Royal Philharmonic Orchestra, Karl Krueger, conductor) 1965; (3) Victor 2059-B (Eastman-Rochester Symphony Orchestra, Howard Hanson, conductor; third movement only); (4) Columbia 11992-D (All-American Youth Orchestra, Leopold Stokowski, conductor; third movement only). Library: de Lerma (1).

———— (orchestra). 1969 revision. London: Novello, 1970, 1962, 1935. 71 p. Novello orchestral scores. Instrumentation: 2 flutes and piccolo, 2 oboes and English horn, 2 clarinets and bass clarinet, 2 bassoons, 4 horns, 3 trumpets, 3 trombones, tuba, timpani, 2 percussion, harp, tenor banjo, strings. Library: Library of Congress (70-263895). Recorded: Columbia M-32782 (London Symphony Orchestra, Paul Freeman, conductor) 1974 (reissued by the College Music Society in 1978 in album P9 19414). Library: de Lerma.

Three Negro songs (medium voice and orchestra). 1921. Manuscript. Contents:

(1) Negro love song; (2) Death song; (3) Song of the backwoods. Duration: 10:00. Withdrawn.

Twelve Negro spirituals (medium voice and piano), arranged by William Grant Still, ed. by Wellington Adams. ca. 1936. New York: Handy Brothers, 1948, 1937. 2 vols. (6 spirituals in each, also published separately): 61, 40 p. Contents: (1) Gwinter sing all along de way; (2) All God's chillun got shoes; (3) Lis'en to de lam's; (4) Keep me from sinkin' down; (5) Lawd, ah wants to be a Christian; (6) Great camp meeting; (7) Great day; (8) Ah gotta home in-a dat rock; (9) Peter go ring dem bells; (10) Good news; (11) Didn't mah Lawd deliver Daniel; (12) Mah Lawd gonna rain down fiah. Duration: 25:00. Includes "William Grant Still, Afro-American composer" by Verna Arvey, and "Literary treatments" for each song by Ruby Berkley Goodwin, illustrated by Albert Barbelle. Library: Library of Congress (37-22232), Schomburg, Spingarn.

———— (medium voice and piano). London: Francis, Day & Hunter, 1937. 2 vols. Contents (reordered): 8, 2, 6, 11, 10, 7, 1, 4, 3, 5, 12, 9. Library: Spingarn.

Winter's approach (high voice and piano). 1928. New York: G. Schirmer, 1928. 5 p. Plate no. 33805. Text: Paul Laurence Dunbar. Duration: 3:00. Library: Columbia, Library of Congress, Spingarn.

Yamekraw: A Negro rhapsody (orchestra), by James P. Johnson, arranged by William Grant Still. New York: Alfred & Co., 1928. Library: Columbia, Library of Congress.

WHITE, CLARENCE CAMERON, 1880–1960

Allegretto energico (violin, violoncello, and piano).

———— (violin and piano).

American Negro folksongs. 1928.

Ballet music, from *Ouanga* (2 pianos and percussion).

Bear de burden (medium voice and piano), by C. Blanco [pseud.]. New York: Carl Fischer, 1921. 5 p. Plate no. 21945. Library: Spingarn.

———— (SATB). New York: Carl Fischer, 1935. Plate no. 2167.

———— (TTBB). New York: Carl Fischer, 1935.

Bend down beloved (violin and piano).

Cabin memories (violin and piano). 1921. New York: Carl Fischer, 1920, 1921. 4 vols. Contents: (1) Nobody knows the troubles I've seen; (2) I'm goin' home; (3) Bear de burden; (4) Down by the ribber side. Library: Library of Congress. Recorded: Brunswick 15107 (Albert Spalding, violin, André Benoist, piano; no. 1 only). Library: de Lerma.

Cabin song, from *From the cotton fields, op. 18, no. 1* (violin and piano). New York: Carl Fischer, 1920. 6 p. and part. Sheet music edition, B-1199. Plate no. 21804. Library: Spingarn.

———— (violin and piano). New York: Carl Fischer, 1927. 5 p. and part. Sheet music edition, P1582. Plate no. 24162. Dedication: Fritz Kreisler. Library: Columbia, Spingarn.

Camp song (Water boy), op. 26, no. 1 (violin and piano). New York: Carl Fischer, 1927. 5 p. Sheet music edition, B.2060. Plate no. 24107-6. Library: Columbia, Library of Congress, Spingarn.

Capriccio (violin and piano).

Caprice, op. 17, no. 2 (violin and piano). New York: Carl Fischer, 1922. 5 p. and part. Sheet music edition, B-1792. Plate no. 22435. Dedication: Pauline Watson. Library: Columbia, Spingarn.

Christmas spirituals. Contents: (1) Poor little Jesus; (2) O Mary, where is your baby?

Concert paraphrases of traditional Negro melodies, op. 26 (violin and piano). New York: Carl Fischer, 1936, 1927. Contents: (1) Camp song (Water boy); (2) Levee dance; (3) Plantation song; (4) Pilgrim song.

Dance caprice, op. 16, no. 3 (piano). Boston: C. W. Thompson, 1919. 7 p. Plate no. T&Co. 2515. Dedication: To my wife. Library: Columbia, Spingarn.

Dance caprice, op. 60, no. 3 (piano). Boston: Boston Music Co., 1919.

Deliverance (violin and piano).

Down by de ribberside (medium voice and piano), by C. Blanco [pseud.]. New York: Carl Fischer, 1921. 5 p. Plate no. 21947. Library: Spingarn.

——— (SATB). New York: Carl Fischer, n.d. [?]. Plate no. 2168.

Forty Negro spirituals (medium voice and piano). Philadelphia: Theodore Presser, 1927. vi, 129 p. Library: Library of Congress, Schomburg.

Four characteristic dances (violin and piano).

From the cotton fields, op. 18 (violin and piano). New York: Carl Fischer, 1920. Sheet music edition B1199. Contents: (1) Cabin song; (2) On the bayou; (3) Spiritual. Dedication: Fritz Kreisler.

——— (band).

——— (orchestra). New York: Carl Fischer, 1927. Duration: 15:00. Instrumentation: 2 flutes and piccolo, 2 oboes, 2 clarinets, 2 bassoons, 2 horns, 2 trumpets, 2 trombones, tuba, timpani, 2 percussion, piano, strings. Library: Spingarn.

——— (piano), arranged by Arthur Friedheim. New York: Carl Fischer, 1927. 3 vols. Plate no. 24162-4. Library: Library of Congress, Spingarn.

Haitian dance (orchestra). New York: Carl Fischer, n.d. [?]. Duration: 4:00. Instrumentation: flute, oboe, 2 clarinets, 2 bassoons, 2 horns, 2 trumpets, trombone, timpani, percussion, strings.

Honey chile (medium voice and piano). Philadelphia: Theodore Presser, 1926. 5 p. Plate no. 23368-3. Text: Alfred Anderson. Library: Library of Congress.

——— (violin and piano). Philadelphia: Theodore Presser, n.d. [?].

Hush, ma honey (low voice and piano). Boston: C. W. Thompson, 1920. 5 p. Plate no. 2601. Text: Helen Boardman Knox. Library: Spingarn.

I know I have another building (SATB with piano reduction). Philadelphia: Theodore Presser, 1925. 11 p. Plate no. 21217-10. Library: Library of Congress.

I'm goin' home (medium voice and piano). New York: Carl Fischer, 1921. 5 p. Plate no. 21946.

——— (SATB). New York: Carl Fischer, n.d. [?]. Plate no. 2169.

Improvisation, op. 16, no. 1 (piano). Boston: C. W. Thompson, 1919. 7 p. Plate no. T&Co. 2318. Dedication: To my mother. *See also* following title. Library: Columbia, Spingarn.

Improvisation, op. 24, no. 1 (piano). Boston: Boston Music Co., 1946, 1919. 7 p. A revision of his op. 16, no. 1.

——— (piano). Boston: Boston Music Co., 1949, 1946, 1919. Revised edition. Plate no. 10170. Library: Columbia, Library of Congress.

Jubilee song, op. 19, no. 1 (violin and piano). Philadelphia: Theodore Presser, 1924. 4 p. and part. Plate no. 19567. Library: Columbia, Library of Congress.

Kashmira: Oriental sketch, op. 16, no. 2 (piano). Boston: C. W. Thompson, 1919. Plate no. T&Co. 2402. Dedication: To William. Library: Spingarn.

Kashmirian dance, op. 60, no. 1 (violin and piano). Boston: Boston Music Co., 1919.

Levee dance, op. 26, no. 2 (violin and piano). 9 p. and part. Sheet music edition, B-1061. Plate no. 27471; 24108-11. Library: Columbia, Library of Congress, Spingarn. Recorded: Brunswick AXL-3017, Decca A-385, Decca DL-5214, and Decca 23387B (Jascha Heifetz, violin, Milton Kaye, piano). Library: de Lerma.

Magnificat (organ).

Mary, do not weep (violin and piano).

Menuet, from *Ouanga* (violin and piano).

Negro folk melodies. Philadelphia: Theodore Presser, 1927.

Negro rhapsody (orchestra).

Night at Sans Souci: Ballet. Scenario: Arthur H. Ryder.

On the bayou, from *From the cotton fields, op. 18, no. 2* (violin and piano). New York: Carl Fischer, 1920. 7 p. and part. Sheet music edition, B-1200. Plate no. 21805. Library: Columbia, Spingarn.

———— (orchestra), arranged by Charles J. Roberts. n.p.: Carl Fischer, 1925. 3 p. (piano-conductor) and parts. Plate no. 2344-20. Library: de Lerma (partial flute part only).

Ouanga: Opera in 3 acts (piano-vocal score). 1932. Fort Wayne: C. C. White, 1955; Chicago: Sam Fox, 1955. 164 p. Text: John Frederick Matheus. Premiere: February 20, 1938, Chicago, WPA Symphony Orchestra (excerpts previously heard November 13, 1932, at the Three Arts Club, Chicago). Won: David Bisphan Memorial Medal, from the American Opera Society. Library: Library of Congress (42-831, manuscript, 124 p.; 75-764022, Sam Fox imprint), Schomburg (piano-vocal score), Spingarn.

Overtones (violin and piano). New York: Sam Fox, n.d. [?].

Patter without chatter: Jazz study (piano). Philadelphia: Theodore Presser, 1926.

———— (piano, 4 hands).

Piece (timpani and orchestra). New York: Sam Fox, n.d. [?]. Duration: 10:00.

Pilgrim song, op. 26, no. 4 (violin and piano). 7 p. Sheet music edition, B.2348. Plate no. 24108; 27471. Library: Library of Congress, Spingarn.

Plantation song, op. 26, no. 3 (violin and piano). 7 p. and part. Sheet music edition, B-2347. Plate no. CC27470-7; 24107. Library: Spingarn.

Poème (violoncello and piano).

Poor little Jesus. Library: Spingarn.

Prelude, from *Ouanga* (orchestra). New York: Sam Fox, n.d. [?]. Duration: 12:00. Instrumentation: 2 flutes and piccolo, 2 oboes, 2 clarinets, 2 bassoons, 2 horns, 2 trumpets, 2 trombones, tuba, timpani, 2 percussion, harp, strings. Library: Yale (manuscript, dated 1942).

Quartet, no. 1, C minor (strings). Revised as *Suite on Negro folk tunes.*

Reflêts (violin and piano). Philadelphia: Theodore Presser, n.d. [?].

Reflêts, op. 24, no. 1 (piano). Philadelphia: Theodore Presser, 1925. 3 p. Plate no. 22928. Library: Columbia, Library of Congress, Spingarn.

Remembrance (violin and piano). New York: Sam Fox, n.d. [?].

Rhapsody (violin and piano).

Scotch idyl, op. 26 (violin and piano). New York: Carl Fischer, 1925. 8 p. Sheet music edition, B-1891. Plate no. 23411. Library: Library of Congress, Spingarn.

Serenade, op. 17, no. 3 (violin and piano). New York: Carl Fischer, 1922. 7 p. and part. Sheet music edition, B-1793. Plate no. 22436-4. Dedication: Irma Seydel. Library: Spingarn.

Sinner, please don't let this harvest pass (SATB with piano reduction). Philadelphia: Theodore Presser, 1935. 1 p. Plate no. 21216-10. Library: Library of Congress.

Spiritual, from *From the cotton fields, op. 18, no. 3* (violin and piano). 6 p. and part. Sheet music edition, B-1201. Plate no. 21806. Library: Columbia, Spingarn.

———— (low voice and piano). New York: Carl Fischer, n.d. [?]. Plate no. 21806. Library: Spingarn.

Symphony, D minor (orchestra).

Tambour: Haitian méringue, op. 34 (piano). New York: Carl Fischer, 1930. 7 p. Sheet music edition P 1881. Plate no. 25819. Used as incidental music to a play of the same name by John Frederick Matheus. Library: Columbia, Library of Congress, Spingarn.

———— (piano). New York: Sam Fox, 1955. Library: Library of Congress.

———— (orchestra). New York: Carl Fischer, 1951. Duration: 8:00. Instrumentation: flute, oboe, 2 clarinets, bassoon, 2 horns, 2 trumpets, trombone, timpani, 2 percussion, piano, strings.

———— (band), arranged by Eric Leidzén. New York: Sam Fox, 1951. Sam Fox national band edition, 28. Library: Library of Congress (condensed score and parts).

To spring (violin and piano). Philadelphia: Theodore Presser, 1924.

Triumphal march, op. 30 (piano). Philadelphia: Theodore Presser, 1927. 5 p. Plate no. 23547. Library: Library of Congress, Spingarn.

———— (band). Philadelphia: Theodore Presser, n.d. [?].

———— (organ).

Twilight, op. 17, no. 1 (violin and piano). New York: Carl Fischer, 1922. 5 p. and part. Sheet music edition, B-1791. Plate no. 22434. Dedication: Mayo Wadler. Library: Columbia, Library of Congress, Spingarn.

Valse coquette, op. 17, no. 4 (violin and piano). New York: Carl Fischer, 1922. Sheet music edition, B-1974. Plate no. 22327. Library: Spingarn.

The violinist's daily dozen: Twelve studies (violin). Chicago: Gamble Hinged Music, 1924. 6 p. Plate no. 697. Library: Spingarn.

Waiting for the trumpet to sound (two voices and piano). Philadelphia: Theodore Presser, 1928. 7 p. Plate no. 24183-5. Library: Library of Congress.

Worship (violin and piano).

WORK, FREDERICK JEROME, 1879–1942

Negro suite. 1936.

Quartet, F major (strings). 12 p. Contents (1 movement): Allegro impetuoso molto con abbandono; Larghetto con moto; Allegro; Moderato con abbandono. Library: Columbia, de Lerma (holograph).

Suite nègre (orchestra). 1936. Library: Fleisher (3081, 3082, 3083, 3084).

WORK, JOHN WESLEY, 1901–1967

For the beauty of the earth (soprano, baritone, SATB, and organ). Glen Rock, N.J.: J. Fischer & Bro., 1936. 8 p. Plate no. J.F.&B. 6851-8. Text: Folliott S. Pierpont. Dedication: Mrs. Charlotte Moulton Brooks. Library: Fisk, Spingarn.

Glory to that new born king (SATB with piano reduction). Bryn Mawr, Pa.: Theodore Presser, 1929. 4 p. Plate no. 312-30885. Library: Fisk.

———— (SATB with piano reduction). Bryn Mawr, Pa.: Theodore Presser, 1935, 1929. 7 p. Plate no. 312-21208. Library: Fisk.

Going home to live with God (soprano, tenor, and SATB, with piano reduction). Glen Rock, N.J.: J. Fischer & Bro., 1962, 1934. 8 p. Part songs for J. W. Work. Plate J.F.&B. 6794-8. Library: Fisk.

———— (tenor and TTBB with piano reduction). New York: J. Fischer & Bro., 1936. 8 p. Fischer edition, 6836. Library: Fisk, Spingarn.

Grace be unto you and peace from God (SATB and organ). 7 p. Text: Colossians. Library: Fisk (manuscript).

Grandmother sings a lullaby (piano). 2 p. Library: Fisk (manuscript).

He never said a mumbaling word (TTBB with piano reduction). Philadelphia: Theodore Presser, 1929. 3 p. Plate no. 20884. Library: Fisk (manuscript).

Holy Bible (SATB).

How beautiful are the mountains (SAATB). New York: Galaxy Music, 1953, 1934. 11 p. Music for the church, 833. Text: Isaiah 52:7–8. Library: Fisk, Schomburg, Spingarn.

———— (TTBB). New York: Galaxy Music, 1953, 1934. 8 p. Plate no. 20884. Library: Fisk.

Into the woods my master went (SATB and organ or piano). New York: Remick Music, 1939. 7 p. Plate no. 5-G1456. Text: Sidney Lanier. Dedication: Charles C. Washburn. Library: Fisk.

Little sister goes to dancing school (piano). 3 p. Library: Fisk (manuscript).

Mandy Lou (medium voice and piano). 1918. New York: Carl Fischer, 1929. 5 p. Sheet music edition, V1064. Plate no. CC 25061-4. Text: John W. Work, Sr. [i.e., II]. Library: Columbia, Fisk.

My Lord, what a morning (soprano, baritone, and SATB with piano reduction). Philadelphia: Theodore Presser, 1929. 4 p. College choral series. Plate no. 312-40622-3. Library: Fisk. Recorded: RCA LSC-7043 (First International University Choral Festival, G. Wallace Woodworth, conductor). Library: de Lerma.

———— (soprano, baritone, and SATB with piano reduction). Bryn Mawr, Pa.: Theodore Presser, 1964, 1929.

———— (TTBB with piano reduction). Philadelphia: Theodore Presser, 1929. 3 p. Plate no. 312-20883.

Sing, O heavens (SATB and organ). New York: Remick Music, 1934. 8 p. Plate no. 1097-7. Text: Isaiah. Dedication: Charles C. Washburn and the Scarritt College Choir. Library: Fisk.

Sittin' down beside of the lamb (TTBB with piano reduction). Philadelphia: Theodore Presser, 1929. 7 p. Plate no. 20 886. Library: Fisk.

Sonata, C minor (piano). Contents: 3 movements. Library: Fisk (manuscript).

Stand the storm (tenor and TTBB with piano reduction). Glen Rock, N.J.: J. Fischer & Bro., 1931. 13 p. Fischer edition, 6514. Plate J.F.&B. 6514-13. Dedication: Roy Tibbs. Library: Fisk, Spingarn.

This ol' hammer killed John Henry (low voice and piano). New York: Galaxy Music, 1948. 7 p. Dedication: Kenneth Spencer. Library: Fisk, Library of Congress.

—— (TTBB). New York: Galaxy Music, 1950, 1933. 16 p. Plate no. GM 629-15. Dedication: John W. Whittaker. Library: Fisk, Library of Congress (1933 imprint).

Variations on an original theme (piano). 1934. Library: Fisk (manuscript).

Wasn't that a mighty day? (SATB with piano reduction). Glen Rock, N.J.: J. Fischer & Bro., 1962, 1934. Part songs by John W. Work. Plate no. 6835-6. Library: Fisk, Spingarn. Recorded: Silver Crest MOR-111977 (Morgan State University Choir, Nathan Carter, conductor) 1977. Library: de Lerma.

—— (SSA). Rockville Center, N.Y.: Belwin-Mills, 1970, 1962. 7 p. Carols and anthems for Christmastide. Plate no. FEC 6846-6. Library: Fisk.

—— (TTBB with piano reduction). Glen Rock, N.J.: J. Fischer & Bro., 1934. 8 p. Fischer edition, 5616. Dedication: Kemper Harreld. Library: Fisk.

NOTES

1. This compilation was developed with the assistance of the composer, his wife Verna Arvey and their daughter Judith Anne Still.

Index

About the Contributors

RAE LINDA BROWN is an assistant professor of music at the University of Michigan. She is compiler and editor of *Music, Printed and Manuscript, in the James Weldon Johnson Memorial Collection of Negro Arts and Letters, Yale University* (Garland, 1982) and is the author of other works of black music scholarship.

PAUL BURGETT is Vice President and Student Affairs Officer at the University of Rochester. His 1976 doctoral dissertation is titled "Aesthetics of the Music of Black Americans: A Critical Analysis of the Writings of Selected Black Scholars with Implications for Black Music Studies and for Music Education" (Eastman School of Music).

DOMINIQUE-RENÉ DE LERMA is a professor of music at Morgan State University and a member of the faculty of the Peabody Conservatory of Music, Johns Hopkins University. He is the author of the multi-volume *Bibliography of Black Music* (Greenwood Press, 1981–) and numerous other publications in the field of black music.

SAMUEL A. FLOYD, JR., is Director of the Center for Black Music Research at Columbia College Chicago. Among his contributions to black music scholarship are *Black Music in the United States: An Annotated Bibliography of Selected Reference and Research Materials* (Kraus, 1983) and *Black Music Biography: An Annotated Bibliography* (Kraus, 1987).

ALLAN M. GORDON is a professor of art history at California State University at Sacramento. His publications include *Echoes of Our Past: The Narrative Artistry of Palmer C. Hayden* (Exhibition Catalog. The Museum of African American Art, 1988).

JOHN GRAZIANO is a professor of music at City University of New York, New York City. He is editor of the journal *American Music*, and his publications include "Sentimental Songs, Rags, and Transformation: The Emergence of the Black Musical, 1895–1910" in *Musical Theatre in Amer-*

ica: Papers and Proceedings of the Conference on the Musical Theatre in America (Greenwood Press, 1984).

JEFFREY P. GREEN is a British management specialist and businessman who has also served as a bank official in Uganda. His publications include *Edmund Thornton Jenkins: The Life and Times of an American Black Composer, 1894–1926* (Greenwood Press, 1982).

RICHARD A. LONG is Atticus Haygood Professor of Interdisciplinary Studies in the Graduate Institute of Liberal Arts at Emory University, Atlanta, Georgia. He is co-editor of the anthology *Afro-American Writing: Prose and Poetry* (Pennsylvania State University Press, 1985).

GEORGIA A. RYDER is Dean Emeritus, Norfolk State University, Norfolk, Virginia, and is also a former head of the school's Music Department. Her publications include "Another Look at Some American Cantatas" (*The Black Perspective in Music*, 3, no. 2, Special Issue, May 1975).

RAWN SPEARMAN is a professor of music at the University of Lowell, Lowell, Massachusetts. His writings include "The 'Joy' of Langston Hughes and Howard Swanson" (*The Black Perspective in Music*, 9, no. 2, Fall 1988, 121–38).

MARK TUCKER is an assistant professor of music at Columbia University. His writings include a study of Duke Ellington's early years, to be published by the University of Illinois Press, and he recently edited *Jazz from the Beginning*, the memoirs of reed-player Garvin Bushell (University of Michigan Press, 1988).